IT'S ABOUT TIME

MIDDLE SCHOOL INQUIRY™
SCIENCE

INVESTIGATING EARTH SYSTEMS™

Developed by
the American
Geological
Institute.
Supported by
the National
Science
Foundation
and the
American
Geological
Institute
Foundation

SERVING THE GEOSCIENCES WORLDWIDE
AGI
THE AMERICAN GEOLOGICAL INSTITUTE

Ann Benbow

Michael Smith

John Southard

Colin Mably

Mark Carpenter

Matthew Hoover

IT's ABOUT TIME®

HERFF JONES EDUCATION DIVISION

84 Business Park Drive, Armonk, NY 10504
Phone (914) 273-2233 Fax (914) 273-2227
www.its-about-time.com

Investigating Earth Systems

All student activities in this textbook have been designed to be as safe as possible, and have been reviewed by professionals specifically for that purpose. As well, appropriate warnings concerning potential safety hazards are included where applicable to particular activities. However, responsibility for safety remains with the student, the classroom teacher, the school principals, and the school board.

Investigating Earth Systems® is a registered trademark of the American Geological Institute. Registered names and trademarks, etc., used in this publication, even without specific indication thereof, are not to be considered unprotected by law.

It's About Time® is a registered trademark of It's About Time, Herff Jones Education Division. Registered names and trademarks, etc., used in this publication, even without specific indication thereof, are not to be considered unprotected by law.

Printed and bound in the United States of America

ISBN 978-58591-684-9

1 2 3 4 5 VH 11 10 09 08 07

This project was supported, in part, by the National Science Foundation (grant no. 9353035).

Opinions expressed are those of the authors and not necessarily those of the National Science Foundation or the donors of the American Geological Institute Foundation.

Acknowledgements

Ann Benbow is a researcher, curriculum developer, teacher, and trainer. She is currently Director of Education, Development and Outreach at AGI. After teaching science (biology, chemistry, and Earth Science) in high school, elementary school, and two-year college, she taught elementary and secondary science methods at the university level. She worked in research and development for the Education Division of the American Chemical Society for over 12 years. During that time, she directed a number of national educational grants from the National Science Foundation (NSF). Her work in the informal science arena included a period of time as managing editor of *WonderScience* magazine for children and adults, and administrator for the Parents and Children for Terrific Science mini-grant program. Dr. Benbow is currently Principal Investigator of two NSF-supported projects, has co-authored a college textbook on elementary science methods for Wadsworth Publishing, and recently published a book on improving communication techniques with adult learners. Dr. Benbow has a B.S. in Biology from St. Mary's College in Maryland, an M.Ed. in Science Education, and a Ph.D. in Curriculum and Instruction from the University of Maryland, College Park.

Michael Smith is former Director of Education at the American Geological Institute in Alexandria, Virginia. Dr. Smith worked as an exploration geologist and hydrogeologist. He began his Earth Science teaching career with Shady Side Academy in Pittsburgh, PA in 1988 and taught Earth Science at the Charter School of Wilmington, DE. He earned a doctorate from the University of Pittsburgh's Cognitive Studies in Education Program and joined the faculty of the University of Delaware School of Education in 1995. Dr. Smith received the Outstanding Earth Science Teacher Award for Pennsylvania from the National Association of Geoscience Teachers in 1991, served as Secretary of the National Earth Science Teachers Association, and is a reviewer for *Science Education* and *The Journal of Research in Science Teaching*. He worked on the Delaware Teacher Standards, Delaware Science Assessment, National Board of Teacher Certification, and AAAS Project 2061 Curriculum Evaluation programs.

John Southard received his undergraduate degree from the Massachusetts Institute of Technology in 1960 and his doctorate in geology from Harvard University in 1966. After a National Science Foundation postdoctoral fellowship at the California Institute of Technology, he joined the faculty at the Massachusetts Institute of Technology, where he is currently Professor of Geology. He was awarded the MIT School of Science teaching prize in 1989 and was one of the first cohorts of first MacVicar Fellows at MIT, in recognition of excellence in undergraduate teaching. He has taught numerous undergraduate courses in introductory geology, sedimentary geology, field geology, and environmental Earth Science both at MIT and in Harvard's adult education program. He was editor of the *Journal of Sedimentary Petrology* from 1992 to 1996, and he continues to do technical editing of scientific books and papers for SEPM, a professional society for sedimentary geology. Dr. Southard received the 2001 Neil Miner Award from the National Association of Geoscience Teachers.

Colin Mably is a curriculum developer, designer/illustrator, educational television producer, teacher, and trainer. He currently acts as Senior Advisor for Communications to AGI. After ten years as an elementary and middle school teacher, he joined the faculty of Furzedown College of Education and later became Principal Lecturer in the School of Education at the University of East London. Leaving academia to form an educational multimedia company, he developed video-based elementary science and mathematics curricula, in the UK and the USA. He has been a key curriculum developer for several NSF-funded national curriculum projects at middle, high school, and college levels. For AGI, he directed the design and development of the IES curriculum and also training workshops for pilot and field-test teachers. He has also recently co-authored a college textbook on elementary science methods. He received certified teacher status from Oxford University Institute of Education, and an Advanced Diploma in Education from London University Institute of Education.

Mark Carpenter is an Education Specialist at the American Geological Institute. After receiving a B.S. in geology from Exeter University, England, he undertook a graduate degree at the University of Waterloo and Wilfrid Laurier, Canada, where he began designing geology investigations for undergraduate students and worked as an instructor. He has worked in basin hydrology in Ontario, Canada, and studied mountain geology in the Pakistan, and the Nepal Himalayas. As a designer of learning materials for AGI, he has made educational films to support teachers and is actively engaged in designing inquiry-based activities in Earth system science for middle school children in the United States.

Matthew Hoover serves as Education Specialist for the American Geological Institute, developing Earth Science educational resources and curriculum programs at the middle and high school levels. He received a B.S. degree in geology from Boston College, an M.A. degree in Environmental Policy from George Washington University and an M.Ed. in Curriculum and Instruction from George Mason University. As a certified teacher, he has taught elementary and middle school Earth, life, and physical sciences. Prior to joining AGI, he worked for NASA's GLOBE Program, coordinating teacher trainings and designing environmental science investigations and learning activities for K-12 students.

Project Team

Marcus Milling
Executive Director - AGI, VA

Michael Smith
Principal Investigator

Ann Benbow
Director of Education - AGI, VA

Colin Mably
Senior Advisor for
Communications - AGI, VA

Matthew Smith
Project Coordinator

Fred Finley
Project Evaluator
University of Minnesota, MN

Joe Moran
American Meteorological
Society

Lynn Lindow
Pilot Test Evaluator
University of Minnesota, MN

Harvey Rosenbaum
Field Test Evaluator
Montgomery School
District, MD

Robert Ridky
Original Project Director
University of Maryland, MD

Chip Groat
Original Principal Investigator -
University of Texas
El Paso, TX

Marilyn Suiter
Original Co-principal
Investigator - AGI, VA

William Houston
Field Test Manager

Caitlin Callahan - Project
Assistant

Original and Contributing Authors

Oceans
George Dawson
Florida State University, FL

Joseph F. Donoghue
Florida State University, FL

Ann Benbow
American Chemical Society

Michael Smith
American Geological Institute

Soil
Robert Ridky
University of Maryland, MD

Colin Mably - LaPlata, MD

John Southard
Massachusetts Institute of
Technology, MA

Michael Smith
American Geological Institute

Fossils
Robert Gastaldo
Colby College, ME

Colin Mably - LaPlata, MD

Michael Smith
American Geological Institute

Climate and Weather
Mike Mogil
How the Weather Works, MD

Ann Benbow
American Chemical Society

Joe Moran
American Meteorological Society

Michael Smith
American Geological Institute

Energy Resources
Laurie Martin-Vermilyea
American Geological Institute

Michael Smith
American Geological Institute

Our Dynamic Planet
Michael Smith
American Geological Institute

Rocks and Landforms
Michael Smith
American Geological Institute

Water as a Resource
Ann Benbow
American Chemical Society

Michael Smith
American Geological Institute

Materials and Minerals
Mary Poulton
University of Arizona, AZ

Colin Mably - LaPlata, MD

Michael Smith
American Geological Institute

Earth in Space: Astronomy
Ann Benbow
American Geological Institute

Mark Carpenter
American Geological Institute

Matthew Hoover
American Geological Institute

Colin Mably
American Geological Institute

Advisory Board

Jane Crowder
Middle School Teacher, WA

Kerry Davidson
Louisiana Board of Regents, LA

Joseph D. Exline
Educational Consultant, VA

Louis A. Fernandez
California State University, CA

Frank Watt Ireton
National Earth Science Teachers
Association, DC

LeRoy Lee
Wisconsin Academy of Sciences,
Arts and Letters, WI

Donald W. Lewis
Chevron Corporation, CA

James V. O'Connor (deceased)
University of the District of
Columbia, DC

Roger A. Pielke Sr.
Colorado State University, CO

Dorothy Stout (deceased)
Cypress College, CA

Lois Veath
Advisory Board Chairperson
Chadron State College, NE

Field Test Teachers and Specialists

Jenny Soro; Ruby Everage
Daniel Boone Elementary

Joyce Anderson; Maureen
Tucker
Burnside Scholastic Academy

Aimee Ray; Marvin Nochowitz
Haines Elementary

Nicole Hauser; Noreen
Sepulveda
Healy Elementary

Roseann Pavelka; Ann Doyle
Kinzie Elementary

Katherine Lee
McCorkle Elementary

Terri Zachary; Chandra Garcia
O'Toole Elementary

Brenda Armstrong; Delores
McKinney
Overton Elementary

Kathryn Doyle; Patsy Moore
Pirie Magnet Elementary

Veronica Johnson; Constance
Grimm-Grason
Ray Elementary

Mary Pat Robertson; Constance
Grimm-Grason
Raymond Montes; Barbara
Dubielak-Wood
Reilly Elementary

Raul Bermejo; Tammy Valaveris
Columbia Explorers Academy

Kim John-Baptiste; Lillian
Degand
Finkl Elementary

Marie Clouston
Peck Elementary

Facilitators

Linda Carter, Gary Morrissey,
Alan Nelson
Office of Math and Science for
Chicago Public Schools

The American Geological Institute and Investigating Earth Systems

Imagine more than 500,000 Earth scientists worldwide sharing a common voice, and you've just imagined the mission of the American Geological Institute. Our mission is to raise public awareness of the Earth sciences and the role that they play in mankind's use of natural resources, mitigation of natural hazards, and stewardship of the environment. For more than 50 years, AGI has served the scientists and teachers of its Member Societies and hundreds of associated colleges, universities, and corporations by producing Earth science educational materials, *Geotimes*–a geoscience news magazine, GeoRef–a reference database, and government affairs and public awareness programs.

So many important decisions made every day that affect our lives depend upon an understanding of how our Earth works. That's why AGI created *Investigating Earth Systems*. In your *Investigating Earth Systems* classroom, you'll discover the wonder and importance of Earth science. As you investigate minerals, soil, or oceans — do field work in nearby beaches, parks, or streams, explore how fossils form, understand where your energy resources come from, or find out how to forecast weather — you'll gain a better understanding of Earth science and its importance in your life.

We would like to thank the National Science Foundation and the AGI Foundation Members that have been supportive in bringing Earth science to students. The Chevron Corporation provided the initial leadership grant, with additional contributions from the following AGI Foundation Members: Anadarko Petroleum Corp., The Anschutz Foundation, Baker Hughes Foundation, Barrett Resources Corp., Elizabeth and Stephen Bechtel, Jr. Foundation, BPAmoco Foundation, Burlington Resources Foundation, CGG Americas, Inc., Conoco Inc., Consolidated Natural Gas Foundation, Diamond Offshore Co., Dominion Exploration & Production, Inc., EEX Corp., ExxonMobil Foundation, Global Marine Drilling Co., Halliburton Foundation, Inc., Kerr McGee Foundation, Maxus Energy Corp., Noble Drilling Corp., Occidental Petroleum Charitable Foundation, Parker Drilling Co., Phillips Petroleum Co., Santa Fe Snyder Corp., Schlumberger Foundation, Shell Oil Company Foundation, Southwestern Energy Co., Texaco, Inc., Texas Crude Energy, Inc., Unocal Corp. USX Foundation (Marathon Oil Co.).

We at AGI wish you success in your exploration of the Earth System!

Ann Benbow
Director of Education, AGI

Marcus E. Milling
Executive Director, AGI

Unit 1: Our Dynamic Planet

Unit 2: Rocks and Landforms

Unit 3: Fossils

Unit 4: Climate and Weather

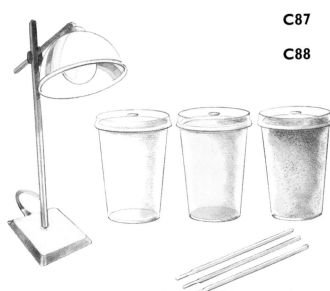

Unit 5: Earth in Space: Astronomy

Unit 6: Water as a Resource

Glossary and Index

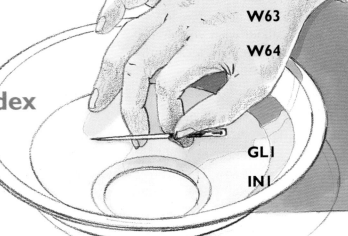

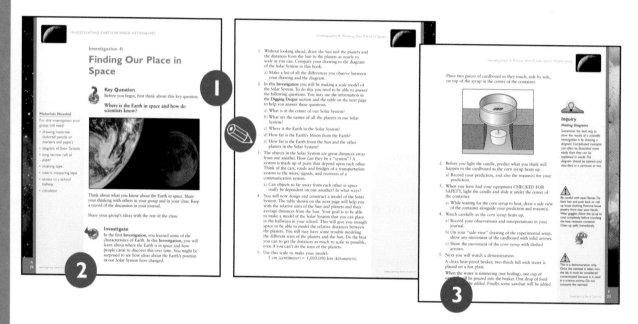

Using Investigating Earth Systems

Look for the following features in this module to help you learn about the Earth System.

1. Key Question

Before you begin, you will be asked to think about the **Key Question** you will investigate. You do not need to come up with a correct answer. Instead, you will be expected to take some time to think about what you already know. You can then share your ideas with your small group and with the class.

2. Investigate

Geoscientists learn about the Earth System by doing investigations. That is exactly what you will be doing. Sometimes you will be given the procedures to follow. Other times you will need to decide what question you want to investigate and what procedure to follow.

Throughout your investigations you will keep your own journal. Your journal is like one that scientists keep when they investigate a scientific question. You can enter anything you think is important during the investigation. There will also be questions after many of the investigate steps for you to answer and enter in your journal. You will also need to think about how the Earth works as a set of systems. You can write the connections you make after each investigation on your *Earth System Connection* sheet in your journal.

3. Inquiry

You will use inquiry processes to investigate and solve problems in an orderly way. Look for these reminders about the processes you are using.

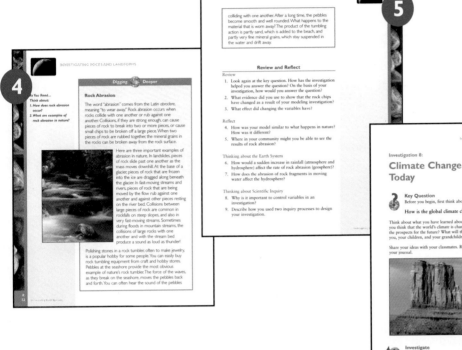

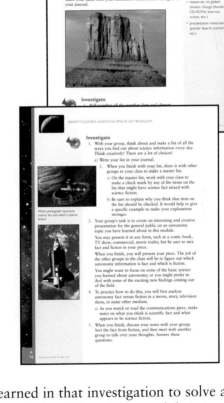

4. Digging Deeper

Scientists build on knowledge that others have discovered through investigation. In this section you can read about the insights scientists have about the question you are investigating. The questions in **As You Read** will help you focus on the information you are looking for.

5. Review and Reflect

After you have completed each investigation, you will be asked to reflect on what you have learned and how it relates to the "Big Picture" of the Earth System. You will also be asked to think about what scientific inquiry processes you used.

6. Investigation: Putting It All Together

In the last investigation of each Unit, you will have a chance to "put it all together." You will be asked to apply all that you have learned in that investigation to solve a practical problem. This module is just the beginning! You continue to learn about the Earth System every time you ask questions and make observations about the world around you.

The Earth System

The Earth System is a set of systems that work together in making the world we know. Four of these important systems are:

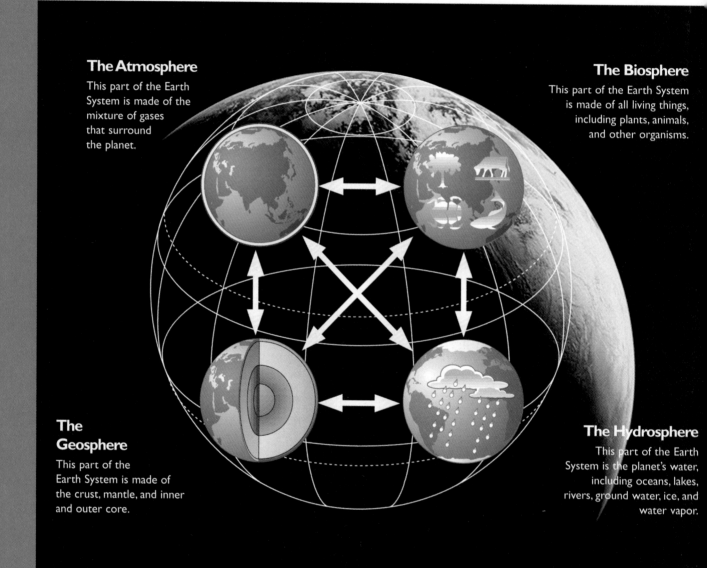

The Atmosphere

This part of the Earth System is made of the mixture of gases that surround the planet.

The Biosphere

This part of the Earth System is made of all living things, including plants, animals, and other organisms.

The Geosphere

This part of the Earth System is made of the crust, mantle, and inner and outer core.

The Hydrosphere

This part of the Earth System is the planet's water, including oceans, lakes, rivers, ground water, ice, and water vapor.

These systems, and others, have been working together since the Earth's beginning more than 4.6 billion years ago. They are still working, because the Earth is always changing, even though we cannot always observe these changes. Energy from within and outside the Earth leads to changes in the Earth System. Changes in any one of these systems affects the others. This is why we think of the Earth as made of interrelated systems.

During your investigations, keep the Earth System in mind. At the end of each investigation, you will be asked to think about how the things you have discovered fit with the Earth System.

To further understand the Earth System, take a look at THE BIG PICTURE at the end of each Unit.

Introducing Inquiry Processes

When geologists and other scientists investigate the world, they use a set of inquiry processes. Using these processes is very important. They ensure that the research is valid and reliable. In your investigations, you will use these same processes. In this way, you will become a scientist, doing what scientists do. Understanding inquiry processes will help you to investigate questions and solve problems in an orderly way. You will also use inquiry processes in high school, in college, and in your work.

During this module, you will learn when, and how, to use these inquiry processes. Use the information below as a reference about the inquiry processes.

Inquiry Processes:

How scientists use these processes

Explore questions to answer by inquiry

Scientists usually form a question to investigate after first looking at what is known about a scientific idea. Sometimes they predict the most likely answer to a question. They base this prediction on what they already know or believe to be true.

Design an investigation

To make sure that the way they test ideas is fair, scientists think very carefully about the design of their investigations. They do this to make sure that the results will be valid and reliable.

Conduct an investigation

After scientists have designed an investigation, they conduct their tests. They observe what happens and record the results. Often, they repeat a test several times to ensure reliable results.

Collect and review data using tools

Scientists collect information (data) from their tests. Data can take many forms. Common kinds of data include numerical (numbers), verbal (words), and visual (images). To collect and manage data, scientists use tools such as computers, calculators, tables, charts, and graphs.

Use evidence to develop ideas

Evidence is very important for scientists. Just as in a court case, it is proven evidence that counts. Scientists look at the evidence other scientists have collected, as well as the evidence they have collected themselves.

Consider evidence for explanations

Finding strong evidence does not always provide the complete answer to a scientific question. Scientists look for likely explanations by studying patterns and relationships within the evidence.

Seek alternative explanations

Sometimes, the evidence available is not clear or can be interpreted in other ways. If this is so, scientists look for different ways of explaining the evidence. This may lead to a new idea or question to investigate.

Show evidence and reasons to others

Scientists communicate their findings to other scientists. Other scientists may then try to repeat the investigation to validate the results.

Use mathematics for science inquiry

Scientists use mathematics in their investigations. Accurate measurement, with suitable units, is very important for both collecting and analyzing data. Data often consist of numbers and calculations.

INVESTIGATING
OUR DYNAMIC PLANET

Unit 1

What you will be investigating in this Unit:

Introducing Our Dynamic Planet

Have you ever seen a volcano erupting?

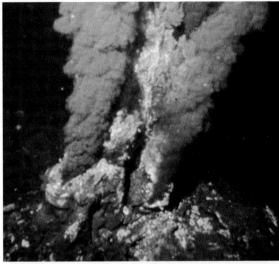

Have you ever heard about hydrothermal vents on the floor of the ocean?

Have you ever wondered how mountains form?

Have you ever seen the effects of an earthquake on a community?

Why Is Our Dynamic Planet Important?

Dynamic means powerful or active. Our dynamic planet is a powerful, active, ever-changing planet. Powerful events like earthquakes and volcanic eruptions have been happening since the Earth formed, over 4.6 billion years ago. Every feature of our planet changes, on time

scales that range from minutes to millions of years. The deepest oceans, the highest mountain peaks—all represent but a page in the volume of Earth's history. Mountains have been destroyed, recycled, and reborn. Oceans have risen and fallen.

These processes are still at work today. Knowledge about present-day volcanic eruptions and earthquakes give clues about the past. Rocks, landforms, and fossils also provide evidence of a long and varied history of the Earth. Knowing about our dynamic planet will help you to understand the past and prepare for the future.

What Will You Investigate?

You will look for evidence and help solve some of the puzzles surrounding Earth processes. Here are some of the things that you will investigate:

- how scientists make and use models;
- what the inside of the Earth is like;
- how the Earth's surface moves;
- how mountains form;
- what causes earthquakes.

You will need to practice your problem-solving skills. You will also need to be good observers and recorders, as you work together with other members of your class.

In the last investigation you will have a chance to apply all that you have learned about our dynamic planet. You will investigate a natural hazard in depth. Then you will design a brochure to provide information to residents of a community on how to prepare for, and protect against, natural disasters.

Investigation I:

Gathering Evidence and Modeling

Key Question

Before you begin, first think about this key question.

How do you make a model of something that you cannot see?

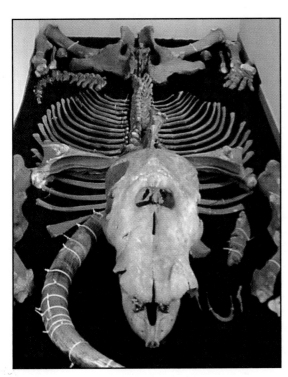

Think about what you know about models. What are some models of things or processes that cannot be seen with the naked eye? How do you think these models were constructed?

Discuss the key question with your group and your class. Record your thoughts in your journal. Be prepared to share your thinking with the rest of the class.

Materials Needed

For this investigation your group will need:

- double-bagged, brown paper bag with "mystery objects" sealed inside

- colored pencils

Investigate

1. Several kinds of objects have been placed into a brown paper "mystery bag," and it has been sealed shut. You will use three senses (smell, hearing, and touch) to gather data about the bag's contents. Then you will design new tests to get more information.

In your journal, write your research question: "What are the contents of the Mystery Bag?" Underneath your research question, write your prediction.

Do not use taste. The items in the bag are safe to smell. Follow safe procedures when smelling unfamiliar materials.

WHAT ARE THE CONTENTS OF THE MYSTERY BAG?	
SMELL **Model** **Evidence**	**HEARING** **Model** **Evidence**
TOUCH **Model** **Evidence**	**FURTHER TESTS**

2. Divide a sheet of paper into four equal sections. Label the four sections as follows:
   - Smell
   - Hearing
   - Touch
   - Further Tests

   Divide the sections for smell, hearing, and touch, into two sections: model and evidence. In the evidence section you will write observations that support your ideas about what you think is in the bag. In the model section you will draw a model of what you think is in the bag.

3. The first sense you will use is smell. Your teacher will place the bag on the center of your table. Smell the bag without touching it.

   a) Record your ideas about what is in the bag in the "model" section of the square, using pictures.

   b) In the other section of the box, record your evidence. This is like a justification, or explanation, of why you drew the picture the way you did.

4. Next, you will use your sense of hearing. One member of your group should pick up the bag and shake it, while walking around to each group member.

   a) Record your model(s) in the correct square, using pictures.

   b) Record your evidence.

5. Next, you will use your sense of touch, using care not to open or damage the bag, or the bag's contents. Allow each group member to touch the bag.

   a) Record your model(s) in the correct square, using pictures.

   b) Record your evidence.

6. Discuss your models and evidence in your group.

   When you have come to an agreement, select a group member to share one of your group's models and evidence with the rest of the class.

7. After discussing your class's findings, compose a list of further tests you could perform to gather more evidence. These do not have to be tests that you will actually try in the classroom, although they could be. The only rule is that you may not look inside the bag.

   a) Write your group's ideas under "Further Tests" in your journal.

   b) Share your ideas in a group discussion.

Inquiry
Using Evidence

Evidence is very important for scientists. They can use evidence to develop conceptual models (what they think something they cannot see might look like). Evidence comes from observation and data. In this investigation you can use the data you collect from your observations as evidence to develop a conceptual model of what is in the brown paper bag.

Have your teacher check your tests for safety if you plan on trying any of them. Wash your hands after the activity.

As You Read...
Think about:

1. *What is the difference between a physical model and a conceptual model?*

2. *What is the difference between a hypothesis and a model?*

3. *How does mathematics help in developing models?*

4. *How do computers help in developing models?*

MODELS

In science there are many kinds of models. Scientists use the words "model" and "modeling" in many different ways.

Physical Models

Physical models are structures that scientists build to represent something else. This kind of model is probably what would pop into your mind first if somebody asked you what a model is. The simplest kind of physical model is just a small-scale structure of what a much larger item looks like, or once looked like but no longer exists. The dinosaurs you might see in a museum are models built by paleontologists (scientists who study fossils and ancient life). They collect the fossilized bones and then make plaster casts of them. They try to fit the bones together in the most realistic way. Then they try to imagine what the flesh and skin might have looked like.

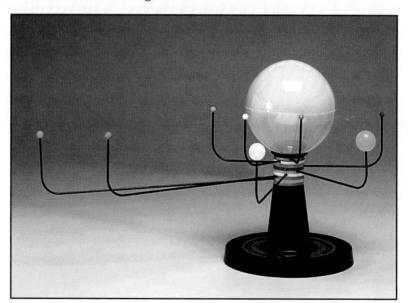

Other physical models simulate some event or process in nature. Very large-scale natural processes like river-flow or ocean waves are difficult to study in the outdoors. Scientists build tanks, channels, or basins to reproduce the processes in a laboratory. Sometimes they are able to adjust the conditions (things like speed of water-flow, or the behavior of water waves). Then what they observe in the model represents what happens in the outdoors. Even if they are not able to do that, then at least they are able to get some valuable qualitative data just by watching what happens in the model.

Conceptual Models

Conceptual models are models that scientists develop in their minds. Scientists often try to develop a concept about how some process works in nature. The basis for the concept is what has already been observed about the process, together with what the scientist knows about basic physical or chemical laws. A conceptual model is a bit like a hypothesis. It is usually broader than a hypothesis, however, because it deals with many things about a complicated natural system. A good example of a conceptual model is the picture scientists have about the nature of atoms. You probably know that atoms consist of a nucleus, and electrons that orbit around the nucleus. The nucleus consists of protons and neutrons. That's the simplest conceptual model of an atom. With the discovery of even more elementary particles, that original conceptual model of an atom has been enlarged and extended.

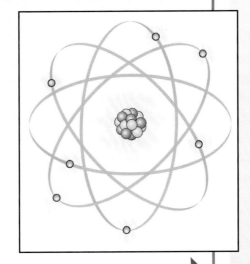

Inquiry

Hypothesis

A hypothesis is a testable statement or idea about how something works. It is based on what you think that you know or understand already. A hypothesis is never a guess. You test a hypothesis by comparing it to observations or data that already exist or that can be gathered in the future. A hypothesis forms the basis for making a prediction, and is used to design an experiment or observation to find out more about a scientific idea or question. Guesses can be useful in science, but they are not hypotheses.

Mathematical Models

Sometimes, scientists are able to write mathematical equations that describe how some process works. The equations express basic physical and chemical laws. Then they solve the equations, in the same way that students in a math class solve equations. The solutions to the equations tell how the process will work, under a variety of conditions. This allows scientists to predict what will happen— which is one of the important things scientists try to do.

Numerical Models

Sometimes, scientists are able to develop a mathematical model, but the model would take too long to fully test by hand. That's where high-speed computers come in. The equations are programmed into the computer. The computer can then compute the model thousands of times. In this way it can quickly simulate what happens either over time, or with changing conditions. As computing power has grown in recent years, the ability of computers to handle numerical models has gotten much greater. Several groups of climatologists (scientists who study global climate) have developed numerical models to study how the Earth's climate might change in the coming decades. As more and more is known about processes of climate, the models are continually being refined.

Review and Reflect

Review

1. Look again at the **Key Question** for this investigation. In your journal, write down what you have learned from your investigation that provides answers.

2. Describe how and why your third model (using touch) is a better model than your first model (using smell).

3. Of the four kinds of models described in the **Digging Deeper** reading section, how would you classify your model of the mystery bag? Explain your answer.

Reflect

4. Explain how time and cost considerations might affect the process of making a model.

5. How does technology affect the ability of scientists to develop models?

6. Describe a situation in which a model is made of something that cannot be observed directly. Use an example that has not been given in this investigation.

Thinking about the Earth System

7. The modeling that you did with the mystery bag can be connected to the Earth's major systems. Provide a connection to each of the Earth systems in this investigation. Remember to write connections, as you find them, on the *Earth System Connection* sheet.

Thinking about Scientific Inquiry

8. What role did evidence play in your group's models?

9. How was communicating findings to others an important scientific process in this activity?

10. In what ways would the process of making a model of the Earth's interior be like the mystery bag activity?

Investigation 2:

The Interior of the Earth

Key Question

Before you begin, first think about this key question.

What is the interior of the Earth like?

Materials Needed

For this part of the investigation your group will need:

- large, flat-bottomed container
- black permanent marker
- plastic metric ruler – 30 cm
- pebble about one centimeter in diameter
- flashlight
- stopwatch
- coiled spring

You now understand how sensory observations and experiments provide the basis for models. Make a drawing of what you think the interior of the Earth is like. What measurements, observations, or instruments would give scientists evidence about the Earth's interior?

Discuss your drawing and your thinking with your group and your class.

Investigate

Part A: Observing Waves and Measuring Wave Speed

1. With the permanent black marker, make a clearly visible dot near one end of the bottom of a container. Make another clearly visible dot near the other end of the container. Measure the distance between the dots, in centimeters.

   a) Record the distance in your journal.

2. Pour water into the container to a depth of 2 to 3 cm. Let the water come to rest, until the water surface is mirror smooth.

3. Have one student hold a pebble 5 cm over one of the marks on the bottom of the container.

4. Have a second student shine a flashlight beam straight down on the other mark. This student should lean directly over the flashlight to see the reflection of the beam from the water surface. This student should also hold a stopwatch and be familiar with how it works.

5. While the second student stares carefully at the reflection of the flashlight beam, the first student drops the pebble into the water. The second student starts the stopwatch when he or she hears the pebble enter the water. The second student stops the watch when he or she first detects motion of the water in the flashlight beam. This motion signals the arrival of the wave.

Inquiry

Conducting an Investigation

After scientists have designed an investigation, they conduct their test. The test must be free from uncontrolled variables. In this case you must be sure that the pebble is dropped from the same height each time, and the stopwatch is started and stopped at the correct time. Tests are often repeated several times to ensure reliable and valid results.

Wear goggles when dropping the pebble. Wash your hands after the activity.

a) Record the time on the stopwatch as the travel time of the wave.

6. Repeat the measurements until your group has at least 10 measurements. If one or two of the measurements are very different from all of the others, they are probably what a scientist would call a "gross error." You can ignore a few bad measurements like that, but be sure you have a large number of "good" measurements.

7. Calculate the average travel time. Add up all the measured travel times and then divide the sum by the number of measurements. Be sure to not include the bad measurements.

   a) In your journal, record the average travel time.

8. Calculate the wave speed in centimeters per second. Use the following equation:

$$\text{average wave speed (cm/s)} = \frac{\text{distance between dots (cm)}}{\text{average travel time (s)}}$$

   a) Record your calculations and your result in your journal.

9. Suppose you had a long pan of water. How long would it take the waves to travel:

   a) 50 cm?

   b) 100 cm?

   c) 200 cm?

10. Suppose you dropped stones into a material through which waves move twice as fast as they do through water.

   a) How would this change the average travel time of the waves?

11. Scientists cannot observe earthquake waves moving through the Earth in the same way you can observe waves moving through water. They can, however, record and study the energy from earthquake waves as the waves arrive at a recording station (seismograph station). They can use information they record about the waves to make models of the interior of the Earth.

   Think about how what you studied relates to how scientists make models of the inside of the Earth. What part of your experiment represented:

   a) An earthquake, which releases energy in the Earth?

   b) The movement of energy waves from the earthquakes (seismic waves) in the Earth?

Inquiry

Using Mathematics

Scientists use mathematics in their investigations. Accurate measurement, with suitable units, is very important when collecting data. In this investigation you made measurements. You then used the measurements to make calculations to interpret the data you collected.

c) The material in the Earth through which seismic waves travel?

d) The arrival of a seismic wave at a seismograph station where earthquakes are detected?

12. Compare your average travel time with those of other groups. Discuss the following questions and record the results of your discussions:

a) What might cause differences in travel times from measurement to measurement within your group?

b) What might cause differences in average travel times among the different groups?

c) What improvements to your measurement technique might decrease the difference in values you obtained?

Part B: Kinds of Seismic Waves

1. With a partner, stretch out a coiled spring on the floor about as far as it can go without making a permanent bend in the metal.

2. Have one partner make waves by holding the end of the coiled spring with a fist, and striking the fist with the other hand, directly toward the end of the spring.

   Observe the direction of wave movement, relative to the coiled spring.

   a) Does it move in the same direction (parallel to the spring) or in the opposite direction (perpendicular to the spring)? Record your observation in your journal.

   b) This kind of wave is called a compressional wave. (To compress means to squeeze together.) From your observations, explain why this is an appropriate name for this wave. You may wish to use diagrams to illustrate your answer.

Materials Needed

For this part of the investigation your group will need:

• two coiled springs

Wear safety goggles throughout. Be sure that neither partner holding the coiled spring lets go while it is stretched out. Wash your hands after the activity.

3. Stretch out the coiled spring again. This time, have one partner make waves by moving the spring from side to side (left to right or right to left).

Again, observe the direction of wave movement, relative to the spring.

a) Does the wave move in the same direction (parallel to the spring) or in the opposite direction (perpendicular to the spring)? Record your observation in your journal.

b) This kind of wave is called a shear wave. (To shear means to slide one thing sideways past another thing.) From your observations, explain why this is an appropriate name for this wave. You may wish to use diagrams to illustrate your answer.

4. To compare the two types of wave motions, stretch out two coiled springs along the floor, about 5 m.

Starting at the same end at the same time, have one student holding the end of the coiled spring strike their fist. Have another student jerk the other coiled spring back and forth. Observe what happens.

Try the movements several times until you are confident in your observations.

a) Which of the two wave types arrives at the other end first (which one is faster)? Explain why you think this happens.

Part C: Refraction of Waves

In **Part A,** you investigated the speed of waves as they pass through one kind of material (water). In **Part B,** you saw that different kinds of waves have different speeds. Next, you will simulate what happens when a seismic wave crosses a boundary between two kinds of materials. It will help if you read all the steps below before you do the activity.

1. One person will be the "marker." That person holds the pieces of chalk. The marker should draw two lines:

• A long, straight line in white chalk across the middle of the area. The white line represents a boundary between two layers in the Earth.

• A long, straight line in red chalk at a 20° angle to the white chalk line. The red line represents the front of a seismic wave that is moving through the Earth.

A stretched spring can move unpredictably when released. Spread out so that you can work without hitting anyone. Do not release the coiled spring while it is stretched. Walk together until the spring is not stretched and then have one person take both ends to put it away.

Materials Needed

For this part of the investigation your group will need:

• large open floor area (paved parking lot or playground)

• piece of white chalk (or masking tape)

• piece of red chalk

• clear container

• long pencil

The marker should also draw an arrow about one meter long and perpendicular to the red chalk line. The result should look like the diagram shown.

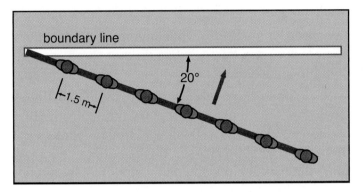

2. Form a line of students along the red line. Stand about 1.5 m apart from one another (arm's length apart).

3. When the marker gives the signal to start, everybody in the line moves forward, taking steps 30 cm long every second. Walk straight ahead as shown by the arrow in the diagram.

4. The instant you cross the white line, keep walking straight ahead, but start to take steps 1m long instead of small steps.

5. After the last person has reached the white chalk line, the marker will tell everybody to stop walking.

6. With the red chalk, the marker will make a long, straight chalk line just in front of everyone's toes. The new red line should connect to the white chalk line. The marker should also draw an arrow about three feet long and perpendicular to the new red line.

7. Stand back and look at the two red chalk lines. Compare the angle of the new red chalk line with that of the old red chalk line.

8. Obtain a copy of the diagram shown above.

   a) Label the region above the boundary "wave speed = 1 m/s" and the layer below the boundary "wave speed = 30 cm/s."

   b) The diagram already shows the old red chalk line. Add the new red line from your results to the diagram. Try to draw the angle accurately, but do not worry if it is not exact.

c) Does the second red chalk line form a different angle with the white chalk line, or the same angle?

d) What is the basic reason for the difference in the angles of the red chalk lines?

e) If the speed of a seismic wave increased after it crossed a boundary in the Earth, what do you think would happen to the wave?

9. With your group, devise a plan to investigate a different kind of change in wave speed. For example, in the original activity, the waves moved (roughly) 30 cm/s and then moved 1 m/s after they crossed the boundary. What would happen if the waves slowed down after crossing the boundary? What would happen if the waves moved four times as fast after crossing the boundary? How would this affect the path of the wave?

a) In your journal, record what you plan to investigate.

b) Predict how you think this would this change the angle of the second red line. Include the reason for your prediction.

c) Record your prediction on a second copy of the diagram. Label the diagram to indicate the relative speeds of waves before and after the boundary.

Have your plan checked by your teacher before you begin.

Clean up spills immediately.

Wash your hands after the activity.

10. Repeat the activity.

a) Record your observations in your journal by drawing the angle of the new red line.

b) How does the angle of the new red line compare with your prediction?

11. Fill a clear container almost full of water. Put the pencil halfway into the water, at an angle. Look at the pencil from above, but slightly to the side.

a) Draw a picture of what you observe.

b) Do you think that light waves travel at the same speed through water as they do through air, or at different speeds? Explain your answer. Relate this to what you discovered about the bending of waves in **Part C.**

12. Imagine a liquid in which light waves travel twice as fast as they do through water.

a) Draw a picture of what the pencil would look like if it were put into this liquid. Explain your drawing.

Part D: Refraction of Earthquake Waves in the Earth

1. Obtain a copy of a diagram similar to the one shown.

   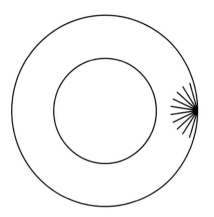

   The large circle represents the Earth. The small circle represents the edge of an inner part of the Earth where earthquake waves move faster than in the outer part. The black dot near the right-hand edge of the large circle represents a place in the Earth where an earthquake happens.

2. The earthquake sends seismic waves in all directions through the Earth. Notice the short lines coming from the dot. These lines show the start of some of the directions in which the waves start to travel (like the arrow that you drew in **Part C**). Your challenge is to show how these directions change when the wave goes through different layers of the Earth.

3. Use your straightedge and pencil to extend the lines through the Earth to the other side. Think about the following before you begin:

   • Some of the lines will go through the Earth without hitting the inner circle.

   • Some of the lines, however, will hit the inner circle. This is a boundary between zones with different wave speeds. Assume that the speed of the waves decreases as the waves cross this boundary. From **Part C** of the investigation, when you pretended you were part of a wave, you then learned what happens.

   • The lines that go into the inner circle also come out of the inner circle. When that happens, the waves will be crossing a boundary again. Think about what will happen to their direction of travel.

4. When you have completed all of the lines, look at where they are when they reach the other side of the Earth.

   a) Describe the pattern shown by the waves when they reach the other side of the Earth.

b) How does the pattern help you to understand how scientists in another part of the Earth can detect an earthquake?

c) How does this help you to understand why scientists in some places would not be able to detect some of the earthquake waves?

d) Scientists used this pattern to argue that the Earth has a core. They claimed that it showed that seismic waves pass through a zone with different wave speeds. Does this conclusion make sense? Explain why or why not.

As You Read...
Think about:

1. What is the difference between compressional (P) waves and shear (S) waves?

2. How do earthquakes produce seismic waves?

3. How would you describe wave refraction?

4. What is the focus of an earthquake?

5. How are earthquake waves detected on the surface of the Earth?

6. How do scientists know that the Earth's mantle is made of solid rock?

7. How do scientists know that the Earth has a core?

Digging Deeper

WHAT EARTHQUAKE WAVES REVEAL ABOUT THE INTERIOR OF THE EARTH

Waves

Shaking a material produces vibrations. Those vibrations move away in all directions in the form of a wave. You saw that clearly with the coiled spring. Speech is another good example. When you speak, you are making your vocal cords vibrate. That makes the air around them vibrate. The vibrations travel out from your mouth and through the air as sound waves. As the waves travel, they carry energy with them. The water waves you made in the pan were given their energy by the falling stone. The waves then delivered their energy to the sides of the pan.

The first kind of wave you made with the coiled spring is called a compressional wave. When you compressed (squeezed together) the end of the coiled spring by hitting it with your fist, it tried to expand again, and when it did, it compressed the material next to it. That part of the coil then expanded again, and so on. The wave of compression and expansion traveled along the coil as a wave.

The second kind of wave you made with the coiled spring is called a shear wave. When you moved the coiled spring sideways, it pulled the material next to it sideways as well. In turn, that material pulled the next part of the coiled spring sideways, and so on down the length of the coiled spring.

Earthquakes and Seismic Waves

During an earthquake, large masses of rock slide past each other, making powerful vibrations. That also happens in human-made explosions. The vibrations move away in all directions through the Earth in the form of waves, called seismic waves. The seismic waves travel all the way through the Earth. When they reach the Earth's surface again, they can be detected with special instruments called seismographs. There are hundreds of seismograph stations all around the Earth.

The Richter Scale is a way of measuring the magnitude of an earthquake using seismograph records. Each whole number increase on the Richter Scale is an increase of 10 times in the size of the vibrations recorded and an increase of 31 times the amount of energy released! To give you some idea of the different magnitudes, anything less than a magnitude 2.5 is too small to be felt by humans. A magnitude 4.5 or over is capable of causing damage near the earthquake, and anything over a magnitude 7 is considered a major earthquake that is potentially very destructive.

Seismic waves weaken as they move through the Earth. That is why the distance from the earthquake must also be considered when calculating the Richter magnitude. There are two reasons that the seismic waves weaken. They spread their energy over a larger and larger area, just like the ripples in the pan of water. Also, they lose energy because they create some friction as they move through the Earth.

Wave Refraction

You saw in **Part C** of the investigation how a wave (the line of students) changes its direction when it suddenly passes from a material with low wave speed ("short steps") to a material with high wave speed ("long steps"). The change in direction is called refraction. Refraction also happens where the wave speed changes gradually rather than suddenly. Suppose you were in a marching band, and the leader yells, "Members on the right take giant steps, members on the left take small steps." You can imagine what would happen. The whole line would gradually curve more and more to the left. The same kind of thing happens with seismic waves in the Earth. The speed of seismic waves generally increases downward in the mantle, so the path of a wave curves upward as the wave passes through the mantle (see the diagram).

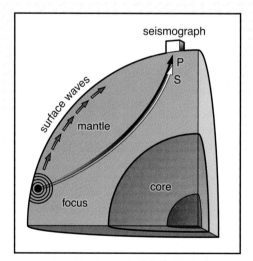

The reason why the speed of seismic waves increases downward in the mantle is complicated, but scientists are able to measure the seismic-wave speed of rocks in the laboratory using special equipment. Using this equipment they can determine how differences in temperature, pressure, and the type of rock affect the speed of seismic waves.

The Interior of the Earth

The main way that scientists know about the interior of the Earth is by studying how seismic waves pass through it. In **Part D** of the investigation, you showed something important about the interior of the Earth. Long ago, scientists noticed that there is a zone where seismic waves from a faraway earthquake do not appear again at the surface. This zone is in the form of a large ring on the Earth's surface, as shown in the diagram. This ring is called

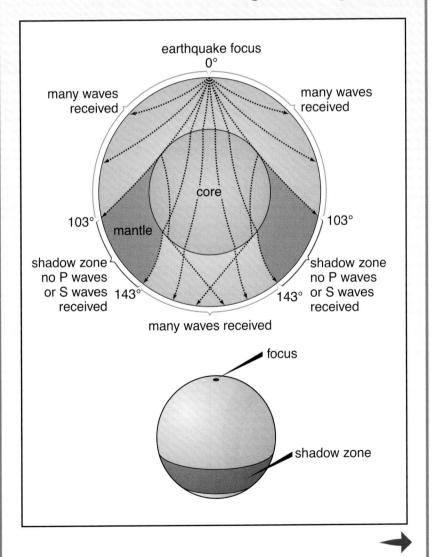

the "shadow zone." This shows that there is a place deep inside of the Earth where there is an abrupt slowing of seismic-wave speeds. How can this be if the seismic-wave speed of the mantle increases with depth? The answer is that there must be an inner shell of the Earth (called the core) that is made of a material that is very different from the mantle.

The core almost certainly consists mostly of iron. You probably know, from using a compass, that the Earth has a strong magnetic field. The only way the Earth can have a magnetic field is for the core to be made of iron. The outer part of the Earth, above the core, is called the mantle. It consists of mostly solid rock. Remember from **Part B** of the investigation that two kinds of seismic waves can go through the Earth: compressional (P) waves, and shear (S) waves. It's known that P waves can pass through solids, liquids, and gases, but S waves can go only through solids. Both P waves and S waves go through the mantle, so it must be solid. On the other hand, only P waves go through the core, so its iron must be melted rather than solid. There is even an inner core within the outer core. The inner core seems to be solid rather than liquid. Scientists discovered the inner core by some very careful detective work, long after the core itself had been discovered. The outermost layer of the Earth, above the mantle, is called the crust. The crust is very thin, not more than about 50 km thick. You will learn more about the Earth's crust in a later activity. The diagram shows the Earth's core, mantle, and crust.

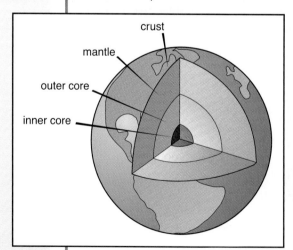

crust

mantle

outer core

inner core

Review and Reflect

Review

1. The direction of wave motion and the direction that a wave travels or propagates are not necessarily the same thing. How were the two types of waves you made in **Part B** of the investigation different from one another?

2. Why do seismic waves follow a curved path through the Earth?

3. How do scientists know that the Earth's core is made of a different material than that of the mantle?

Reflect

4. Think about the **Key Question:** "What is the interior of the Earth like?" Has your answer to this question changed from the beginning of the investigation? Explain.

5. Give an example of how you used a model in this investigation.

6. What have you learned about how scientists investigate the Earth?

Thinking about the Earth System

7. On your *Earth System Connection* sheet, summarize what you have learned about the geosphere.

8. Suppose an earthquake occurred below the ocean floor. How might earthquakes affect the hydrosphere?

Thinking about Scientific Inquiry

9. How did you revise your ideas on the basis of evidence?

10. Why did you repeat the experiment (conduct multiple trials) in **Part A** of the investigation?

Investigation 3:

Forces that Cause Earth Movements

Materials Needed

For this investigation, each group will need:

- candle
- small heat-resistant container
- corn syrup
- two pieces of thin cardboard, I cm square
- two small bricks
- lighter or matches
- hot plate
- oatmeal
- food coloring
- sawdust

Key Question

Before you begin, first think about this key question.

Does the rock of the Earth's mantle move?

In the previous investigation you learned that the outer part of the Earth, above the core, is called the mantle. It consists mostly of solid rock. Is it possible that this rock moves?

Share your thinking with others in your class. Keep a record of the discussion in your journal.

Investigate

1. Set up the experiment as shown on the opposite page. Place a small heat-resistant container where it can receive heat from a candle.

   Pour one centimeter of cold corn syrup into the container.

Place two pieces of cardboard so they touch, side by side, on top of the syrup in the center of the container.

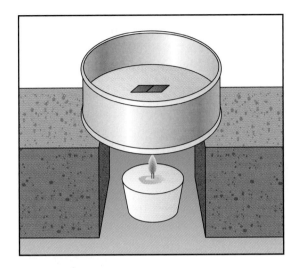

Inquiry

Making Diagrams

Sometimes the best way to show the results of a scientific investigation is by drawing a diagram. Complicated concepts can often be illustrated more easily than they can be explained in words. The diagram should be labeled and described in a sentence or two.

2. Before you light the candle, predict what you think will happen to the cardboard as the corn syrup heats up.

   a) Record your prediction, and also the reason(s) for your prediction.

3. When you have had your equipment CHECKED FOR SAFETY, light the candle and slide it under the center of the container.

   a) While waiting for the corn syrup to heat, draw a side view of the container alongside your prediction and reason(s).

4. Watch carefully as the corn syrup heats up.

   a) Record your observations and interpretations in your journal.

   b) On your "side-view" drawing of the experimental setup, show any movement of the cardboard with solid arrows.

   c) Show the movement of the corn syrup with dashed arrows.

5. Next you will watch a demonstration.

   A clear, heat-proof beaker, two-thirds full with water is placed on a hot plate.

   When the water is simmering (not boiling), one cup of oatmeal will be poured into the beaker. One drop of food coloring will be added. Finally, some sawdust will be added.

Be careful with open flames. Tie back hair and push back or roll up loose clothing. Remove loose jewelry from near your hands. Wear goggles. Allow the syrup to cool completely before touching the heat-resistant container. Clean up spills immediately.

This is a demonstration only. Once the oatmeal is taken into the lab, it must be considered contaminated because it is used in a science activity. Do not consume the oatmeal.

a) Write a prediction about what you think will happen to oatmeal, food coloring and sawdust when they are added to the water. Give a reason for your prediction.

When the hot plate is turned on and the water begins to warm, carefully observe what happens when oatmeal, food coloring, and sawdust are added.

b) Describe what you observe. Draw a series of diagrams to record your observations.

6. Below is a simple cross-section diagram of a mid-ocean ridge, showing both what is above and below the Earth's surface.

Think about how the corn syrup model and the oatmeal model behaved, especially the cardboard and sawdust, as the liquid heats up.
Compare this to the diagram.

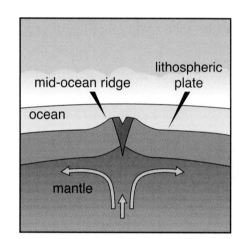

a) What evidence can you find from your models that might be similar to what you see in the diagram?

7. What parts or processes within the Earth do you think each of the following parts of your model represent?

a) the heat source;

b) the upward movement of water/syrup;

c) the horizontal movement of water/syrup;

d) the separation of the cardboard by syrup;

e) the horizontal movement of the cardboard/sawdust.

8. Hold a whole-class session where each group in turn posts and explains its diagrams to others. Look for similarities and differences and try to reach some overall agreements about the Atlantic Ocean's mid-ocean ridge.

Digging Deeper

FORCES THAT DRIVE OUR DYNAMIC PLANET

Convection Cells

Convection is a motion in a fluid that is caused by heating from below and cooling from above. The corn syrup and oatmeal in your investigation were convecting. When a liquid is heated, it expands slightly. That makes its density slightly less. The fluid with lower density then rises up, in the same way that a party balloon filled with helium rises up. With the balloon, you can even feel the upward tug on the string! When the heated liquid reaches cool surroundings, it shrinks again, making its density greater. It then sinks down toward where it was first heated. This circulation, which you observed in the corn syrup, and in the water/oatmeal mixture, is called a convection cell.

Convection in the Earth's Mantle

In **Investigation 2** you learned that the Earth's mantle extends down to the hot iron core. It is known that P waves can pass through solids, liquids, and gases, but S waves can go only through solids. Both P waves and S waves go through the mantle, so it must be solid. On the other hand, only P waves go through the core, so its iron must be melted rather than solid. Scientists are now sure that the mantle convects, in the form of gigantic convection cells. How can that be, if the mantle is solid rock?

As You Read...
Think about:
1. *What are the conditions that cause convection cells in a fluid?*
2. *How can the mantle convect if it is a solid?*
3. *What is the typical speed of mantle convection?*
4. *What is the reason for volcanic activity along mid-ocean ridges?*
5. *What kinds of forces drive sea-floor spreading?*

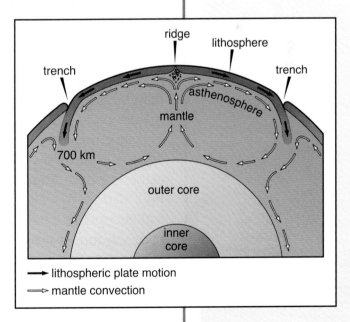

lithospheric plate motion
mantle convection

Many materials act like solids on short time scales but like liquids on much longer time scales. If you've ever played with stretchy polymer clay, you know all about that. Ordinary glass is also a good example. You know that it breaks easily. But if you were to take a long glass rod and hang it horizontally between two supports, it would gradually sag down in the middle. It would have flowed, to take on a new shape, even though it seems like a solid. The Earth's mantle behaves in just the same way. The speeds of flow in the mantle are only a few centimeters per year, but over millions of years of geologic time, that adds up to a lot of movement. Here's a comparison that will give you a good idea of how fast the convection cells in the mantle move: about as fast as your fingernails grow!

The Lithosphere and the Asthenosphere

The outermost part of the Earth, down to a depth of 100 to 200 km in most places, is cooler than the deeper part of the Earth. Because this outermost part of the Earth is relatively cool, it stays rigid, and it does not take part in the convection of the mantle. It is called the lithosphere ("rock sphere"). The lithosphere is made up of the crust and the uppermost part of the mantle. Below the lithosphere is a zone where the mantle rocks are just hot enough and under enough pressure that they will deform and change shape. This zone is right below the lithosphere and is called the asthenosphere. You can think of the lithosphere as a rigid slab that rides on top of the convecting asthenosphere. That is much like the cardboard that rode on top of the syrup in your model. The lithosphere consists of several pieces, each in a different part of the world. These pieces are called lithospheric plates.

Mid-Ocean Ridges

All the Earth's oceans have a continuous mountain range, called a mid-ocean ridge. These ridges are greater than 80,000 km long in total. The Earth's mid-ocean ridges are located above rising currents in mantle convection cells. You might think that the ridges are formed by the upward push of the rising mantle material, but that's not the reason. The ridges stand high because they are heated by the hot rising material. Like most materials, rocks expand when they are heated.

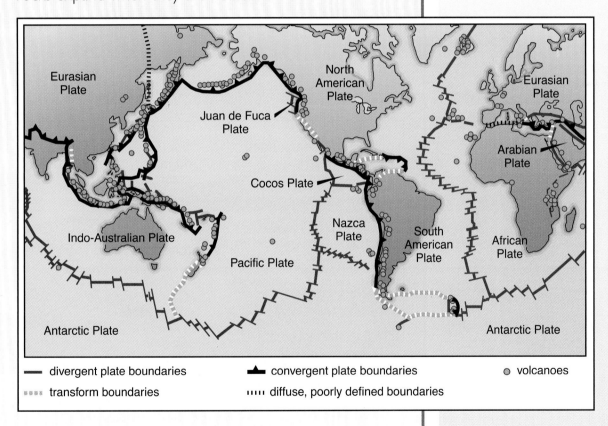

- ▬▬▬ divergent plate boundaries
- ••••• transform boundaries
- ◣▬◣ convergent plate boundaries
- ıııı diffuse, poorly defined boundaries
- ◎ volcanoes

As the hot mantle rock rises up toward the mid-ocean ridge, some of it melts, to form molten rock called magma. The magma is less dense than the surrounding rocks, so it rises up to form volcanoes along the ridge. The reason for the melting is not obvious. As the rock →

rises, it stays at about the same temperature, but the pressure on it decreases, because there is less weight of rock above it. It's known, from laboratory experiments, that the melting temperature of most rocks decreases as the pressure decreases. That's why some of the rising rock forms magma.

When the magma reaches the surface of the ridge, it solidifies to form a rock called basalt. That's how new crust is formed in the oceans. As soon as the new crust is formed, it moves away from the crest of the ridge. The movement is partly from the force of the moving mantle below. It is also partly because of the downhill slope of the ridge away from the crest. The movement of new oceanic crust in both directions away from the crest of a mid-ocean ridge is called sea-floor spreading.

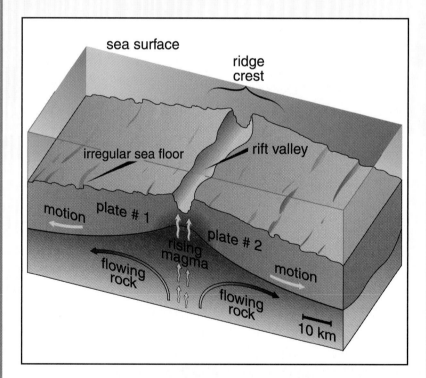

Review and Reflect

Review

1. Think back on the **Key Question:** "Does the rock of the Earth's mantle move?" Answer this question again, based on what you learned in this investigation.

2. Why is the mid-ocean ridge made of volcanic rock?

3. Is the rock that makes up the mid-ocean ridge young or old? Explain your answer.

Reflect

4. Give at least one example of where a convection cell could be formed. Use an example different from any that are presented in this investigation. Describe why the convection occurs.

5. Do you think that a convection cell would be formed in a fluid that is heated at the surface rather than at the bottom? Explain your answer.

Thinking about the Earth System

6. What connections did you discover between convection in the mantle (geosphere) and the oceans (hydrosphere)?

7. How does convection in the Earth's mantle help to shape the geosphere?

8. Describe the flow of energy in the geosphere. Think about the movement of heat energy during mantle convection.

Thinking about Scientific Inquiry

9. a) What hypothesis did you form in this investigation?

   b) Was your hypothesis proven right or wrong by your investigation?

   c) If your hypothesis was wrong, are the results of the investigation still valid? Explain.

10. Explain why a diagram was a good way to show your observations in this investigation.

Investigation 4:

The Movement of the Earth's Lithospheric Plates

Key Question
Before you begin, first think about this key question.

What happens where lithospheric plates meet?

To think about what might happen where plates meet, do these simple demonstrations. Place your hands together palms down, in front of you with your fingers pointing forward and the sides of your thumbs touching. What do you think happens when plates move toward one another? (Push your hands together.) What do you think happens when plates move away from each other? (Move your hands apart.) What might happen when plates slide past one another? (Slide your hands past one another.)

Share your thinking with others in your class. Keep a record of the discussion in your journal.

Materials Needed

For this investigation your group will need:

- scissors
- thick corrugated cardboard
- thin cardboard like a cereal box
- duct tape
- foaming shaving cream
- metric ruler

Investigate

Part A: Modeling Plate Convergence

1. In your group, discuss what you expect would happen when two plates move toward each other. On the next page are some questions to help your discussion.

Using what you already know about mountains, volcanoes, and earthquakes, work together to find the most reasonable answers to these questions. Record your answers in your journal.

a) How might mountains form there?

b) Might volcanoes develop where plates meet? If so, why?

c) Could there be earthquakes where plates collide? Why?

2. You are now going to model what happens when two plates move toward one another.

With scissors, cut out two pieces of corrugated cardboard. Make each piece about 8 cm wide and about 20 cm long.

Also cut out one piece of cereal-box cardboard, about 8 cm wide and about 15 cm long.

Assemble the pieces of cardboard as shown in the diagram.

When you are ready to run your model, you will be squirting some shaving cream onto the cereal-box cardboard to make a layer about 3 mm thick.

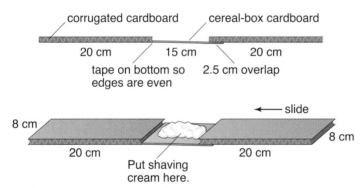

3. You have set up a model of what happens when two plates move toward each other. The process you are modeling is called plate convergence. (The motion of two things toward one another is called convergence.)

The two pieces of corrugated cardboard represent continental plates, and the cereal-box cardboard represents an oceanic plate. The shaving cream represents ocean-floor sediment.

a) Predict what you think will happen when you push the two pieces together until one of the pieces of corrugated cardboard has moved 5 cm beneath the other piece of corrugated cardboard. Also record the reason(s) for your prediction.

b) Draw a side-view diagram of your prediction. On this drawing, use arrows to show the direction of plate movements.

4. Make a data table to record your observations.

Use this example or design your own.

MEASUREMENTS OF CONVERGENT PLATE MOVEMENT			
Distance plates moved together	Shape (drawing)	Height (cm)	Width (cm)
2.5 cm			
5.0 cm			
7.5 cm			
10.0 cm			
12.5 cm			
15 cm			
17.5 cm			

5. When you are ready, apply the layer of shaving cream, as described in **Step 2**.

Now push the two pieces of cardboard together slowly, 2.5 cm at a time. Let the model run until one of the corrugated-cardboard continents has moved under the other corrugated-cardboard continent about 5 cm.

a) Describe what happens as the pieces of cardboard move toward one another.

b) In your notebook, make a sketch of what the model looks like after the two continents have collided and the one has moved underneath the other.

c) How did your results compare to your predictions?

6. Now look at this map, which shows the plate boundaries. The arrows show the direction the plates are moving.

Wash your hands after the activity.

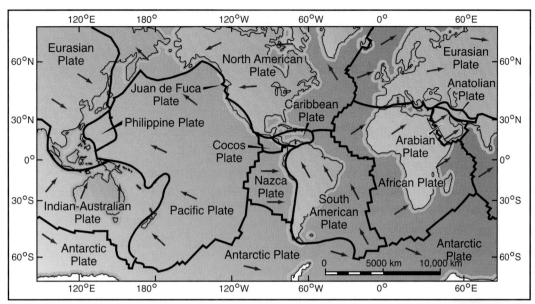

Look closely at those points where an oceanic plate is touching a continental plate. A good example is South America, where the Nazca Plate and the South American Plate are moving toward each other.

a) Where else can you find oceanic plates and continental plates moving toward each other?

b) At a convergent plate boundary, two plates are moving toward each other. How do you think your model might relate to convergent plates like these?

c) What kind of pattern would you expect to see in the locations of earthquakes under the continental plate of South America?

d) Note the places where you think earthquakes or volcanoes might occur.

7. Share your ideas with your group and the rest of the class.

Part B: Modeling Plate Boundaries

1. In **Part A** of this investigation you modeled a convergent plate boundary between continental crust and oceanic crust.

    Read the **Digging Deeper** section that describes other plate boundaries.

    Choose one type of plate boundary to model. You may wish to model a convergent plate boundary between continental and oceanic crust as in **Part A**, using different materials.

    a) Record in your journal the boundary you have decided to model. Write your investigation in the form of a question.

    b) Based on the information you have, predict what you think will happen at the boundary and explain why.

2. In your group discuss the best way to model the boundary you have selected. Consider the materials that are available to you.

    a) List the materials you plan to use. Explain why you chose the materials that you did.

    b) Outline the steps that are required to set up and run your model.

    c) Record all safety factors you need to consider.

3. With the approval of your teacher, demonstrate your model to the class.

Digging Deeper

The Earth's Lithosphere

In the previous investigation you learned that the rock of the Earth's mantle flows slowly in gigantic convection cells. The uppermost part of the mantle, however, does not take part in the convection. That's because its rock is not as hot, and it remains rigid while the rest of the mantle flows. Here's a similar example, on a much smaller scale. If you squeeze stretchy polymer clay at room temperature, it flows as you squeeze it in your hand. If you cool it in the refrigerator, it stays hard and rigid when you try to squeeze it. In **Investigation 3**, you found that this outermost rigid part of the Earth is called the lithosphere. The thickness of the lithosphere varies from place to place, but mostly it is a hundred or so kilometers. That's still fairly thin, compared to the thickness of the whole mantle, which is about 3000 km. The lithosphere has two parts: the Earth's crust, and the uppermost part of the mantle. The material below the lithosphere is called the asthenosphere ("weak sphere"). Unlike the lithosphere, the asthenosphere does take part in the convection of the mantle. The boundary between the lithosphere and the asthenosphere is really a temperature boundary. Below the boundary the rocks are hot enough to flow. Above the boundary they are cooler and rigid.

In the ocean basins the uppermost part of the lithosphere consists of the basalt that is formed by volcanoes along the mid-ocean ridges. This material is called the oceanic crust. It's only 4 to 8 km thick. The oceanic lithosphere gradually thickens as it moves away from the hot mid-ocean ridge. This is because the temperature boundary where the lithosphere turns into asthenosphere gets deeper in the Earth (see the diagram on the following page).

The Earth's continents form another part of the crust. The continental crust is very different from the oceanic crust.

➡️

As You Read...
Think about:
1. *What is the difference between crust and lithosphere?*
2. *What is the difference between oceanic crust and continental crust?*
3. *What is the difference between a subduction zone and a continent–continent collision zone?*
4. *Why do continents not go down subduction zones?*

It is thicker (mostly 30 to 50 km), its rock is less dense, and it is mostly very much older than the oceanic crust.

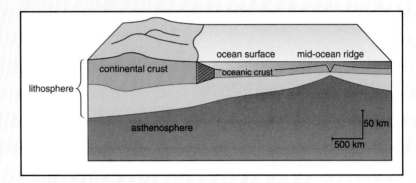

Lithospheric Plates

The lithosphere is not one continuous piece. Instead, it is made up of several very large pieces and a lot of smaller pieces. These pieces are called lithospheric plates (or just plates, for short). They fit together a bit like the pieces of a jigsaw puzzle. The line on the Earth's surface where two plates are in contact with each other is called a plate boundary.

Everywhere on Earth, the plates are in motion relative to one another. Along some boundaries, called divergent boundaries, plates are moving away from each other. Along other boundaries, called convergent boundaries, plates are moving toward one another.

The mid-ocean ridges, which you learned about in the last investigation, are divergent plate boundaries. As the plates move away from each other, new plate material is produced on either side of the ridge.

There is also a third kind of boundary, called a transform boundary, where the plates are moving neither towards one another nor away from one another. Instead, they are simply moving past one another like two cars in different lanes on the highway (only much slower!)

An example of a transform boundary is the San Andreas Fault in California. It appears as a line in the aerial photo to the right. There, the Pacific Plate is moving northwest relative to the North American Plate. Lithosphere is neither created nor destroyed at transform boundaries. For this reason, transform boundaries are sometimes called conservative.

Subduction

Scientists have determined that the surface area of the Earth is not changing over time. Therefore, there must be plate boundaries where plates are consumed, as well as plate boundaries where plates are created. Plate boundaries where one plate dives down underneath another are called subduction zones. The downgoing plate consists of oceanic lithosphere. The other plate, the one that stays at the surface, can also consist of oceanic lithosphere, or it can be a continent. The place where the downgoing plate bends downward is marked by a deep trench on the ocean floor. Earthquakes and volcanoes are very common along subduction zones. The downgoing plate is eventually absorbed into the mantle, but scientists are just beginning to understand how that happens.

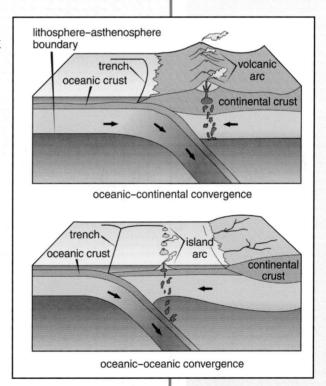

oceanic–continental convergence

oceanic–oceanic convergence

Continent–Continent Collision

Subduction zones can make an ocean basin close up completely. When that happens, two continents meet at the subduction zone. Continents are less dense than the mantle, so they do not go down the subduction zone. It is like pushing a wooden board down into the water: the board tries to float up to the surface again. When the two continents meet, one of the continents is pushed horizontally beneath the other continent. The movement eventually stops, when the force of friction between the continents becomes large enough.

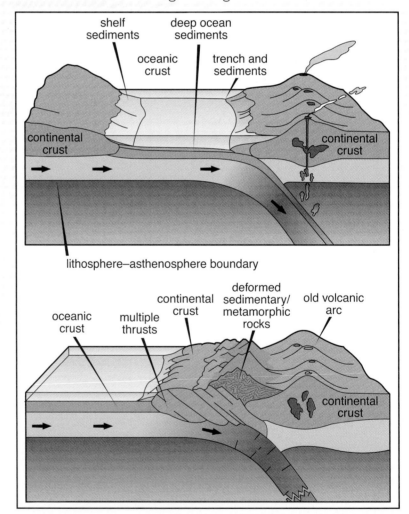

Continent–continent collision zones are places where continents are thickest. Where a continent is thicker, it extends deeper down in the mantle, and its surface stands higher above sea level. There is one place on the Earth today where continent–continent collision is happening: India is slowly being pushed under southern Asia. That collision has produced the Himalayas, which are the highest mountains on Earth, and the Tibetan Plateau, which is the highest large plateau on Earth.

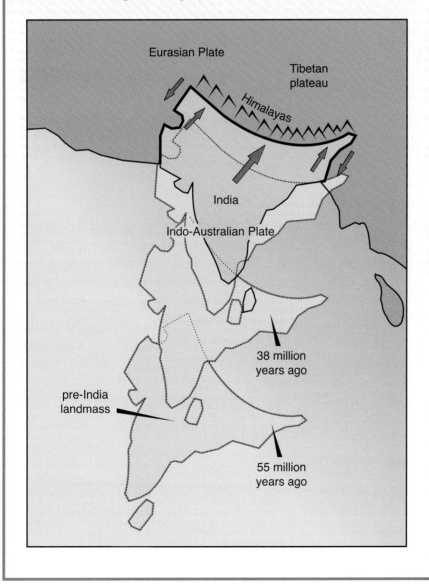

Review and Reflect

Review

1. What types of plate boundaries are found in or along the continental United States?

2. Why are folded mountain ranges found where plates converge? Why are folded mountains uncommon where plates move apart?

3. The Appalachian Mountains in the eastern United States are made up of folded rocks. Do you think that this suggests that this region was once the front edge of colliding plates, spreading plates, or sliding plates? Explain your reasoning.

Reflect

4. Why does the surface of a thicker continent stand higher above sea level than the surface of a thinner continent?

5. Would you expect volcanoes to form where plates slide past one another? Would you expect earthquakes? Explain your answers.

Thinking about the Earth System

6. Movement of the Earth's plates can create and destroy ocean basins. It can change the shape of oceans, the circulation of ocean water, and the depth of water in the ocean. Give an example of how plate tectonics might affect life on land or in the oceans (the biosphere).

7. When an oceanic plate is subducted beneath another plate, some water-rich sediment from the ocean crust descends into the mantle. There is also some water that is trapped within parts of the subducting plate that underlie the sediments. How does this process connect the hydrosphere and the geosphere?

Thinking about Scientific Inquiry

8. Why are models useful in scientific inquiry?

9. What are some problems associated with the use of models?

10. Describe how you used mathematics for science inquiry in this investigation.

Investigation 5:

Earthquakes, Volcanoes, and Mountains

Before you begin, first think about this key question.

How are earthquakes, volcanoes, and mountains related?

In **Investigation 2** you discovered how earthquakes helped shed light on what is inside the Earth. You also found that earthquakes and volcanoes occur along subduction zones. Is that the only place that you find earthquakes and volcanoes? What makes them happen? How are mountains related to earthquakes and volcanoes?

Share your thinking with others in your group and with your class. Keep a record of the discussion in your journal.

Materials Needed

For this investigation your group will need:

• colored pencils (3 different colors)

• copy of a world map

Investigate

1. Discuss the questions on the next page in your group. Be sure to explain your answers. Record the results of your discussion in your journal.

a) Can any mountain have a volcano erupt from it?

b) Do earthquakes and volcanoes always occur in the same area?

c) Do earthquakes and volcanoes always occur at the same time?

2. Look closely at *Table 1*. The data table shows recent earthquakes from around the world. The data was collected at regional seismograph stations.

Discuss the terms used in the table. Describe in your journal what the following terms mean and how they relate to the table.

a) Latitude   c) Depth

b) Longitude   d) Magnitude

Table I: Subset of Seismograph Station Results for One Week				
Latitude	Longitude	Depth (kilometers)	Magnitude (Richter Scale)	Occurrence Region
47°N	151°E	141	5.2	Kuril Islands
28°S	178°W	155	5.0	Kermadec Islands
30°N	52°E	33	4.2	Iran
36°N	140°E	69	4.7	Honshu, Japan
34°N	103°E	33	4.3	Gansu, China
40°S	177°E	27	4.8	New Zealand
0°N	36°E	10	4.6	Kenya, Africa
38°N	21°E	33	4.6	Ionian Sea
16°N	47°W	10	4.7	N. Mid-Atlantic Ridge
6°S	147°E	100	4.4	New Guinea
55°N	164°W	150	4.5	Unimak Island, Alaska
24°S	67°W	176	4.1	Argentina
13°N	91°W	33	4.2	Guatemala coast
4°N	76°W	171	5.6	Colombia
40°N	125°W	2	4.5	N. California coast
5°S	102°E	33	4.4	S. Sumatra, Indonesia
44°S	16°W	10	4.6	S. Mid-Atlantic Ridge
51°N	179°E	33	4.4	Aleutian Islands
15°S	71°W	150	4.2	Peru
49°N	128°W	10	4.7	Vancouver, Canada
35°N	103°E	33	4.3	Gansu, China

3. Use a copy of the world map shown.

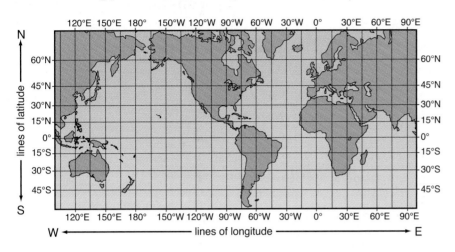

a) Plot the locations of recent earthquakes shown in
Table 1, using a colored dot for each earthquake.

b) Make a key at the bottom of the map to show what
the dot represents.

4. Use your copy of the map
with the earthquakes plotted.

a) Plot the locations of recent
volcanoes shown in
Table 2 on the next page.
Use a different color and
symbol than you did
when plotting
earthquakes.

b) Make sure your key
reflects this new
information.

Inquiry

Using Maps and Data Tables as Scientific Tools

Scientists collect and review data using tools. You may think of tools as only physical objects such as shovels and hand lenses, but forms in which information is gathered, stored, and presented are also tools for scientists. In this investigation you are using scientific tools: data tables and maps.

Table 2: Global Volcanic Activity Over One-Month Period			
Latitude	**Longitude**	**Location**	**Region**
1°S	29°E	Nyamuragira	Congo, Eastern Africa
38°N	15°E	Stromboli	Aeolian Islands, Italy
37°N	15°E	Etna	Sicily, Italy
15°S	71°W	Sabancaya	Peru
0°	78°W	Guagua Pichincha	Ecuador
12°N	87°W	San Cristobal	Nicaragua
0°	91°W	Cerro Azul	Galapagos, Ecuador
19°N	103°W	Colima	Western Mexico
19°N	155°W	Kilauea	Hawaii, USA
56°N	161°E	Shiveluch	Kamchatka, Russia
54°N	159°E	Karymsky	Kamchatka, Russia
43°N	144°E	Akan	Hokkaido, Japan
39°N	141°E	Iwate	Honshu, Japan
42°N	140°E	Komaga-take	Hokkaido, Japan
1°S	101°E	Kerinci	Sumatra, Indonesia
4°S	145°E	Manam	Papua, New Guinea
5°S	148°E	Langila	Papua, New Guinea
15°S	167°E	Aoba	Vanuatu
16°N	62°W	Soufriere Hills	Montserrat, West Indies
12°N	86°W	Masaya	Nicaragua
37°N	25°W	Sete Cidades	Azores

5. Use your map to answer the following questions:

   a) List several locations where an earthquake happened close to a volcanic eruption.

   b) List several locations where an earthquake happened far from the nearest volcanic eruption.

   c) Describe any pattern or patterns in the locations of earthquakes and volcanoes.

   d) How might additional data help you to find patterns, trends, and relationships between volcanoes and earthquakes?

6. The next map shows the major mountain chains of the world.

a) Add this information to your map. Use a different color and a symbol to represent the mountains.

b) Make sure your key reflects this new information.

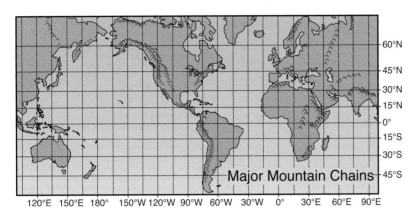

Major Mountain Chains

7. You now have a map showing the correlation between earthquakes, volcanoes, and major mountain chains in the world. Compare your map to the map of plate boundaries on P27. Discuss and record your ideas about the following. Share your observations and discuss your ideas with the rest of the class.

a) List three places where earthquakes, volcanoes, and mountains occur together.

b) List three volcanic mountain chains.

c) Explain the relationship you think there is among earthquakes, volcanoes, and mountains.

8. The *IES* web site lists several eathquakes and volcanoes. Each group should choose one volcano and one earthquake to investigate. You may wish to divide this task so that each group takes responsibility for a different information source. These might include:

• Earth science textbooks and reference books.

• Encyclopedias.

• CD-ROMs.

• The *IES* web site at www.agiweb.org/ies.

Work together to use what you've learned about plate tectonics to explain why these earthquakes and volcanoes occurred. Discuss your findings with the rest of the class.

a) Record the results of your discussions in your journal.

Inquiry

Correlations as Evidence

A correlation is a relationship or connection between two or more things. Correlations are often the first kind of evidence gathered when trying to explain an occurrence.

EARTHQUAKES, VOLCANOES, AND MOUNTAINS

The Nature of Earthquakes

As You Read...
Think about:

1. What is the cause of earthquakes?
2. How are faults and earthquakes related?
3. What is the cause of volcanoes?
4. How does gas content affect how a volcano erupts?
5. How is volcanism at a hot spot different from volcanism at a mid-ocean ridge. How are they similar?
6. Why are mountains found in regions where the lithosphere is thick?

Like all solids, rocks have strength. It takes a large force to break them. Plate movements cause large forces to build up within the lithosphere, and at certain times and places, the forces become greater than the strength of the rock. The rock then breaks, along a fracture surface that sometimes extend for tens of kilometers. This surface is called a fault. Faults are fractures in the Earth's surface along which there has been rupture and movement in the past. When the rocks break, the rocks on either side of the fracture plane slide past one another, until the forces are relieved. Strong vibrations are produced as the rock masses slide past one another. Those vibrations are felt as an earthquake. The vibrations travel away in all directions in the form of seismic waves, which you learned about earlier. Over time, the fracture "heals," making the strength of the rock greater again. For this reason, faults tend to slip, then stick, then slip again, and so on. As the rocks on either side of a fault slide past one another, they produce strong vibrations.

Earthquakes and Plate Movements

Many of the largest earthquakes occur along subduction zones, as the downgoing plate slides downward. The pattern of forces within the plate that cause the earthquake fracture is very complicated. The result of those forces, however, is the occurrence

of earthquakes that range from very shallow to as deep as hundreds of kilometers. Earthquakes are also very common in continent–continent collision zones, as one continent is pushed beneath another.

Along transform boundaries, the two plates slide parallel to one another along a surface called a transform fault. If the fault becomes locked for a long period of time and then suddenly slips, a major earthquake results. Along some transform boundaries, however, the fault slips continuously, causing nothing more than very minor earthquakes. The San Andreas Fault, in California, is an unusually long transform fault. It is locked in southern California, in the vicinity of Los Angeles. It is also locked in central California, in the vicinity of San Francisco. That is why the earthquake hazard is great in both of those cities.

The Nature of Volcanoes

A volcano is a place where molten rock, and also solid volcanic fragments and volcanic gases, are erupted at the Earth's surface. At certain times and places, rock deep in the Earth is melted, to form magma. The magma rises upward, because it is less dense than the surrounding rock. It does not always reach the surface before it crystallizes to rock again, but when it does, it forms a volcano.

Volcanoes vary a lot in how they erupt. The most important factor is the gas content of the magma. All magmas have gases dissolved in them, in the same way that soft drinks have carbon dioxide dissolved in them to make them fizzy. As the magma gets close to the surface, the pressure on the magma decreases. That causes some of the gas to bubble out of the magma. Magma with low gas content comes out of the volcano without violent explosions and then flows peacefully down the sides of the volcano. Magmas with high gas content cause powerful explosions when they approach the surface.

The explosions blow globs of magma and pieces of broken rock high into the atmosphere. Large explosive volcanic eruptions are the most serious hazard humankind faces, except for extremely rare impacts of large meteorites.

Volcanoes and Plate Movements

In **Investigation 3** you learned how volcanoes are formed along mid-ocean ridges. Those volcanoes are very numerous, but most of them are deep in the ocean. In some places, however, volcanic activity on a mid-ocean ridge is strong enough to build an island above sea level. Iceland is a good example of that.

Most large volcanoes occur along subduction zones. Certain scientists think that some volcanoes near subduction zones are caused when parts of the subducting ocean crust reach a certain depth and begin to melt. Many scientists, however, believe that the cause of most subduction zone volcanoes has to do with the water that is contained in the rocks of the ocean crust. At a certain depth down the subduction zone, the water is released from the rocks. The water rises up into the mantle above the subducted plate. Laboratory experiments have shown that adding water lowers the melting point of the mantle rocks. Whichever way the magma is generated, it rises up to feed volcanoes along the subduction zone.

There is another kind of volcano called a hot spot volcano. It is caused by a hot spot in the mantle that generates magma for long periods of time. Scientists think that hot spots don't move, and so a line of volcanoes forms as the plate moves over the hot spot. The orientation of that line and ages of the volcanoes that make it up reveal the direction and speed of plate movement. Unlike most other volcanoes, hot spot volcanoes can occur far from plate boundaries. The Hawaiian Islands and Yellowstone Park are good examples of hot spot volcanism.

The Association of Earthquakes and Volcanoes

Along subduction zones, major earthquakes and large volcanoes are both common. Most of the Pacific Ocean is rimmed with subduction zones. That's why earthquakes and volcanoes are so common in countries that border the Pacific. You might have heard that the Pacific Rim is called the "Ring of Fire." In continent–continent collision zones, as in southern Asia, earthquakes are common but volcanoes are not formed. Countries like China, India, Iran, and Turkey experience major earthquakes but not volcanoes.

Mountain Building

Most of the world's large mountain ranges are formed where two lithospheric plates collide. Where two plates converge at a subduction zone, enormous volumes of material are added to the region. Some of this material is sediment that is scraped off from the downgoing plate. Also, magma from deep in the subduction zone rises up to feed volcanoes on the plate that isn't subducting. Some of the magma stays below the surface to form deep igneous rocks. As the crust near the subduction zone grows in volume, its base becomes lower and its top becomes higher. It's very much like a block of wood floating in water: the thicker the block, the lower its base, and the higher its top. The rocks of the Earth's lithosphere float on the denser mantle below, so when the lithosphere becomes thicker, mountains are formed. The Andes, along the west coast of South America, have been formed in that way. The same thing happens when two continents collide. As one of the continents is shoved beneath the other, the lithosphere becomes thicker, so it rises up to form a mountain range. The Himalayas, in southern Asia, have been formed in that way.

Review and Reflect

Review

1. Review your answers to **Investigate, Step 1**. Answer the questions again, using what you learned in this investigation. Be sure to explain your answers.

   a) Can any mountain have a volcano erupt from it?

   b) Do earthquakes and volcanoes always occur in the same area?

   c) Do earthquakes and volcanoes always occur at the same time?

2. Where do most earthquakes occur in the United States? Why?

3. Where in the United States are most volcanoes found? Why?

Reflect

4. How does the gas content of a magma affect the shape of a volcano?

5. Dynamic means powerful or active. How has this investigation added to your understanding of Earth as a dynamic planet?

Thinking about the Earth System

6. How does the hydrosphere influence the nature of volcanic eruptions?

7. How do volcanic eruptions affect the atmosphere?

8. How are volcanoes, earthquakes, and mountains (geosphere) linked to the biosphere?

   Remember to write in any connections that you have made between volcanoes, earthquakes, mountains, and the Earth System on your *Earth System Connection* sheet.

Thinking about Scientific Inquiry

9. When did you form your hypotheses in this investigation?

10. What scientific tools did you use in this investigation?

Investigation 6:

Earth's Moving Continents

Key Question
Before you begin, first think about this key question.

Have the continents and oceans always been in the positions they are today?

In **Investigation 4** you learned that the Earth's lithospheric plates move relative to one another. Do they go anywhere? How far do they move? Have they always been moving? Have there always been the same number of plates?

Share your thinking with others in your class. Keep a record of the discussion in your journal.

Materials Needed

For this investigation your group will need:

• a copy of the world map cutout showing the continents and the continental shelf

• scissors

• construction paper

• glue

Investigate
1. Look at the map of the world on the following page, centered on the Atlantic Ocean. Look especially at the edges of the African and South American continents.

The dashed lines show the continental shelf, a shallow platform along the edge of all the continents.

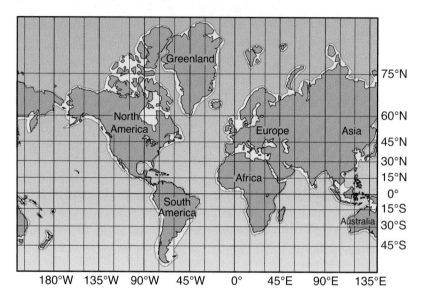

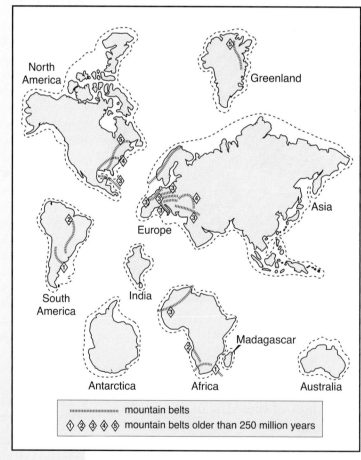

a) Describe the match between the East Coast of South America and the West Coast of Africa.

b) Describe the match between the bulge of West Africa and the outline of the East Coast of North America.

2. Examine the figure to the left that has all of the continents separated from one another so that they can be cut out with a pair of scissors.

Get a copy of this map. Use scissors to cut out the continents along the outer edges of the continental shelves, along the dashed lines.

3. Use the cutouts of the continents like pieces of a jigsaw puzzle.

    On a sheet of construction paper, try to arrange the continents as one large landmass.

    a) Describe the locations of any overlapping areas.

    b) How confident are you that the continents were linked together at some time in the past?

4. Several of the world's mountain ranges that appear on a continent today are similar in age and form to mountain ranges that today are on another continent. Some of these mountain ranges are shown in the continent cutouts. They are numbered according to those that have similarities with one another.

    a) Do the mountain ranges with common features line up with one another in your arrangement of the continents?

Inquiry

Using Evidence Collected by Others

In this investigation you are using evidence that you have been provided to formulate your ideas about how the continents may have fit together. Scientists must often rely on evidence gathered by others to develop their hypotheses.

b) Does this information give supporting evidence for your arrangement of the continents, or does it argue against your arrangement of the continents?

c) Make changes in your model in light of the evidence you have.

5. Several fossils are found on particular landmasses but not on others. Review the following evidence:

Cynognathus was a reptile that lived in what are now Brazil and Africa.

Lystrosaurus was found in Central Africa, India, and Antarctica.

Mesosaurus was found in the southern tip of South America and the southern tip of Africa.

Glossopteris was a fern found in Antarctica, Australia, India, southern Africa, and southern South America.

The map shows the locations of the fossils.

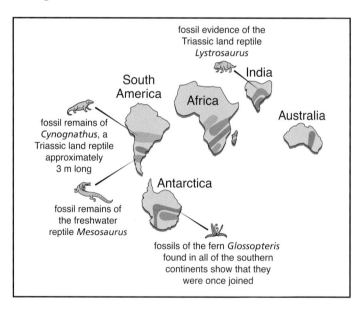

a) Add this information to the landmasses you are arranging on your construction paper.

b) Does this new information strengthen or weaken your model? Explain.

c) Make changes in your model in light of the new evidence you have.

d) What new information might change your model?

6. Evidence produced by glaciers from long ago provides geoscientists with ideas about the movement of continents. Imagine a bulldozer plowing a pile of soil, then stopping, backing up, and driving away. Like a bulldozer, a glacier plows a large pile of rock and sediment. When the glacier melts, the "plowed" deposit, called a terminal moraine, is left at the front of the glacier.

Examine the map below, which shows where evidence of ice sheets 300 million years old has been found in the Southern Hemisphere. The red line on the map connects all the places where terminal moraines from this time have been found on the continents, and the arrows show the direction of glacier movement.

Inquiry

Sharing Findings

An important part of a scientific experiment is sharing the results with others. Scientists do this whenever they think that they have discovered scientifically interesting information. In this investigation you are sharing your ideas with other groups.

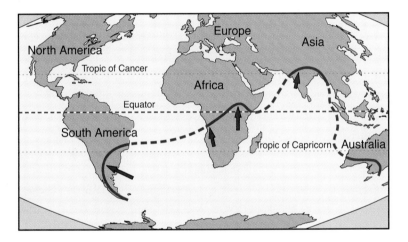

a) Add the information to your tracing-paper landmasses, including the extent of glacial ice and the direction of its movement.

b) How do you think this evidence might support the idea that these continents were once joined together?

c) Make changes in your model in light of the new evidence you have.

7. When you are satisfied with the model you have created, glue your landmasses onto the construction paper. Include a key or legend for all the information you have added.

a) What additional new information would you need in order to improve the model?

8. Share your model with the class. Discuss the evidence behind the model.

As You Read...

Think about:

1. *In your own words, explain the theory of continental drift.*
2. *What was Pangea?*
3. *How is a suture zone formed?*
4. *Why is the Pacific Ocean shrinking?*

SUPERCONTINENTS

Continental Drift

When you tried to assemble the continents like jigsaw-puzzle pieces, it probably seemed natural to you that Africa and South America fit together fairly well if you remove the ocean. This is one of the pieces of evidence that caused scientists 100 years ago to think that the two continents were once a single continent. The idea is that the single continent broke apart and the pieces drifted away from each other, to form the Atlantic Ocean. The fit of the continents is not the only evidence that supports the theory of continental drift. For example, you saw in your investigation that fossils of the same plants and animals are found in areas that are now separated by wide oceans and are in very different climatic zones.

Does it surprise you that it took a long time for most geoscientists to accept the theory of continental drift, even with the good evidence you worked with? The main reason was that no one could think of a way that the continents could plow along through the mantle beneath. When the theory of plate tectonics was developed in the 1960s, however, it gave a natural explanation for continental drift. Plate tectonic theory proposes that the outermost layer of the Earth, the lithosphere, behaves as a rigid layer. The lithosphere is broken into plates. These plates move relative to one another at their boundaries. Nowadays nearly all geoscientists believe in the reality of continental drift.

Supercontinents

In **Investigation 4** you learned that subduction can lead to the closing of an ocean and then continent–continent collision. When that happens, two separate continents

become one large continent. Geoscientists are now sure that about 250 million years ago all of the Earth's continents were gathered into a single very large "supercontinent." That happened by a long series of continent–continent collisions. That supercontinent has been named Pangea (*pan* means "all," and *gea* means "land"). The diagram below is a map that shows geoscientists' the best estimate of what Pangea looked like.

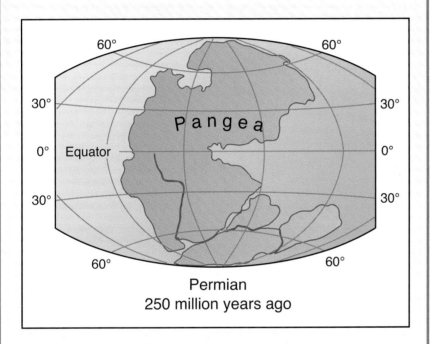

Permian
250 million years ago

You've already learned about some of the evidence for the existence of Pangea: For example, the fit of continents like Africa and South America, and similar fossils that are now far apart but must have been together in the past. Another important kind of evidence is the existence of former continent–continent collision zones, called suture zones, in the interiors of today's continents. These suture zones are the places where the earlier continents came together to form Pangea. The Appalachian Mountains, in eastern North America, are an example of these suture zones.

The Breakup of Pangea

About 200 million years ago the pattern of convection cells in the mantle changed, for reasons geoscientists are not yet sure about. This change caused Pangea to slowly split apart into several pieces. This process is called continental rifting. The pieces, which we know as today's continents, gradually drifted apart. That caused the Atlantic Ocean and the Indian Ocean, and the Antarctic Ocean to grow larger. The rifts didn't develop in exactly the same places where Pangea

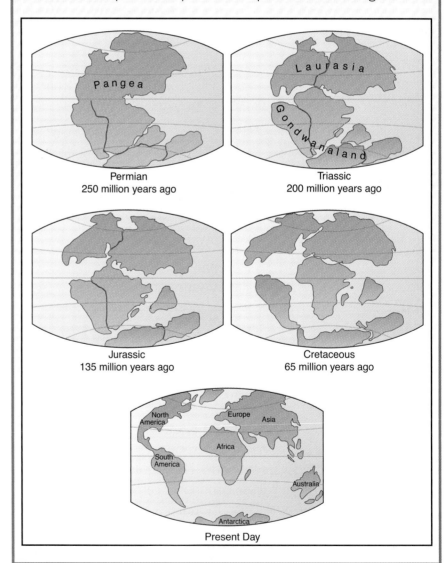

Permian
250 million years ago

Triassic
200 million years ago

Jurassic
135 million years ago

Cretaceous
65 million years ago

Present Day

was first sutured together. For example, the rift that formed the Atlantic Ocean was located to the east of the present Appalachian Mountains. That's why you sometimes hear that areas along the East Coast of the United States were once part of Africa! What does that really mean? They were on the **east** side of the ocean that vanished when northern Africa and North America were sutured together, but they were left on the **west** side of the new Atlantic Ocean that formed when Pangea was rifted apart.

There's evidence of earlier supercontinents, much farther back in geologic time. There seems to have been a supercontinent that formed and then rifted apart about 600 million years ago. Not nearly as much is known about the nature of that earlier supercontinent, because of the later movement of the continents while Pangea was being assembled.

At the time of Pangea, the Pacific Ocean was the world's only ocean! As the new oceans (the Atlantic, Indian, and Antarctic Oceans) have widened after Pangea was rifted apart, the Pacific Ocean has shrunk, although it's still the largest ocean. As you saw in **Investigation 4**, today's Pacific Ocean is surrounded by subduction zones. Those are the places where the floor of the Pacific Ocean is being consumed. What's going to happen in the geologic future? Will the Pacific continue to shrink, until all of today's continents collect there to form a new supercontinent? Or will the Pacific expand again, and the new oceans close up again to form a supercontinent where Pangea once existed? Most geoscientists think that the latter will happen.

Today scientists can actually measure how the plates are moving. They use orbiting satellites to directly measure the plates' movements as they happen. Only since the development of the satellite-based global positioning system (GPS) has this direct measurement of continental drift been possible.

Review and Reflect

Review

1. Look again at the **Key Question** for this investigation: "Have the continents and oceans always been in the positions they are today?" In your journal, write down what you have learned from your investigations that provides an answer.

2. What kinds of evidence can be used to identify the former existence of a supercontinent?

3. In your own words, explain the theory of continental drift.

Reflect

4. Why do you think it took so long for most geoscientists to accept the theory of continental drift?

5. What additional evidence would you like to have to prove that the Earth's surface has moved and is moving?

6. What additional questions would you like to be answered and explained?

Thinking about the Earth System

7. What connections has your investigation revealed about the dynamic planet and the geosphere?

8. What links to the biosphere did you make in this investigation?

9. How was the hydrosphere connected to the evidence that you used?

   Don't forget to write any connections you uncover on the *Earth System Connection* sheet.

Thinking about Scientific Inquiry

10. How did you use evidence to develop scientific ideas?

11. How did you communicate your findings to others in a way that could be seen and understood?

Investigation 7:

Natural Hazards and Our Dynamic Planet

Key Question

Before you begin this final investigation, first think about this key question.

What natural hazards do dynamic events cause?

Think about the movement of Earth's lithospheric plates. What hazards can they pose to humans? Think about all you have learned in the previous investigations. Share your thinking with others in your class. Keep a record of the discussion in your journal.

Materials Needed

For this investigation, each group may need:

• reference materials

• access to computer word processing and desktop publishing (if possible)

• range of general craft materials required to make a brochure

Investigate

1. Consider what might happen if an earthquake or volcanic eruption occurred in or close to a community. In your group, brainstorm the ideas that you have about the questions on the next page:

a) What would happen to local dams, reservoirs, or water supply stations?

b) What would happen to schools, homes, and government buildings?

c) What would happen to electrical power plants?

d) What would happen to local hospitals?

2. Share your ideas in a class discussion.

Do not be too concerned at this point whether or not your initial ideas are correct. Just ensure that all ideas are given. The goal of this investigation is to learn about natural hazards. Pay careful attention to what your classmates contribute to this discussion.

3. Here are just some of the hazards that can be caused by volcanoes and earthquakes.

Event	Effect	Examples
Volcanoes	Eruption with lava flow	• lava streams burn all in their path
	Eruption with ash fall	• aircraft endangered, roofs collapse
	Lahar (mud flow)	• Large, fast-moving river of mud
	Pyroclastic flow	• hot mobile flow of volcanic material
	Lateral blast	• explosive wave knocks down all in its path
	Volcano collapses	• land drops away— homes threatened
	Volcanic gases	• volcanic pollution
Earthquakes	Ground motion	• buildings and bridges collapse
	Fault displacement	• roads crack, rail tracks split
	Fires	• ruptures in gas lines cause building fires
	Landslides	• shaking causes rock to slide downhill
	Liquefaction	• ground becomes like quicksand
	Failures of dams	• flooding

4. Using the resources available in your class, school media center, public library, and home, select one of the terms to research. Find out:

- what the hazard is;
- how it forms and works;
- how it affects living and non-living things;
- what steps citizens can take to prepare for such hazards;
- what people can do to protect themselves once the hazards start;
- where people can get further information.

Here are some of the factors you could consider when assessing potential earthquake hazards for a particular area, or designing an investigation into earthquake hazards:

- closeness to active earthquake faults;
- seismic history of the region (how often earthquakes occur; time since last earthquake);
- building construction (type of building and foundation; architectural layout; materials used; quality of workmanship; extent to which earthquake resistance was considered by the designer);
- local conditions (type and condition of soil; slope of the land; fill material; geologic structure of the Earth beneath; annual rainfall).

Inquiry

Dividing Tasks

This investigation provides you with an opportunity to mirror the teamwork that often happens in scientific studies. Different scientists often take on responsibility for different parts of a study.

Presenting Information

Scientists are often asked to provide information to the public. In doing so, they need to consider both the message they want to communicate and the persons or groups that will be using the information. Once they are clear about the message and the audience, they can then decide on the best method of presenting the information. These are decisions you also will need to make in this investigation.

Here are some of the factors you could consider when assessing potential volcanic hazards for a particular area:

- volcanic history of the area (how often eruptions occur; time since last eruption?);
- population of the area around the volcano (are there towns and villages in high risk areas?);
- prevailing wind directions (where will most of the volcanic ash settle?);
- topography of the land (where are there valleys and ridges that will direct where the lava and hot gasses flow out of the volcano?).

5. It is important that you find out all you can about your chosen hazard.

   To do this, you may want to divide up the tasks, with each member of your group specializing in a particular aspect, using all information sources available.

   a) List the responsibilities of each group member in your journal.

6. When you are sure you have organized your research in a reasonable way, begin your investigation.

   When each person has conducted his or her research, share and discuss your findings in your group.

   You may think that you need to experiment further, to establish clearly how your hazard works. If necessary, design and model your hazard, using readily available materials.

7. Once you have assembled all the information you need, and completed any tests you think necessary, design a brochure.

   The job of the brochure is to provide information to residents of a community that is close to a potential earthquake or volcano hazard site. Be sure the brochure addresses all the points in **Step 4.**

   Discuss the best way to organize your information to cover these points.

   Here are a number of ideas to consider when designing your brochure:

   - the shape and size of the brochure;

- the color of the paper or card that can be used;
- computer programs that have templates for brochure design;
- artwork, diagrams, charts, or drawings that you can use or create;
- the various talents members of your group have.

Keep in mind that the brochure has size limits and that you may need to find creative ways to include all the information you think is essential.

Work together to produce the best brochure you can, keeping in mind the audience for which it is intended.

8. When all groups' brochures are complete, arrange a session where groups look at each brochure in turn.

Digging Deeper

EARTHQUAKE HAZARDS

Earthquakes happen when there is sudden movement of two rock masses along a fracture plane called a fault. Because of large-scale movements of the Earth's lithospheric plates, great forces can build up in rocks. Eventually, when the forces become greater than the strength of the rocks, long fractures form, and the rocks on either side of the fracture surface shift relative to one another. This motion is jerky and irregular, which causes strong vibrations. The vibrations travel away from the fault in the form of seismic waves. Above the fault, the vibrations cause up-and-down motions and side-to-side motions of the ground surface. Those motions are what you feel as an earthquake. Earthquakes vary greatly in their strength. Most earthquakes are so small that they can be detected only with special instruments. Some earthquakes, however, release an enormous amount of energy. They can cause ground motions so strong that people who are out in the open can't even stand up! ➡

As You Read...
Think about:
1. *What causes earthquakes?*
2. *What effects can earthquakes have on buildings?*
3. *What is the hazard associated with liquefaction?*
4. *What is the difference between an ash fall and an ash flow?*
5. *What warning signs make volcanic eruptions easier to predict than earthquakes?*

The most serious hazard associated with earthquakes is the collapse of buildings. If a large building is not carefully designed to withstand the shaking of an earthquake, the floors can collapse upon one another in a kind of "pancaking." If the foundation of a building is not adequate, the building can tip over sideways during a strong earthquake. Structural engineers continue to make careful studies on how to design buildings to withstand earthquakes. Cities in areas of the United States that are prone to earthquakes have building codes that builders are required to follow. Loss of life in earthquakes in the United States is much less than in some other countries where buildings are not designed to withstand large earthquakes.

Earthquakes can cause many other kinds of serious damage. In areas with steep land slopes, earthquakes can trigger large and fast-moving landslides. Water mains can be broken, making it difficult to fight fires, which are often caused by earthquakes. In areas where the soil is porous and saturated with water, the earthquake vibrations sometimes cause the material to settle into closer packing of the soil particles. When that happens, the soil can flow like a liquid. The process is called liquefaction. Liquefaction can cause buildings to sink into the ground!

Volcano Hazards

Lava flows from volcanoes are not especially hazardous to human life, because they flow slowly enough for people to get out of their way. Of course, they burn buildings that are in their path! Explosive volcanoes are far more dangerous. Such volcanoes throw enormous quantities of rock and mineral particles, called volcanic ash, high into the atmosphere. The ash settles back to the ground for distances of tens to hundreds of miles. The ash fall forms a blanket as thick as several meters on the ground surface. Even a thin blanket of ash can collapse roofs and kill crops. By far the worst hazard associated with explosive volcanoes, however, is an ash flow. Sometimes, volcanoes erupt ash in such large quantities that it collapses back downward over the volcano and rushes down the slopes of the volcano as a thick mixture of hot ash and volcanic gases. Ash flows move at express-train speeds of hundreds of meters per second. They can travel for tens or hundreds of miles, killing and burying everything in their path.

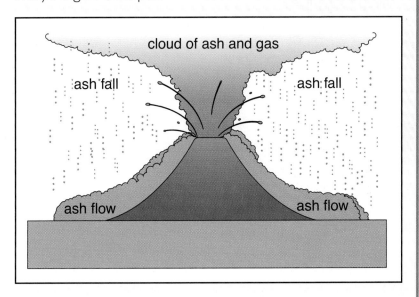

Predicting Earthquakes and Volcanoes

Many attempts have been made to develop ways of predicting earthquakes. So far, no reliable method has been developed. Geoscientists are not sure whether they will ever be successful in predicting earthquakes with a high degree of certainty. If a weather forecast of a major snowstorm is wrong, and it rains instead, that's not a big problem. If there is a forecast of a major earthquake, large numbers of people might be evacuated from a city. If the earthquake didn't happen, think of all the unnecessary economic disruption there would be.

Volcanic eruptions are easier to predict, because most volcanoes give warnings of an eruption. Gases begin to escape from around the volcano. Minor earthquakes in the area beneath the volcano become much more common. Often, the surface of the volcano swells upward enough to be measured by surveying methods. At that point, a major eruption is likely, although not certain. Evacuations based on such observations have saved many lives.

Review and Reflect

Review

1. Describe an example of an earthquake hazard.

2. Describe an example of a volcanic hazard.

3. How do ash falls and ash flows from volcanic eruptions pose hazards to humans?

Reflect

4. What are the advantages and disadvantages of attempting to predict earthquakes and volcanoes?

5. The movement along a fault that causes an earthquake can also damage gas lines and water lines. Why does this pose a problem after an earthquake?

6. Why do you think people live in regions that are prone to volcanic eruptions and earthquakes?

7. Why is the kind of information that you provided for your report useful to the public?

Thinking about the Earth System

8. How might a volcanic eruption affect the biosphere, hydrosphere, or atmosphere in a negative way?

9. How do volcanic eruptions benefit the biosphere, hydrosphere, or atmosphere?

Thinking about Scientific Inquiry

10. Why do scientists present their findings to others?

11. What are some of the advantages to doing scientific work as a team?

12. What inquiry processes did you use in this final investigation? Name at least three processes, where you used them, and how they helped you complete this assignment.

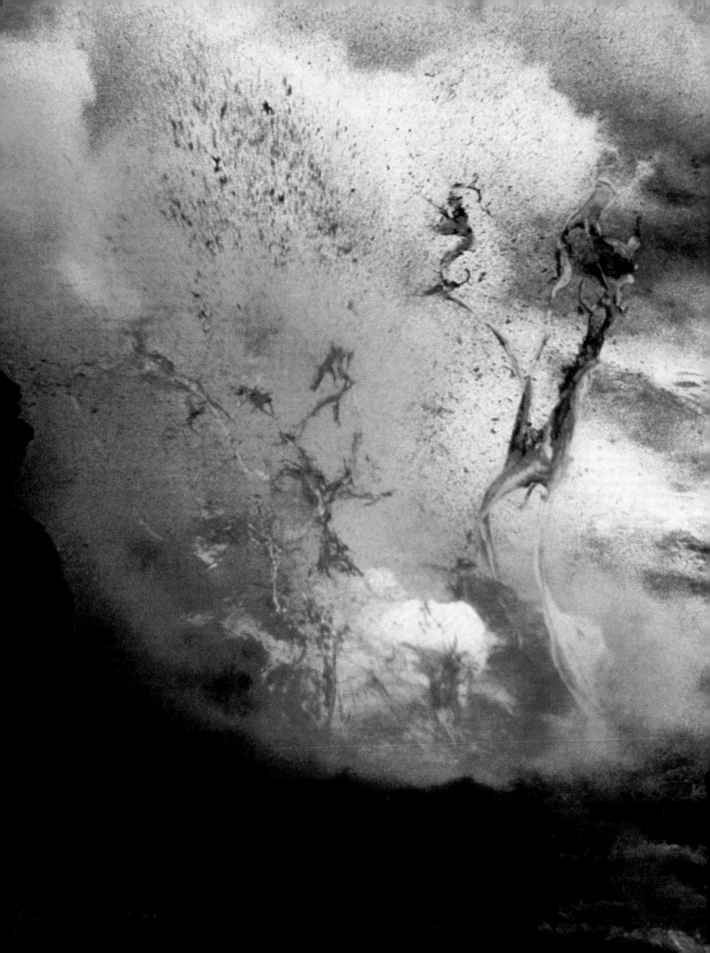

Reflecting

Back to the Beginning

You have been investigating Our Dynamic Planet in many ways. How have your ideas changed since the beginning of the investigation? Look at the following questions and write down your ideas in your journal:

- What are volcanoes and why do they occur where they do?
- What are earthquakes and what causes them?
- How are earthquakes and volcanoes related?
- How do mountains form?

How has your thinking about earthquakes, volcanoes, and mountains changed?

Thinking about the Earth System

At the end of each investigation, you thought about how your findings connected with the Earth system. Consider what you have learned about the Earth system. Refer to the *Earth System Connection* sheet that you have been building up throughout this module.

- What connections between Dynamic Planet and the Earth system have you been able to find?

Thinking about Scientific Inquiry

You have used inquiry processes throughout the module. Review the investigations you have done and the inquiry processes you have used.

- What scientific inquiry processes did you use?
- How did scientific inquiry processes help you learn about the Dynamic Planet?

A New Beginning!

Not so much an ending as a new beginning!

This investigation into *Our Dynamic Planet* is now completed. However, this is not the end of the story. You will see the importance of Earth's dynamic events where you live and everywhere you travel. Be alert for opportunities to observe the importance of *Our Dynamic Planet* and add to your understanding.

The Big Picture

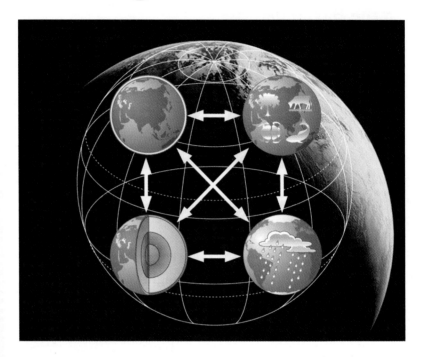

Key Concepts

Earth is a set of closely linked systems.

Earth's processes are powered by two sources: the Sun, and Earth's own inner heat.

The geology of Earth is dynamic, and has evolved over 4.6 billion years.

The geological evolution of Earth has left a record of its history that geoscientists interpret.

We depend upon Earth's resources—both mined and grown.

INVESTIGATING
ROCKS
AND LANDFORMS

Unit 2

What you will be investigating in this Unit:

Introducing Rocks and Landforms

Have you ever wondered how falling snow builds up to become a glacier?

Have you ever seen a river meandering over a fertile plain?

Have you ever wondered what different kinds of rocks there are?

Have you ever looked at the way seashores are shaped?

Why Are Rocks and Landforms Important?

You live on the topmost layer of the Earth, the crust, which is made of solid rock. Structures are constructed on this rocky crust. Sometimes rocks are even used to make these structures. Useful mineral resources are also obtained from rocks through mining.

Three-quarters of the Earth's crust is covered by liquid water. The rest is land. Land can be different in different places. Mountains, valleys, hills, plains, marshlands, cliffs, shorelines, and dry desert are just some of the many landforms you can see.

Understanding how rocks and landforms change over time will help you to appreciate how the past is a key to the future, and how to better manage your environment.

What Will You Investigate?

You will examine the rocks and landforms in your region. You will study how land is shaped and why it looks the way it does today.

Here are some of the things that you will investigate:

- different types of rock;
- how rocks are formed, and how they are worn away;
- different types of landforms created by the removal and the deposition of rock and soil;
- the effect of glaciers on landforms.

You will need to practice your problem-solving skills and be good observers and recorders as you work together with other members of your class.

In the last investigation you will have a chance to apply all that you have learned about rocks and landforms. You will design and make a landform information product for local people, or visitors to your area.

Investigation 1:

Different Types of Rock

Key Question

Before you begin, first think about this key question.

What kinds of rocks are there?

Think about what you already know about rocks. What are rocks made of? How are they formed? Are all rocks formed in the same way? Do you know the names of any rocks?

Share your thinking with others in your group and with your class.

Materials Needed

For this investigation your group will need:

- samples of rocks
- hand lens
- index cards (one per student)

Investigate

1. You will be given a rock sample.

    Observe your rock sample very closely. You can use a hand lens to make your observations. Try to notice every detail about it. Use your senses of sight and touch to do so.

    a) Write down your name and all your observations on one side of an index card.

Inquiry

Recording Observations

Good observations are vital in scientific inquiry. It is important that all observations you make are clearly and accurately recorded, so that others can see, understand, and interpret the data. In this investigation others will rely on your observations to find the correct rock sample.

2. All the rock samples will be collected and placed in a long line.

   When everything is ready, go over and look at the line of rocks.

   Use your previous observations to find your rock. When you have found it, take it back to your work station.

3. In your group, discuss how easy or difficult it was to find your rock. Consider what you could add to your description to make it more accurate. Think about whether there is a better method of recording your description. Review your observations to see if you included features such as color, size and arrangement of crystals or grains, fractures or breaks in the rock, layering, or relative hardness.

   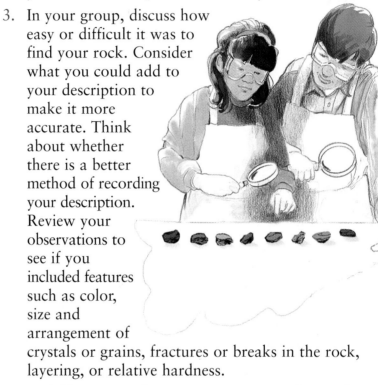

   a) Add any new descriptions to your index card.

4. The rocks will be collected again and placed in a long line.

   This time you will be given another person's index card.

   Use the information on the card to find the rock it describes.

   As a class, discuss the following questions, then answer each in your journal:

   a) How easy or difficult was it to find another person's rock using their index card? What does this tell you about making and recording observations?

   b) What can you now say about rocks based on the evidence you have collected?

5. The types of rock samples you have been observing are sedimentary rock.

   a) What kind of evidence do you have that suggests that these rocks should all be placed in one group?

6. You will now be given samples of a different rock type. These are called igneous rocks. Observe them closely. Look to see how they are different from, and similar to, the sedimentary rock samples.

   a) List the differences and similarities that you find.

7. Finally, you will be given samples of another different rock type. These are called metamorphic rocks. Observe them closely. Look to see how they are different from, and similar to, the sedimentary and igneous rock samples.

   a) List the differences and similarities that you find.

Wash your hands after the activity.

Digging Deeper

Types of Rocks
Sedimentary Rocks

Sediment is made up of loose pieces of minerals and rocks (in the form of gravel, sand, silt, and clay). Often, it contains the remains of living things as well. The pieces of minerals and rocks come from solid rock exposed at the Earth's surface. The solid rock is broken down very slowly by weathering. The loose pieces are then eroded and moved by running water, wind, waves, or ice, to be deposited somewhere else, sometimes thousands of miles away. Sediment can also form from material left behind by the evaporation of seawater, or from the remains of animals and plants in oceans, lakes, or swamps.

In certain conditions, and over a very long period of time, sediment becomes compacted and cemented into sedimentary rock. Usually, this happens as sediment is buried more and more deeply beneath new layers of sediment that are deposited later. Burial increases the ➡

As You Read...
Think about:
1. *What are the three types of rocks and how is each type of rock formed?*
2. *What is the difference between intrusive and extrusive igneous rock?*
3. *Describe the processes in the rock cycle.*

Sedimentary Rocks

a) conglomerate

b) sandstone

c) limestone

d) shale

Igneous Rocks

a) basalt

b) basalt seen through a microscope

c) granite

temperature in the sediment, and the pressure on it. As that happens, new minerals are deposited around the grains of sediment, cementing them into solid rock. There are two ways to tell if a rock sample is sedimentary. One is to see if it is in layers. The second is to see if it contains partially worn grains.

Igneous Rocks

Igneous rocks are made of minerals. The atoms that make up the minerals are arranged in a well-ordered structure. Rocks consist of grains or crystals of one or more minerals. Crystals or mineral grains are solids with geometric shapes and smooth, flat surfaces. Most rocks are mixtures of more than one kind of mineral. Just as apples, butter, flour, and sugar are the ingredients of apple pie, minerals like quartz, mica, and feldspar are the ingredients of an igneous (from the Latin word for fire) rock called granite.

Igneous rocks come from melted rock material, called magma. Magma is formed deep beneath the Earth's surface at certain times and places. As magma moves upward toward the surface, some of it is often forced out to the surface in the form of lava and ash, which in turn form a volcano.

There are two categories of igneous rocks. When magma becomes solid slowly under the Earth's surface, it produces intrusive igneous rock. The crystals that you can see in this type of rock are large. When magma solidifies rapidly on the Earth's surface, it produces extrusive igneous rock. The crystals of extrusive igneous rock are too small to see without a magnifying glass or microscope. Most igneous rocks are very hard and are made of interlocking crystals. Layering in igneous rocks is not as common as in sedimentary or metamorphic rocks.

Metamorphic Rocks

Sedimentary rocks and extrusive igneous rocks, which are formed at the Earth's surface, can become buried deep in the Earth's crust by various processes. A metamorphic rock is a rock that has become changed from some original rock by high temperature or pressure (usually both) as it is buried. During the metamorphic process (called metamorphism), the rock does not melt. Instead, new minerals grow in the rock at the expense of some of the original minerals, while the rock remains solid.

Sometimes metamorphism happens just because a body of very hot magma moves next to solid rock. That raises the temperature of the rock, and new minerals grow in it.

Eventually, the metamorphic rock might arrive back at the Earth's surface for you to see, if the Earth's crust is uplifted and then worn down by erosion to expose deep rocks. Metamorphic rocks are often layered, with different layers having different mineral composition. Often, minerals such as micas, that have shapes like plates or flaky layers, tend to be lined up all parallel.

The Rock Cycle

The rock cycle is the combination of all the processes that act to break down rocks, move sedimentary materials from place to place, and produce new rocks. It is expressed best in the form of a diagram like the one shown. The processes in the rock cycle operate very slowly, over times that range from tens of thousands of years to many millions of years, or even longer. Times that long are hard for humans to appreciate.

Metamorphic Rocks

a) marble   b) quartzite

c) marble seen   d) quartzite
through a   seen through
microscope   a microscope

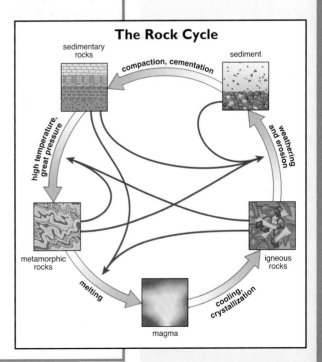

The Rock Cycle

sedimentary rocks — compaction, cementation — sediment

high temperature, great pressure

weathering and erosion

metamorphic rocks

melting

magma

cooling, crystallization

igneous rocks

Review and Reflect

Review

1. What are the three different types of rocks that you observed in this investigation?

2. How can you tell the different rock types apart?

3. Start with one of the three types of rocks. Describe a journey through the rock cycle through time. Note the processes that act to change the rock in each stage of its journey.

Reflect

4. What processes in the rock cycle can you observe in nature? Explain why.

5. What processes in the rock cycle must be inferred?

Thinking about the Earth System

6. To what part of the Earth system are rocks directly related?

7. Write any connection that you have discovered in this investigation to connect rocks to the geosphere, hydrosphere, atmosphere, and biosphere. You can record this information on your *Earth System Connection* sheet.

Thinking about Scientific Inquiry

8. How did you use a question as a starting point for inquiry?

9. What tools did you use to collect evidence in this investigation?

10. Why do you think the careful recording of observations is important?

Investigation 2:

Rocks and Landforms in Your Region

Key Question

Before you begin, first think about this key question.

What kinds of rocks are in your area?

In the last investigation you discovered that there are different kinds of rocks, each of which is formed in a different way. Think about the kinds of rocks you might find in the part of the Earth's crust on which you live (in your community, district, or state).

Share your thinking with others in your group and with your class.

Materials Needed

For this investigation your group will need:

- topographic map of your region
- geologic map of your region
- tracing paper
- examples of rocks from your region
- rock identification sheets or guidebook
- hand lens
- colored pencils, markers, or crayons

Investigate

1. On the following page is an example of a topographic map. Topography is the term used to describe the shape of the land surface (hills, valleys, and other landforms). To complete this investigation you will need to be able to interpret maps of this kind.

Look at the map and answer the following questions. (The **Digging Deeper** section will help you.)

a) What do the contour lines (curves) on the map connect?

b) How can you tell by the contour lines whether a slope is steep or gentle?

c) What do each of the following colors on the map represent: blue, green, black?

d) How can you determine the real-life distance between two locations shown on the map?

e) What on the map indicates what section of the United States this map represents?

Inquiry

Using Maps and Data Tables as Scientific Tools

Scientists collect and review data using tools. You may think of tools as only physical objects such as shovels and hand lenses. However, forms in which information is gathered, stored, and presented are also tools for scientists. In this investigation you are using scientific tools: topographic and geologic maps and a data table.

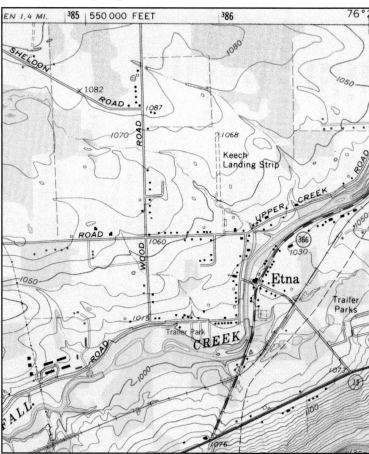

Topographic map of Etna, NY.

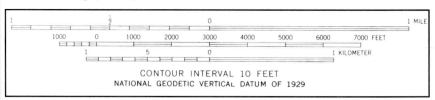

CONTOUR INTERVAL 10 FEET
NATIONAL GEODETIC VERTICAL DATUM OF 1929

2. Look at a topographic map of your region. Use what you learned in step 1 to interpret the map. Answer the following. Explain each answer:

   a) Where are the high elevations found in your region?

   b) Where are the low elevations found in your region?

   c) Where are the steepest slopes in your region?

   d) Where are the gentlest slopes in your region?

3. Geologists do field work in a region and describe and name each kind of rock they find. (Below is a data table showing major rock types.) They put this information on a geologic map.

Major Rock Types			
		Igneous Rocks	
Sediments and Sedimentary Rocks	Metamorphic Rocks	Intrusive Igneous (magma)	Extrusive Igneous (lava/ash)
breccia	anthracite coal	anorthosite	andesite
chert	gneiss	diabase	basalt
clay/claystone	greenstone	diorite	dacite
coal	hornfels	dunite	obsidian
diatomaceous earth	marble	gabbro	pumice
dolomite	phyllite	granite	rhyolite
gravel/conglomerate	quartzite	migmatite	scoria
limestone (crushed)	serpentinite	pegmatite	tuff (ash)
mudstone	schist	peridotite	
outwash	slate		
sand/sandstone			
shale			
silt/siltstone			
till			

Geologic maps show the boundaries, or contacts, between the rock bodies that are present in the area of the map. An example of a geologic map is shown below. Look at the legend to see the different kinds of rocks on the map. Compare the rocks on the legend to the names given in the data table.

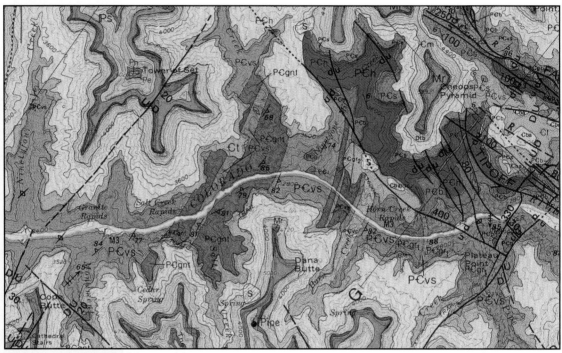

Geologic map of the Grand Canyon, Arizona.

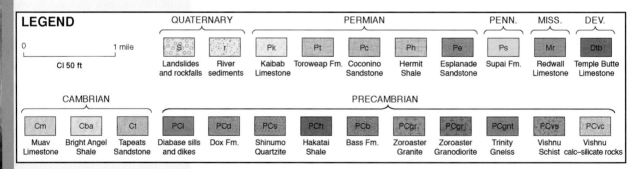

LEGEND	QUATERNARY		PERMIAN					PENN.	MISS.	DEV.
0 ———————— 1 mile CI 50 ft	S Landslides and rockfalls	r River sediments	Pk Kaibab Limestone	Pt Toroweap Fm.	Pc Coconino Sandstone	Ph Hermit Shale	Pe Esplanade Sandstone	Ps Supai Fm.	Mr Redwall Limestone	Dtb Temple Butte Limestone

CAMBRIAN			PRECAMBRIAN								
Cm Muav Limestone	Cba Bright Angel Shale	Ct Tapeats Sandstone	PCi Diabase sills and dikes	PCd Dox Fm.	PCs Shinumo Quartzite	PCh Hakatai Shale	PCb Bass Fm.	PCgr₁ Zoroaster Granite	PCgr₂ Zoroaster Granodiorite	PCgnt Trinity Gneiss	PCvs Vishnu Schist	PCvc Vishnu calc–silicate rocks

4. Look closely at a geologic map of your area. Compare the names of the rocks in your region to the data table. Consider the following:

   - Where are sediments and sedimentary rocks found in your region?

   - Where are igneous rocks found in your region?

   - Where are metamorphic rocks found in your region?

5. Place a piece of tracing paper over the map. Anchor the tracing paper so that it will not move but will be easy to remove when you are done.

   Make an overlay showing the major kinds of rocks in your region. One way to do this is to assign each of the rock types a separate color. On the tracing paper, shade in the different colors for each rock type. In places having mixtures of two kinds of rocks, use lines of two colors to show this.

   a) Keep a record of your overlay map.

6. Look at the examples of the rocks from your region. Identify each type of rock sample. You may find a rock identification guidebook helpful.

   a) Record the type of rock samples you have identified from your region.

7. Match any local rock samples you have identified with the traced geologic map of your region.

   Discuss the connections that you find between the kinds of rocks found in your region and the landforms that you found.

   a) In your journal record any patterns and relationships that you find.

8. Discuss ways in which you can turn this information into a display.

   a) Make a display to share your findings with others in your class.

9. Present your display and findings to the class.

   Listen carefully to the findings of other groups. Notice if other groups have different information or different ideas.

Wash your hands after the activity.

Inquiry

Representing Information

Communicating findings to other scientists is very important in scientific inquiry. In this investigation it is important for you to find good ways of showing what you learned to others in your class. Be sure your maps and displays are clearly labeled and well organized.

Also, think about how you can give constructive feedback to other groups.

a) In your journal record any new information you learned from other groups.

b) Record the types of constructive feedback, if any, that you provided to others in your class.

As You Read...

Think about:

1. What is topography?

2. What do the curves on a topographic map represent?

3. How can you use color to interpret a topographic map?

Digging Deeper

Topographic Maps

Topography is the shape of the physical features of the land surface. Scientists and engineers who study landforms, and anyone else who wants to know about the topography of the land surface, need a way of showing what the shape of the land is like. The best way to do this is with topographic maps. Topographic maps are maps that show the topography of the land surface in various areas.

Topographic maps exist for almost all of the United States. They show you the elevations of topographic features like hills and valleys. The hills and valleys are marked with a series of curves called contour lines. A contour line connects all the points on the land surface that are at the same elevation (height above sea level). The difference between each contour line is called the contour interval. The contour interval used on a

topographic map depends upon the region's relief (the difference between the lowest and highest points). The lower the relief, the smaller the contour interval, and vice versa.

Colors and symbols on topographic maps are used to show natural and human-made features such as rivers, mountains, orchards, forests, roads, schools, and industries. For example, blue is used to show water, green to show vegetated areas, and black squares are used to show buildings. Each topographic map shows latitudes and longitudes across the region by marks along the edges of the map. Every topographic map also has a key or legend that shows the map scale, the meaning of the symbols on the map, and the date the map was made.

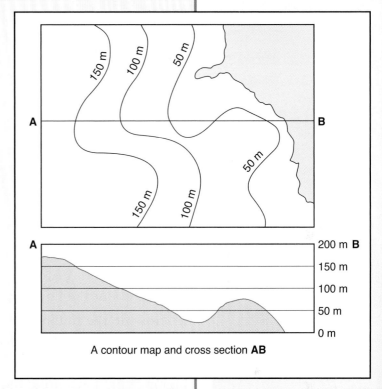

A contour map and cross section **AB**

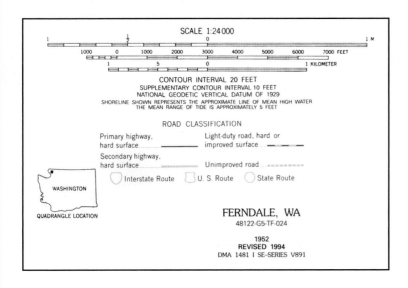

Review and Reflect

Review

1. What rock types are most common in your region?

2. How are the various kinds of rocks or sediment related to any major landforms in your region?

3. What information did you obtain from a topographic map that helped you with your investigation?

Reflect

4. What further questions about rocks in your region could you investigate?

5. What new information about the three different categories of rocks did you discover in this investigation?

Thinking about the Earth System

6. How do the findings from your investigation relate to Earth's crust, or the geosphere?

Thinking about Scientific Inquiry

7. Explain why maps and data tables are considered scientific tools.

8. How did you use evidence to develop your ideas in this investigation?

9. What other inquiry process(es) did you use in this investigation?

Investigation 3:

Rocks and Weathering

Key Question
Before you begin, first think about this key question.

How do different rock types weather?

In the last two investigations you learned that there are three major kinds of rocks. Although they are different, they are all related to each other as they pass through the rock cycle. Think about how rocks are eroded. What processes are responsible for breaking up and wearing away rocks? Do all rocks wear away at the same rate?

Share your thinking with others in your group and with your class.

Materials Needed

For this investigation the materials your group will need depends on which part of the investigation your group will be doing.

Investigate

Part A: Preparing for the Investigation

1. In this investigation you will be forming your own hypotheses (plural form of hypothesis) and designing ways to test them. In your group

Inquiry

Hypothesis

When you make a prediction and give your reasons for that prediction, you are forming a hypothesis. A hypothesis is a statement of the expected outcome of an experiment or observation, along with an explanation of why this will happen.

A hypothesis is never a guess. It is based on what the scientist already knows about something. A hypothesis is used to design an experiment or observation to find out more about a scientific idea or question. Guesses can be useful in science, but they are not hypotheses.

Dependent and Independent Variables

In all experiments, there are things that can change (vary). These are called variables. In a "fair test", scientists must decide which things will be varied in the experiment and which things must remain the same. In this investigation you will make measurements to determine whether or not rocks (or models of rocks) have changed. This is the dependent variable. The kinds of rocks you test or the different temperatures you use are called the independent variables. All other variables must be controlled; that is, nothing else should change.

discuss what a hypothesis means. You may wish to read the information about hypotheses in the **Inquiry** box. Then answer the following questions:

a) Why is a hypothesis not the same as a guess?

b) Why do you think a hypothesis is useful in setting up a fair test?

c) Do you think that a hypothesis has to be correct? Why or why not?

2. There are several different parts to this investigation:

Part A: Preparing for the Investigation

Part B: Chemical Weathering

Part C: Climate and Weathering

Part D: Water and Weathering

Part E: Biological Weathering

Part F: Sharing Your Results

All groups will do **Parts A** and **F.** Your group will be assigned to do one other part. Your teacher may decide that you should do some parts as a class.

Your group will be responsible for the following:

• forming a hypothesis to test the effects of weathering on rocks;

• designing a "fair" test (a test that is objective and systematic) using the materials available;

• deciding what measurements you will make, how you will make your measurements, and when you will make measurements;

• carrying out your test and recording the data along the way.

Once you have been assigned your part of the investigation, find out which other groups are working on the same part. Work together as you form your hypothesis and conduct your tests.

Part B: Chemical Weathering

1. You will be given samples of several different kinds of rocks.

   Examine the rocks closely and decide what kinds of observations to make using the materials you are provided. Be careful not to break the rocks. It is important that the rocks be roughly equal in size at the start of the experiment.

   a) Make a list of observations for each rock. Include similarities and differences among the rocks. Keep in mind that a very thorough description of the rocks will be important if you are to detect any changes as a result of your experiment.

2. On your own, think about the following questions:

   • Will these rocks weather in the same way when placed in vinegar (a mild acid)?

   • Why or why not?

   a) Write down your thinking in your journal.

3. Look at what you have written down as an answer to the first question in step 2. In your group, work together to predict what will happen to each rock sample if it is placed in vinegar and left there for 24 hours.

   Next, as a group, decide why you think this will happen.

   a) Record your group's hypothesis (your group's prediction and the reasons).

4. Decide what your independent and dependent variables will be and which variables you must control in your test of the hypothesis. For example, the vinegar will be one of the controls because it will be the same for every rock.

   a) Record your independent and dependent variables, and all the controlled variables in your journal.

Materials Needed

For this part of the investigation your group will need:

- 500 mL vinegar
- 2 or 3 small chips of the following rocks: marble, granite, rock salt, chalk, limestone
- 5 small plastic cups (100 mL)
- tweezers (to handle rock samples)
- balance scales
- magnifying glass
- paper towels

The vinegar used in this investigation should be treated as a chemical reagent. Vinegar is an irritant. Report any contact with eyes and rinse immediately with clean water. Clean up any spills immediately. Store any containers with rocks and vinegar loosely covered, carefully labeled, and in an area not easily accessible. Wash your hands after the activity.

Materials Needed

For this part of the investigation your group will need:

• 4 steel-wool pads

• 4 jars with lids

• water (for high rainfall)

• access to a refrigerator (for cold climate)

• sunny window or lamp (for warm climate)

• balance scales

• magnifying glass

• plaster of Paris

• 2 milk cartons

5. Complete your design of the experiment. Decide on the steps you will take from start to finish. Be sure to include any safety precautions you will take.

Also, provide a data table in which you can record your observations. You can use a table similar to the following or make up your own to suit your test design.

a) Include your procedure and data table in your journal.

Observations and Measurements						
Rock Sample	Before	Time 1	Time 2	Time 3	Time 4	After
1						
2						
3						
4						
5						

6. With the approval of your teacher, conduct your investigation.

You are going to measure changes over a 24-hour period, so make sure that you have labeled your samples and have stored them in a safe place.

a) Record all observations in your data table.

Part C: Climate and Weathering

1. On your own, think about the following questions:

• Does chemical weathering happen faster in a warm climate or a cool climate? Why?

• Does chemical weathering happen faster in a dry climate or a wet climate? Why?

Discuss your ideas with your group.

a) Write down your thinking in your journal.

2. Next you will use a steel-wool pad, which contains iron, to model a rock containing iron. Iron is found in many sedimentary, igneous, and metamorphic rocks. When rocks containing iron undergo chemical weathering, the iron combines with oxygen to form iron oxide compounds, which are usually orange colored. Ordinary rust is an example of such a compound.

Consider the materials you are provided for this investigation. Discuss how you could use these materials in an experiment to find out more about how climate may affect the weathering of rocks.

3. Working with your group, decide upon a question to test. The question should relate to the effect of climate on chemical weathering.

As a group, agree on a prediction of what will happen to the steel wool. Decide why you think this will happen.

a) Record your group's question and hypothesis (your prediction and the reasons).

What do you think causes the red color in this sandstone?

4. Decide what your independent and dependent variables will be and which variables you must control in your test of the hypothesis. For example, if you decide to test cold versus warm, then temperature will be your independent variable.

a) Record your independent and dependent variables, and all the controlled variables in your journal.

Handle steel wool with extreme care. Metal slivers can puncture skin. Keep hands that have handled steel wool away from your face. Steel wool is flammable. Wash your hands after the activity.

5. Examine the steel wool closely and decide what kinds of observations to make using the materials you are provided. Because your goal is to measure change over time, your first observations are important.

a) Make a data table to keep track of your observations. You can use a data table similar to the following, or you can make up your own to suit your test design. You may wish to add other categories.

Title		
Time	Situation 1 Observations	Situation 2 Observations

b) Record your initial observations.

6. Complete your design of the experiment. Decide on the steps you will take from start to finish. Be sure to include any safety precautions you will take.

a) Include your procedure in your journal.

7. With the approval of your teacher, conduct your investigation.

You are going to measure changes over a period of about a week, so make sure that you have labeled your samples, and have stored them in a safe place.

a) Record all your observations in your data table. You may also wish to record observations that you did not expect.

Part D: Water and Weathering

1. On your own, think about the following questions:

   • How can water break rocks into small pieces?

   • When water enters a crack in a rock, what happens if the water freezes?

   Discuss your ideas with your group.

   a) Write your thoughts in your journal.

2. In this investigation you will use plaster of Paris blocks to model rocks.

   Consider the materials you are provided for this investigation. Think about and discuss how you could use these materials in an experiment to find out more about how freezing water can weather a rock.

3. In your group, work together to agree on a prediction of what will happen to a plaster of Paris block if a water balloon placed inside freezes.

   Next, as a group, decide why you think this will happen.

   a) Record your group's hypothesis (your group's prediction and the reasons).

4. Decide what your independent and dependent variables will be and which variables you must control in your test of the hypothesis. For example, the amount of plaster of Paris you use should be the same for both milk cartons, and therefore is a controlled variable.

   a) Record your independent and dependent variables, and all the controlled variables in your journal.

Materials Needed

For this part of the investigation your group will need:

• plaster of Paris

• water

• stirring stick

• 2 bottom halves of 500 mL (pint-size) milk cartons

• paper towels

• small balloons

• access to a freezer

Use caution when mixing plaster. Dry powder can irritate eyes and nostrils. Wipe up any spills immediately. Wash your hands after the activity.

Materials Needed

For this part of the investigation your group will need:

• 2 plaster of Paris "rocks"

• soil

• water

• mustard seeds

5. Complete your design of the experiment. Decide on the steps you will take from start to finish. Be sure to include any safety precautions you will take.

a) Include your procedure in your journal.

6. With the approval of your teacher, conduct your investigation.

You are going to observe the changes the following day. Make sure that you have labeled your samples, so that others know what they are.

a) Record all your observations.

Part E: Biological Weathering

1. On your own, think about the following question:

• How can the roots of plants cause rocks to weather?

Discuss your ideas with your group.

a) Write down your thinking in your journal.

2. In this investigation you will use a plaster of Paris model of a rock. Some small crevices have been made in your model rock.

Consider the materials you are provided for this investigation. Think about and discuss how you could use these materials in an experiment to find out more about how plant roots can weather a rock.

3. In your group, work together to agree on a prediction of what will happen to a plaster of Paris rock if mustard seeds are allowed to sprout in the crevices.

Next, as a group, decide why you think this will happen.

a) Record your group's hypothesis (your group's prediction and the reasons).

4. Decide what your independent and dependent variables will be and which variables you must control in your test of the hypothesis. For example, the size and shape of the plaster of Paris rocks you use should be the same, and therefore they are controlled variables.

a) Record your independent and dependent variables, and all the controlled variables in your journal.

5. Complete your design of the experiment. Decide on the steps you will take from start to finish. Be sure to include any safety precautions you will take.

a) Include your procedure in your journal.

6. With the approval of your teacher, conduct your investigation.

You are going to observe the changes for several days. Make sure that you have labeled your samples, so that others know what they are.

a) Record all your observations.

Part F: Sharing Your Results

1. When you have finished your test, examine your data. As a group discuss and answer the following questions:

a) Does the evidence you have gathered support the hypothesis?

b) Which data in particular support your hypothesis?

c) Are there any data that are not clear? Why do you think this is so?

d) Has anything occurred during your test that raises new questions? If so, what new hypothesis can you form?

2. Put all your information together into a form that others can see and understand.

Prepare to share your findings with other groups.

Wash your hands after the activity.

Inquiry

Sharing Findings

An important part of a scientific experiment is sharing the results with others. Scientists do this whenever they think that they have discovered scientifically interesting and important information that other scientists might want to know about. In this investigation it is important that other groups learn about what you discovered.

As You Read...
Think about:
1. What is the difference between chemical and physical weathering?
2. What are some of the different types of physical weathering?
3. How are chemical conditions on the Earth's surface different from those inside the Earth?

Digging Deeper

Weathering

If you were to sit and watch a rock surface for a day, or a month, or even a year, it might seem to you that rocks do not change. Yet rocks exposed at the Earth's surface do not stay the way they are forever. Over tens to hundreds of years, many processes that act in the surface environment of the Earth cause solid rocks to be broken down into loose pieces of minerals and rocks. These processes, taken together, are called physical weathering.

Also, some of the minerals in rocks at the surface can be easily changed into other chemicals. Rocks form deep in the Earth, at much higher temperatures and pressures, and in a very different chemical environment. When these rocks are brought near the surface, the change in conditions makes some of their minerals chemically unstable. This chemical breakdown of some minerals when they are exposed at the Earth's surface is called chemical weathering. Physical weathering and chemical weathering act together, but they are easier to understand by considering them separately.

Physical Weathering

Physical weathering breaks rocks apart without changing their mineral composition. Here are some examples of processes that are important in physical weathering:

Ice Wedging

Water seeps into cracks in rocks near the surface. When the temperature drops below freezing, the water freezes. As it freezes, it expands. The expansion puts enormous pressures on the surrounding rocks. The frozen water acts like a wedge, making cracks wider. After repeated freezing and thawing, the rock breaks apart. This expansion and contraction is also a major cause of potholes in streets.

Plant Roots

Plants can take root in cracks in rock. As the plant grows, the root becomes larger. The pressure exerted by a confined growing root can be very great. These pressures make the cracks in the rocks larger. As the roots continue to grow, they can break rocks apart.

Chemical Weathering

As you may have found in your investigations, water is important to chemical weathering. Water dissolves the minerals in rock (just like when you put salt into water, but much more slowly). Water can also dissolve gases, like the gas that is dissolved in your soda pop. When gases in the atmosphere dissolve in water (for example, in rain), they form a weak acid. The acidic water makes some rocks dissolve even faster. Rocks made of the mineral calcite (like limestone) are the most easily dissolved by

acidic water. Without water, chemical reactions that cause rocks to weather happen much more slowly. You probably know that a piece of iron or steel stays the same for long times in dry air but rusts rapidly when it is in contact with water.

The Sphinx, found in Giza, Egypt, weathers very slowly. Can you explain why?

Biological Processes in Weathering

Lichens are among the first living things that establish themselves on bare rock. Lichens produce a diluted acidic solution that causes some minerals in rock to break down slowly.

Once rock is weathered into soil, microorganisms (very small plants and animals) begin to establish themselves there. They are present in the soil in amazingly large numbers. Larger animals like earthworms and rodents also live in the soil. As the plants and animals die, they add organic matter to the soil. As this organic matter decays, it is converted into carbon dioxide. The carbon dioxide dissolves in water making a weak acid called carbonic acid. This promotes further weathering of the mineral material of the soil.

The Earth System and Weathering

The formation of karst landforms by chemical weathering is an excellent example of the Earth systems in action. Animals exhale carbon dioxide into the atmosphere. Humans also burn fossil fuels to power cars, heat buildings, and run machinery. The burning of fossil fuels also releases carbon dioxide into the atmosphere. As organic matter decays in the soil, it also releases carbon dioxide. Some of this carbon dioxide is dissolved in surface waters, making the water more acidic and more capable of dissolving limestone. In areas with pure limestone bedrock and lots of rainfall, a kind of topography called karst topography often develops. This happens both on rock surfaces and in cracks and fractures in the limestone, as acidic groundwater percolates downward. This often leads to large underground networks of caverns. Now and then a cavern will collapse, forming a sinkhole. Sometimes whole blocks of homes will fall into a sinkhole. The atmosphere, the hydrosphere, the biosphere, and the geosphere all interact to produce karst topography.

Karst topography is clearly seen in Monroe County, Illinois.

Review and Reflect

Review

1. What are ways in which rocks can weather?

2. What effects can climate have on weathering?

3. Do all rocks weather the same way? Explain your answer.

Reflect

4. Why is weathering an important part of the Rock Cycle?

5. Explain two ways that weathering affects your life.

Thinking about the Earth System

6. How does the weathering of rocks affect landforms?

7. Explain how the hydrosphere is connected to the weathering of rocks.

8. How is the biosphere connected to the weathering of rocks?

9. Acid rain can have an effect similar to vinegar on rocks. How does this type of weathering relate to the atmosphere?

10. Write any connection that you have discovered in this investigation to connect rocks to the geosphere, hydrosphere, atmosphere, and biosphere. You can record this information on your *Earth System Connection* sheet.

Thinking about Scientific Inquiry

11. How did you form a testable hypothesis for your investigation?

12. Use an example to explain what a dependent variable, an independent variable, and a controlled variable are.

13. How did you use mathematics in your inquiry?

Investigation 4:

Rock Abrasion

Key Question

Before you begin, first think about this key question.

What happens when rocks collide in water?

In the previous investigation you modeled various forms of weathering of rock. Think about weathering of rocks by water. What happens when rocks collide with one another in water?

Share your ideas with others in your class.

Materials Needed

For this investigation your group will need:

- 1-L plastic bottle
- presoaked chips of three rock types (granite, sandstone, limestone or marble)
- nontoxic, permanent marker
- water
- balance
- sieve
- paper towels

Investigate

1. Discuss with your group how you think rocks will change when they rub together over a long time. Here are questions to get you started:

   - Where and when might rocks collide in the natural world?

   - How could you model some of these rock collisions?

   - When rocks collide and rub together, what parts are most likely to break off?

- How might the size of the rocks affect what happens when they collide?

- Do you think all rocks would react the same way to rubbing and collision? Why or why not?

a) Make a list of the ideas you generated.

2. Gather the rock chips and other materials available for your group.

First, study the equipment. Consider the following:

- How could you use these items to model rocks colliding into each other?

- How could you measure the amount of rock abrasion?

- How could you record your observations and results clearly?

Look at the rock chips.

- What do you observe about them?

- How are they the same? How are they different?

- How could you measure the rock chips?

- What do you expect will happen to the chips when you put them through a rock-abrasion test?

a) Record your ideas about these questions in your journal.

3. Work together in your group to design an experiment on rock abrasion.

You may wish to test parts of the model to see how well they work.

Share your ideas with the rest of the class. Listen carefully to their points.

a) Review your experimental design and record it in your journal.

Rock dust may be produced in this activity. Avoid exposure to eyes. Wipe up spills immediately.

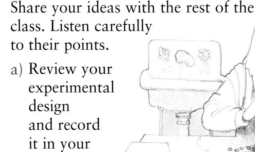

4. In your group, think about the question or questions you are investigating.

   Predict the most likely outcome of your experiment.

   a) Write down the investigation question(s) on which you all agree.

   b) Record your prediction and the reasons for your prediction.

5. With the approval of your teacher conduct your investigation.

   As you proceed, you may need to adjust or change parts of your plan. Make sure you present any changes to your teacher for approval.

   a) Write down any changes you make to your plan and the reasons for the changes.

   b) Record your observations.

   c) What patterns and relationships can you see in your data?

6. Discuss how you could change your model to get a more useful set of data. What do you think might happen if you changed the following variables:

   • the number of rock chips;

   • the volume of water;

   • the duration of the test;

   • the strength of the test?

   Pick one of the possible variables and make a change. Have different groups in the class change different variables.

   Conduct your investigation.

   a) What differences does this produce in your data?

   b) What additional information does this give you about rock abrasion?

7. Prepare your report.

   Share your report with other groups.

Inquiry

Adjustments and Changes

Scientists sometimes change their investigation designs, if the changes do not affect the overall validity of the test. However, they must document their changes and the reasons for them.

Wash your hands after the activity.

As You Read...
Think about:
1. *How does rock abrasion occur?*
2. *What are examples of rock abrasion in nature?*

Rock Abrasion

The word "abrasion" comes from the Latin *abradere*, meaning "to wear away." Rock abrasion occurs when rocks collide with one another or rub against one another. Collisions, if they are strong enough, can cause pieces of rock to break into two or more pieces, or cause small chips to be broken off a large piece. When two pieces of rock are rubbed together, the mineral grains in the rocks can be broken away from the rock surface.

Here are three important examples of abrasion in nature. In landslides, pieces of rock slide past one another as the mass moves downhill. At the base of a glacier, pieces of rock that are frozen into the ice are dragged along beneath the glacier. In fast-moving streams and rivers, pieces of rock that are being moved by the flow rub against one another and against other pieces resting on the river bed. Collisions between large pieces of rock are common in rockfalls on steep slopes, and also in very fast-moving streams. Sometimes during floods in mountain streams, the collisions of large rocks with one another and with the stream bed produce a sound as loud as thunder!

Polishing stones in a rock tumbler, often to make jewelry, is a popular hobby for some people. You can easily buy rock tumbling equipment from craft and hobby stores. Pebbles at the seashore provide the most obvious example of nature's rock tumbler. The force of the waves, as they break on the seashore, moves the pebbles back and forth. You can often hear the sound of the pebbles

colliding with one another. After a long time, the pebbles become smooth and well rounded. What happens to the material that is worn away? The product of the tumbling action is partly sand, which is added to the beach, and partly very fine mineral grains, which stay suspended in the water and drift away.

Review and Reflect

Review

1. Look again at the key question. How has the investigation helped you answer the question? On the basis of your investigation, how would you answer the question?

2. What evidence did you use to show that the rock chips have changed as a result of your modeling investigation?

3. What effect did changing the variables have?

Reflect

4. How was your model similar to what happens in nature? How was it different?

5. Where in your community might you be able to see the results of rock abrasion?

Thinking about the Earth System

6. How would a sudden increase in rainfall (atmosphere and hydrosphere) affect the rate of rock abrasion (geosphere)?

7. How does the abrasion of rock fragments in moving water affect the hydrosphere?

Thinking about Scientific Inquiry

8. Why is it important to control variables in an investigation?

9. Describe how you used two inquiry processes to design your investigation.

Investigation 5:

Erosional Landforms

Key Question

Before you begin, first think about this key question.

How can moving water create and change landforms?

In the last investigation you learned that rock surfaces wear away slowly by weathering. Think about ways that water can cause the wearing away of rocks. How does water in rivers and streams change the landforms? How do waves crashing on a shore result in changed landforms?

Share your thinking with others in your group and with your class.

Materials Needed

For this investigation all groups will need:

- stream table or similar container
- fine sand
- water reservoir
- water
- books or blocks of wood to elevate the stream table
- eraser
- paper towel
- container for collecting overflow
- small, thin block of wood
- index card cut to a 3 cm by 15 cm strip
- ruler or meter stick
- stopwatch or watch with second hand

Investigate

1. In this investigation different groups will be studying different forms of water erosion.

    The goal of your group will be to find out how your form of water erosion works. Then you will invent a way of demonstrating it to others.

Here are the questions you will be investigating:

Part A: Erosion by Rivers and Streams

Station A: How does a fast-moving stream erode the land?

Station B: How does a slow-moving stream erode the land?

Station C: How does erosion happen at river bends?

Station D: What erosion takes place where two rivers meet?

Part B: Erosion by Waves at Shorelines

Station E: How does coastal erosion form cliffs?

Station F: How does erosion happen in bays?

Station G: How does wave erosion affect islands?

Station H: How does wave erosion affect spits?

In your group, discuss what you already know about each question. Think about what you have seen and what you have learned.

a) Record your ideas in your journal.

2. Your teacher will provide you with a stream table, or something similar to it. One possible setup is shown to the right.

Obtain the equipment you will need.

Follow the procedures outlined for your station.

Inquiry
Modeling

To investigate your particular erosion process you will set up and use a model. Models are very useful scientific tools. Scientists use models to simulate real-world events and processes. They do this when it is difficult to study the real thing in a controlled way. It is important that you try to model what happens in the real world as accurately as possible.

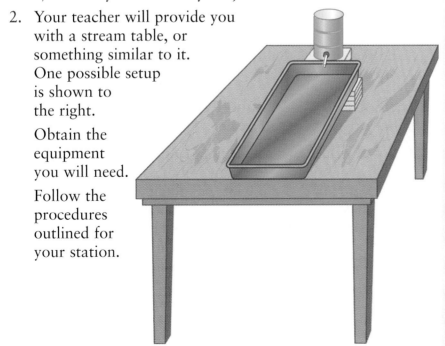

Part A: Erosion by Rivers and Streams
Stations A to D: Model Preparation

1. Place about 3 cm of fine sand in the stream table.

2. Wet the sand thoroughly and smooth out the surface until it is close to being a plane (flat).

3. Set up one end of the stream table in a way that will allow you to raise it from 1 through 10 cm. To do this, put one or two thin wooden blocks or books under one end. Be prepared to adjust the slope of the stream table to a value that will be suggested for your particular station. The slope of the stream table is the height of the high end of the stream table, divided by the horizontal distance along the stream table. See the diagram shown.

4. Set up the water reservoir so it will feed into the high end of the stream table. Be prepared to adjust the rate of flow of the water.

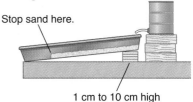

Stop sand here.

1 cm to 10 cm high

5. Follow the instructions and suggestions below for each group to run its test.

   a) In your journal, record the question you are investigating.

   b) Record the conditions of your experiment and the results you observe. Use both words and sketches.

Stations A to D: Running the Test
Station A: Fast-Moving Stream

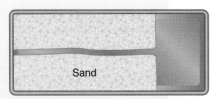

Sand

With your finger, carve a narrow, fairly straight stream through the sand, as shown in the diagram. Make the stream about 1 cm wide and about 1 cm deep. Set the slope of the stream table to be about 0.4. Run a small stream of water down the channel. If necessary, increase the rate of flow until you can see sand moving. Observe how erosion proceeds. If your reservoir is small, you can continue the test by adding more water to the reservoir. Describe how the sand is eroded and moved, and how the size and shape of the channel change with time.

Do not let fine sand get into eyes. Wipe up any spills immediately.

Station B: Slow-Moving Stream

With your finger, carve a wide, fairly straight stream through the sand, as shown in the diagram. Make the stream about 3 cm wide and about 1 cm deep. Set the slope of the stream table to be about 0.1. Run a small stream of water down the channel. If necessary, increase the rate of flow until you can see sand moving. Observe how erosion proceeds. If your reservoir is small, you can continue the test by adding more water to the reservoir. Describe how the sand is eroded and moved, and how the size and shape of the channel change with time.

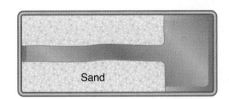

Station C: River Bends

With your finger, carve two sweeping river bends in the sand, as shown in the diagram. Make the stream about 2 cm wide and about 1 cm deep. Set the slope of the stream table to be about 0.1. Run a small stream of water down the channel. If necessary, increase the rate of flow until you can see sand moving. Observe how the bends change their size and shape as the water flow erodes, moves, and deposits sand. If your reservoir is small, you can continue the test by adding more water to the reservoir. Describe how the sand is moved by the flow, and how the size and shape of the bends change with time.

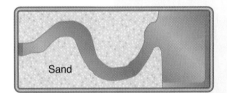

Station D: Where Two Rivers Meet

With your finger, carve two streams that meet to form one stream halfway down the stream table. See the diagram. The channels should be about 2 cm wide and about 1 cm deep. Set the slope of the stream table to be about 0.1. Run a small stream of water down each of the upstream channels. Try to make the flows in the two channels about equal. If necessary, increase the rate of flow until you can see sand moving. Observe how the flowing water erodes the sand and shapes the channel where the two channels meet. If your reservoir is small, you can continue the test by adding more water to the reservoir. Describe how the sand is moved by the flow, and how the geometry develops where the streams meet.

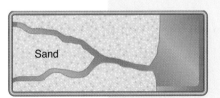

Wash your hands after the activity.

Do not let fine sand get into eyes. Wipe up spills immediately.

Part B: Erosion by Waves at Shorelines
Stations E to H: Model Preparation

1. Place the stream table on a flat surface.

Make a shoreline "bluff" by placing several handfuls of wet sand at one end of the stream table. Flatten the top of the material.

Place boards against the bluff to protect it as you slowly pour water into the container to a depth of 2 to 3 cm.

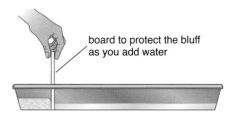

board to protect the bluff as you add water

Use the board at the other end of the stream table to make small waves that move toward the bluff. The waves should be just large enough to move your bluff material a little bit. Start small. Practice your wave-making technique.

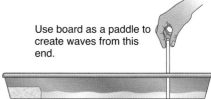

Use board as a paddle to create waves from this end.

2. Set up your station as described below.

Station E: Cliffs

Make a cliff like the bluff you made before. This time make it 8 cm high.

Gently place an index card along the top, parallel to the width of the cliff and with the edge of the card about 2 cm from the edge of the cliff.

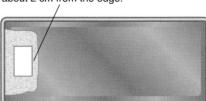

Place index card here, about 2 cm from the edge.

Station F: Bays

Make a bay shape about 5 cm high at one end of your stream table. Gently place an index card on top of the bay.

Station G: Islands

Make an island about 5 cm high at one end of the stream table.

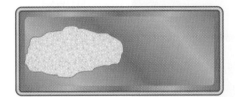

Station H: Spits

Make a spit about 5 cm high, as shown in the diagram.

3. Follow these steps to test your model:

Stations E to H: Running the Test

As in the preparation steps, use boards to protect your landform. Gently pour water into the stream table to a depth of about 2 to 3 cm.

Remove the boards slowly and carefully when the water is still.

a) In your journal record the question you are investigating.

b) Make a sketch of the landforms in your stream table for later comparison.

Use the board to create small waves that move toward the landform.

Have one member of your group count the number of waves you produce.

Gradually increase the strength of the waves to model the wind becoming stronger.

c) As this happens, record your observations.

After 60 waves, stop and make your observations of the condition of your landform.

d) Record your observations. Make another sketch.

Review your results. If necessary, repeat the experiment to get more reliable results. Note all observations clearly.

Wash your hands after the activity.

Inquiry

Preparing a Learning Center

A key part of this investigation is to educate all groups about each station. In effect, you are creating a "learning center" based on your investigation. In this way you are mirroring what scientists do. Think carefully about how you will do this. Other groups are dependent on you for their understanding.

As You Read...
Think about:

1. How are most landscapes formed?

2. What types of landscapes are formed by moving water?

3. What are some structures that people have developed to prevent erosion along a shoreline?

Part C: Demonstrating Your Results

1. Decide the best way to prepare your model for a demonstration that will show the other groups what you have discovered.

   Keep in mind that you will only be able to do this once, so you will need to construct a model that clearly shows erosion.

2. Hold a session in which each group, in turn, demonstrates its model to other groups.

   As you watch each demonstration, note carefully the erosion processes. Look for events that are similar, and different, to your own.

   a) Record your observations of each demonstration in your journal.

Digging Deeper

Moving Water and Landscapes

Would you have guessed that most landscapes are formed by moving water? Almost all the land surface of the Earth is above sea level. Everyone knows that water runs downhill, because of the pull of gravity. At first the part of the rain that does not immediately sink into the ground runs off as broad sheets of water, called sheet flow or overland flow. You probably have seen this on a broad and gently sloping parking lot during a heavy rain. As the overland flow collects downslope on the land surface, it eventually forms itself into narrower and deeper channels. The water flows much faster. Flow in these channels can erode the soil to form gullies, canyons, and valleys. The scale of the features formed varies greatly. The flowing water can form little rills a few centimeters deep on highway cuts, or great canyons the size of the Grand Canyon.

Most canyons and valleys are not vertical slots in the landscape. Instead, they have sloping sides. That's

because gravity is pulling the rock and soil material on the slopes downward, too. This downslope force moves the material down the slope, toward the stream or river in the bottom of the valley. These movements vary greatly in their scale and speed.

Rivers and the Rock Cycle

Rivers carry the eroded sediment to the ocean. There it is deposited as sediment and eventually buried to make new sedimentary rocks. Rivers are thus an important part of the rock cycle, which you learned about in an earlier investigation. If rivers have been removing rock and soil material from the continents through long periods of geologic time, why haven't the continents long since been worn down to low plains? The answer is that the land of the continents is raised up, usually very slowly, by various kinds of Earth movements, providing new high land for rivers to erode. That's also an important part of the rock cycle.

Waves and Shorelines

Rivers are not the only places where moving water shapes the landscape. Ocean waves that move toward the shoreline deliver their energy to the shoreline in the form of breaking waves. When waves break, they exert enormous forces on the sediment and rock at the ➤

shore. Even the solid rock of sea cliffs is worn back slowly by those forces.

Beaches are masses of sand (or, in some places, gravel) that are shaped by breaking waves. Each wave, when it breaks, sends a sheet of water up the beach, carrying sand up the beach. The water then turns and flows back down the beach, carrying sand back down the slope. In this way, grains of sand can travel enormous distances without getting anywhere! When waves approach the shore at an angle, however, they carry the sand not just up and down the beach but also along the beach. Currents flowing parallel to the beach, called longshore currents, also move sand along the beach, if they become strong enough. Over time, large volumes of sand can be moved along the beach in this way.

Engineers have devised many ways to try to protect beaches and human-built structures from coastline erosion and keep shipping channels from being blocked by sand moving along coastlines. Examples include groins, jetties, and breakwaters.

Sand is deposited on the up-current side of a groin.

Groins are long, wall-like structures along beaches that extend into the ocean. Their purpose is to act as barriers to longshore currents in order to control or change sand movement. A longshore current loses speed as it meets the groin. This causes the current to deposit sand on the up-current side of the groin. This builds up the sand on the beach. Whenever sand on one beach increases, however, other beaches downcurrent lose a lot of sand.

Jetties are similar structures designed to keep sand from moving into a ship channel and making it too shallow for ship traffic. Often, two jetties are used, one on each side of the channel.

Jetties are often built in pairs.

Breakwaters are barriers that are built offshore to protect part of a shoreline. They act as a barrier to waves, preventing erosion and allowing the beach to grow. However, the beach behind the breakwater often grows at the expense of the shoreline that is not protected. Seawalls are sometimes built in places where the shoreline is retreating because of coastal erosion.

A breakwater.

Structures built to stop coastal erosion tend to work well for some period of time. However, they often fail during especially large storms, and have to be rebuilt. As you can imagine, there is a great difference of opinion about whether such structures should continue to be built, or whether the coastline should be allowed to develop naturally.

Review and Reflect

Review

1. How do streams and rivers change the shape of the land?

2. What would happen to a landscape without streams and rivers?

3. In what different ways can lake or ocean water move land material and shape the shoreline?

4. How can shorelines be protected from erosion?

Reflect

5. What types of land material are most likely to erode quickly? What do you think erodes slowly? Why do you think this is so?

6. How can human actions affect the natural process of erosion?

7. Do you think humans should interfere with the natural processes of erosion? Explain your answer.

Thinking about the Earth System

8. Explain why erosion is a key process in the geosphere.

9. How do erosion processes you studied in this investigation involve the hydrosphere?

10. How is the atmosphere involved with the erosion process?

11. What connection did you find in this investigation between erosion and the biosphere?

Thinking about Scientific Inquiry

12. Why was modeling an important tool to use in this investigation?

13. Which variables did you need to control in your station?

14. Which parts of the real world were you not able to include in your models?

Investigation 6:

Deltas and Floodplains

Key Question

Before you begin, first think about this key question.

Where do rivers deposit sediment?

In the last investigation you modeled the erosion of land by moving water. You were able to observe how land materials are worn and carried away by streams and rivers and by model ocean waves. Think about where this eroded material, called sediment, finally ends up.

Share your thinking with others in your group and with your class.

Materials Needed

For this investigation your group will need:

- 300-mL clear, plastic cup
- water supply
- sand supply
- stir stick
- paper towel
- topographic map of river flowing into ocean
- aluminum-foil baking tray
- stream table or something that can be used as a stream table
- 1-L container with a pour spout
- clay soil
- container for collecting overflow
- stopwatch
- ruler
- graph paper

Investigate

1. In your group, take a 300-mL clear, plastic cup. Fill it two-thirds full of water.

   Put in about 15 mL of dry sand. Stir the water.

   Think of the water as a stream and the sand as sediment.

   a) Record your observations until the water stops moving.

2. In your group, study a topographic map of a river flowing to the ocean. Look closely at the landforms on either side of the river valley, and where the river enters the ocean.

Think about water carrying sediment down a stream or river. What questions would you like to investigate about where streams and rivers may deposit sediment?

Make a group list of ideas and questions.

a) Record your group's list.

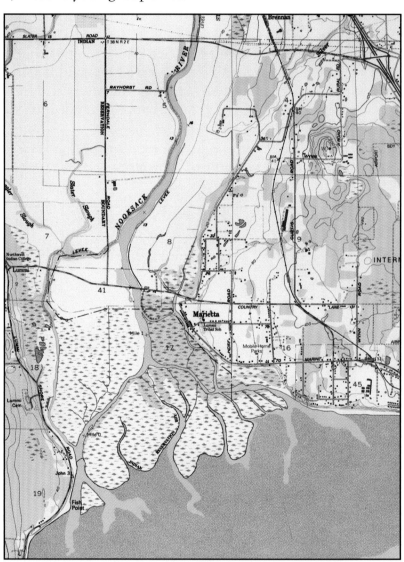

Topographic map of the Nooksack River near Bellingham, Washington.

3. Share your group's list with other groups. Together, agree on the key questions to investigate.

a) Make up one list of questions for the class.

4. Design an investigation to answer your question.

   a) Write your question in a way that it can be investigated clearly.

   b) Form a prediction and write down a reason for your prediction. Review making a hypothesis in Investigation 3.

   c) Which variables will you control in your test?

   d) Make a diagram showing how you will set up the stream table and sand to test your question.

   e) How will you record what happens?

   f) How many times will you repeat your test to be sure of your results?

5. Setting up your stream table will take time and a lot of sand. Before setting up your full-scale model, you will want to run a pilot.

   You can pilot your test design using an aluminum-foil tray.

   Experiment until you are sure that you have a good design, one that will work on a larger scale in the stream table.

   When you think you have the best design, check and compare it with other groups. If necessary, make adjustments.

   Before you proceed with the stream table, have your teacher approve your final pilot test.

6. Build your model in the stream table.

   Before you pour your water, you need to add some clay soil to it to act as sediment. Stir in a good amount and mix it around until the water becomes cloudy with particles.

Inquiry

Pilot Testing

Piloting a test means trying it out on a small scale first to see if it works and how well it answers the question. You can pilot your stream-table test by doing it in miniature. Scientists often pilot their test designs. A pilot helps to save time and money. It can also redirect your thinking about the nature of the problem and your hypothesis about it.

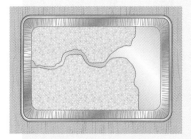

 Do not let fine sand get into eyes. Wipe up any spills immediately. Wash your hands after the activity.

Inquiry

Using Mathematics

Mathematics is a key tool for scientists. Accurate measurement with suitable units is very important for collecting and analyzing data. Your test will be greatly enhanced if you can figure out a way to make measurements.

Wash your hands after the activity.

You will probably need to "flood" your model of a broad, river valley several times.

Run your test.

a) Record your observations. You may wish to make diagrams to record the changes that happen over time.

7. After you have tried your test once, think about how you could make measurements of any changes you observed. You could use graph paper, a ruler, and a stopwatch.

Run your test again, and make the measurements your group has decided upon.

a) Record the measurements you make.

8. Gather, review, and organize your findings. Think about the following questions:

   • What answers and explanations do your data give?

   • What evidence do you have that tells you how sediment is deposited on the broad, flat areas, called floodplains, next to streams and rivers?

   • What evidence do you have that tells you how sediment is deposited in the form of a delta at the mouth of a stream or river where it flows into a lake or ocean?

   • What evidence do you have about sediment once it enters a large body of water?

   a) Record your findings in a way that you can show them to others.

9. Present your findings to other groups.

   Listen carefully as others present their findings to you. Think about these questions:

   • How are other groups' results similar to and different from your own?

   • What common patterns of deposition can you find?

   • What can you all agree upon about the ways in which sediment becomes deposited in a river floodplain, a river delta, and where the river water moves into an ocean or lake?

   a) Use everyone's ideas to record clear statements about depositional landforms formed by rivers.

Digging Deeper

Movement of Sediment by Rivers

Along their upstream courses, rivers pick up sediment from their banks and from valley slopes and carry it downstream. The sediment can range in size from fine mud, through sand, to coarse gravel. Sediment that is being carried by the river is called the sediment load of the river. The very fine particles of the mud are mostly raised upward from the bed by the turbulent swirls and little whirlpools in the river. They are carried for long distances while they are suspended above the bed. The coarser part of the sediment load, the sand and gravel, is usually moved more slowly along the bed of the river.

Most rivers are usually curvy rather than straight. Also, the geometry of the curves changes through time, because rivers tend to shift sideways in their position, by eroding on one bank and depositing on the other bank. Changes like that happen fast enough that the course of the river can be very different, even within a human lifetime.

River Valleys and Floodplains

As rivers continually shift sideways through time, they eat away at the walls of their valleys, making the valleys wider and wider. After a river has widened its valley, it has a

As You Read...
Think about:
1. How is sediment carried along by a river?
2. How do floodplains form?
3. What is a delta, and how does it form?

broad, almost flat plain, called a floodplain, outside of its banks. When the river is in flood, usually every year or two, the river water spills over the banks and spreads out over the floodplain. The water on the floodplain moves more slowly than in the river channel, so some of the fine suspended mud settles out onto the floodplain. It's unpleasant for people whose homes are on a floodplain to have to clean up a layer of silt from their living room floor after the flood waters subside. However, the silt that is deposited adds to the soil, and causes many floodplains to be very rich land for growing crops.

Deltas

A delta is a body of river sediment that is deposited at the mouth of the river, where it flows into the ocean. Where a river reaches the ocean, the fast-flowing water meets the ocean water and slows down. Most of the sediment carried by the river is deposited at the mouth of the river, because that is where the river current slows down, although much of the fine suspended mud drifts out to sea, where it settles slowly to the ocean bottom over large areas. Over long periods of time, as the mass of deposited sediment becomes larger, a river delta is formed. Deltas also form where a river flows into a large lake. Most large rivers divide their flow into a number of separate channels, called distributary channels, before they actually reach the ocean.

Deltas have many different shapes, depending mainly on how strong the river is versus how strong the ocean waves and currents are. Deltas formed by large, strong rivers like the Mississippi, which empty into areas of the ocean where waves and currents are usually not too strong, form deltas with complicated shapes. In deltas like that, the distributary channels build outward into the ocean in the form of long "fingers." If the ocean waves and currents are very strong compared to the river flow, the front of the delta becomes blunted or rounded off.

Review and Reflect

Review

1. What is a depositional landform?

2. What kinds of landforms are created by rivers and streams?

3. In what ways is sediment carried by a river?

Reflect

4. With many trials, how might the floodplain and the delta in your model change?

5. How many times a year do you think the stream nearest your community floods?

6. If you wanted to model 1000 years of floods in a real stream, how many times would you have to do your tests?

Thinking about the Earth System

7. How can human actions affect the natural processes by which sediment is carried by water?

8. How can severe weather affect the formation of landforms created by sediment from rivers and streams?

9. From where does the sediment that is carried by streams and rivers come?

10. Write any connection that you have discovered in this investigation to connect rocks to the geosphere, hydrosphere, atmosphere, and biosphere. You can record this information on your *Earth System Connection* sheet.

Thinking about Scientific Inquiry

11. How did you use modeling as a tool in this investigation?

12. Why was piloting your test useful?

13. How did you use evidence you collected to find explanations?

14. Name one other inquiry process you used in this investigation. Explain where and how you used it.

Investigation 7:

Glaciers, Erosion, and Deposition

 Key Question

Before you begin, first think about this key question.

How can glaciers create landforms?

Think about what makes glaciers change (get larger or smaller) over time. What do you think happens to the land as a glacier advances? What do you think happens to the land as the glacier retreats?

Share your thinking with others in your group and with your class.

Materials Needed

For this investigation your group will need:

- stream table or something that can be used as a stream table
- soil
- sand
- gravel
- block of ice
- hair dryer
- graph paper
- reference materials

Investigate

1. In this investigation you will once again use the stream table, this time to model the advance, standstill, and retreat of a continental ice sheet. You will be using a block of ice with sand frozen into the base to represent a glacier.

Set up your stream table as shown in diagram.

2. In each of these tests, you will be using a hair dryer to melt the terminus of the glacier (the front edge of the ice block). Hold the heat source well away from the ice block, and wave it slowly from side to side to melt the front of the ice block slowly and evenly.

3. Develop hypotheses that will fit the kinds of changes that you think might happen during the following events:

   • A glacier advance during a long period of snowy winters and cool summers: Slide the ice block forward very slowly while using the heat source to melt the ice at the front end of the ice block. Adjust the speed of movement of the ice block so that it is slightly faster than the speed of melting back of the front end of the ice block (terminus of the glacier). As a result, the terminus will advance slowly.

   • A glacier retreat during a long period of less snowy winters and warm summers: Slide the ice block forward very slowly while using the heat source to melt the ice at the front end of the ice block. Adjust the speed of movement of the ice block so that it is slightly slower than the speed of melting back of the front end of the ice block (terminus of the glacier). As a result, the terminus will retreat slowly.

   • A glacier standstill during a long period when removal of glacier ice by melting is just balanced by addition of glacier ice from snowfall: Slide the ice block forward very slowly while using the heat source to melt the ice at the front end of the ice block. Adjust the speed of movement of the ice block so that it is the same as the speed of melting back of the front end of the ice block (terminus of the glacier). As a result, the terminus will stay in almost the same place for a long period of time.

   a) To make your predictions, think about where erosion and where deposition might take place in each event. Record your predictions and your reasons.

4. Consider carefully how you will make measurements and record your observations. You may wish to use drawings.

5. Have your model approved by your teacher. Then run your tests.

   a) Record your observations.

Prepared Ice Block

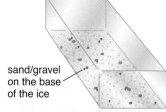

sand/gravel on the base of the ice

The materials at the base of the ice block represent the sediment and rock that either falls onto, or is picked up by, glaciers and carried at their base.

Continental Landscape

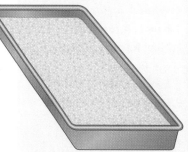

For your model of a continental glacier, prepare a broad, fairly flat surface of wet sand.

Do not let fine sand get into eyes. Wipe up spills immediately. Wash your hands after the activity.

Inquiry

Gathering Evidence

Evidence is very important for scientists. Scientists use evidence they collect themselves. They also look at evidence collected by other scientists. They use all this evidence to develop ideas. By doing research, you are using the work of other scientists to help you develop your ideas.

6. Research to find information on glaciers. Resources can include library reference books, videos, CD-ROMs, encyclopedias, and the Internet. Try searching the Internet using these key words: glaciers, glacial landforms, glacial erosion, glacial deposition, continental glaciers, ice sheets, valley glaciers, or alpine glaciers.

a) Record your findings. Then share your results with the class.

As You Read...

Think about:

1. *What is a glacier, and how is it formed?*

2. *How has the climate of the Earth changed over long periods of time?*

3. *How do glaciers affect landforms?*

Digging Deeper

GLACIERS

A glacier is a large mass of ice on the land surface, which moves by flowing under its own weight. It might surprise you that a material as solid as ice can flow like a liquid, but many materials, like ice, can do that when they are under great pressure. A glacier forms over a very long period of years wherever there is so much snow in winter that not all of it melts during summer. In places like that, the old snow gradually builds up to be so thick that it slowly becomes compacted and turns into solid ice. After the ice reaches a thickness of many tens of meters, the pressure on it is great enough to make it flow. Some glaciers, called valley glaciers, form in high mountains and flow down valleys like "rivers of ice." Much larger glaciers, called ice sheets or ice caps, form over large areas of the land and flow outward from the highest part of the ice mass. Ice sheets are far larger than valley glaciers; they can cover a large part of a continent. The Antarctic ice sheet, at the South Pole, covers almost all of the continent of Antarctica. It is the largest glacier on Earth today.

It may be difficult to imagine, but the Earth's climate has changed greatly over time. The Earth has gone through many cycles of warmer and colder average temperature. The overall change in temperature is as much as several

degrees Celsius. Suppose, for example, that the Earth goes through a cooling cycle of several thousand years. In many regions of the Earth, more snow falls than melts, and glaciers grow over time. In the past one million years, ice sheets have advanced and then shrunk back for great distances (thousands of kilometers) at least four times. Each of these advances was enough to cover vast areas of North America with ice sheets that must have been a few kilometers thick.

The ice of glaciers is moving forward all the time, toward the front end of the glacier, called the terminus. When it reaches the terminus, it melts. If the glacier becomes larger in its volume, during a period of years when winter snowfall is greater and summer melting is less, the terminus of the glacier shifts forward on the land surface. If, however, the glacier becomes smaller in volume, during a period of years when snowfall is less and melting is greater, then the terminus shifts backward on the land surface—but the ice of the glacier is always moving toward the terminus, even though the terminus is shifting slowly backward.

Glacial Sediment and Glacial Landforms

When you first take ice cubes out of the refrigerator they are dry and not very slippery. When they warm up to the melting temperature, however, they are wet and much more slippery. Glaciers are like that too. In some glaciers, especially in very cold regions, the ice at the base of the glacier is below the melting temperature. Glaciers like that are frozen solid to the bedrock underneath, so they do not do much geological work of eroding and moving rock material. Other glaciers are at the melting temperature at their base. They slide along the bedrock, so they are able to erode the bedrock and carry enormous amounts of material, ranging in size from fine clay to gigantic boulders.

→

Some of the material eroded and carried by a glacier near its base is plastered onto the bedrock somewhere farther along the path of the glacier. This leaves an irregular sheet of very compacted glacial sediment after the glacier finally disappears. The rest of the material is dumped onto the land surface by the glacier when the ice reaches the terminus and melts. If the terminus is gradually shifting forward, the glacier just rides over this material and picks it up again. If the terminus stays in about the same place for a long period of many years, a ridge of glacial sediment, called an end moraine, is built. Many other kinds of local hills and ridges of glacier sediment can also be deposited at or near the terminus of the glacier. During the warm season of the year, streams of water are produced by melting of glacier ice and snow. This water, called glacial meltwater, flows out from beneath the terminus of the glacier. Meltwater streams carry glacial sand and gravel for long distances before depositing it in river valleys.

Review and Reflect

Review

1. How is fluffy snow transformed into glacier ice?

2. Why is "river of ice" a good name for a valley glacier?

3. Explain how glaciers form both erosional and depositional landforms.

Reflect

4. How might human activities affect the advance or retreat of glaciers?

5. What evidence is there of the action of glaciers in your community?

Thinking about the Earth System

6. In what part of the Earth system would you put glaciers? Why?

7. How do glaciers affect the geosphere?

8. Explain how changes in the atmosphere can affect glaciers.

9. Write any connection that you have discovered in this investigation to connect rocks to the geosphere, hydrosphere, atmosphere, and biosphere. You can record this information on your *Earth System Connection* sheet.

Thinking about Scientific Inquiry

10. How did you use evidence in this investigation to find explanations?

11. What tools did you use to help you answer the key question?

Investigation 8:

Rocks, Landforms, and Human Activity

Putting It All Together

Key Question

Before you begin, first think about this key question.

How do rocks and landforms affect what we do?

In this last investigation you will have a chance to apply all that you have learned about landforms. You will design and make a landform information product for local people or visitors to your area. Think about why landforms are important to many people. Why would engineers, farmers, miners, athletes, tourists, or truck drivers be affected by the local landforms?

Share your thinking with others in your group and with your class.

Materials Needed

In this investigation your group may need:

- topographic map of your area
- geologic map of your area
- road map or tourist map of your area
- samples of tourist information materials
- access to a variety of materials and equipment needed to make your product

Investigate

1. To design and produce an information product about rocks and landforms for local people or visitors, you will first need to consider the following two groups of questions. In your group discuss these questions and ways in which you might find the answers.

What are the main landform features in your area?

- What is the general topography?

- What different types of rocks are there in your area?

- Where are these rocks found, and how do they affect the landforms?

- Where is there evidence of erosion now and in the past?

- Where is there evidence of deposition now and in the past?

- Where is there water (ocean, lakes, rivers, streams) found in your area?

- How have the landform features in your area formed over time?

- How are the landforms in your area changing?

How do the landforms in your area or region affect the way in which people live, work, and play?

- How do the landforms affect where people live in your area?

- How do the landforms affect the work people do in your area?

- How do the landforms affect the kinds of buildings, bridges, roads, highways, railways, and other structures in your area?

- What different recreational activities do the landforms in your area make possible?

- What landform features may be of interest to visitors in your area?

a) Write a brief summary of your group discussion in your journal.

2. Develop a list of items that you think will be important to include in your product. Remember that you will need to provide all the landform evidence you can find to explain why these items are the way they are.

a) In your journal, begin an outline plan for your product. List the items you plan to include.

3. Discuss who your users will be and how you will package the information.

Inquiry

Ways of Packaging Information

Scientists are often asked to provide information to the public. In doing so, they need to consider both the message they want to communicate and the persons or groups that will be using the information. For example, they may be providing the same kind of information to a group of civil engineers or a group of interested tourists. Once they are clear about the message and the audience, they can then decide on the best method of packaging and delivery. These are decisions you also will need to make in this investigation.

There are many alternatives. Here are a few:

- Booklet
- Brochure
- Poster
- Tourist map
- Photograph collection
- Video program
- Radio program
- Guided tour
- Trail for people to follow
- Web site.

a) To your outline plan, add a description of how you will present your information.

4. Discuss how you will make your product attractive to the users. Be as creative as possible. Think about how you can make your product exciting as well as informative for your users.

If possible, discuss your form of presentation with a specialist in creative design.

a) Add your creative ideas to your outline plan.

5. Consider how much time you will have to complete the task.

Think about how the tasks will be shared among the members of your group.

a) Include a schedule in your outline plan.

6. Check your outline plan with other groups. Then have your plan approved by your teacher.

Once you have done this, complete your product.

7. Show your completed product to other groups.

Observe carefully as others present their products to you. Think about:

• how attractive the product will be to visitors;

• how well the product explains the relationship between local landforms and human activities.

Review and Reflect

Review

1. What have you discovered about your local rocks and landforms?

2. How are human activities (jobs and recreation) in your area affected by the landforms?

Reflect

3. Think about areas in other parts of the United States or the rest of the world. What kinds of landforms would you like to see if you have a chance? Explain why.

4. Are there any actions by humans on landforms that you think may cause problems in the future? If so, what are they and why are they a problem?

5. Which local organizations might be interested in a product of the kind you created? How could they use it?

Thinking about the Earth System

6. Add any new connections that you have discovered in this investigation to connect rocks to the geosphere, hydrosphere, atmosphere, and biosphere. You can record this information on your *Earth System Connection* sheet.

7. Look closely at all the connections you have made since you began this module. List any questions you still have about the Earth system.

Thinking about Scientific Inquiry

8. What inquiry processes did you use in this final investigation? Name at least three processes, where you used them, and how they helped you complete this investigation.

Reflecting

Back to the Beginning

How have your ideas about *Rocks and Landforms* changed from when you started? Look at the following questions and write down your ideas now:

• What are rocks made of?
• How do rocks change over time?
• What causes the shape of the land to change over time?
• What questions do you have about rocks and landforms?

How has your thinking about *Rocks and Landforms* changed?

Thinking about the Earth System

Consider what you have learned about the Earth system. Refer to the *Earth System Connection* sheet that you have been building up throughout this module.

• What connections between *Rocks and Landforms* and the Earth system have you been able to find?

Thinking about Scientific Inquiry

Review the investigations you have done and the inquiry processes you have used.

• What scientific inquiry processes did you use?
• How did scientific inquiry processes help you learn about *Rocks and Landforms*?

A New Beginning!

Not so much an ending as a new beginning!

This investigation into *Rocks and Landforms* is now completed, but that is not the end of the story! As time goes by, you will see many different examples as you travel to different parts of the United States, or abroad. Be alert for opportunities to add to your knowledge and understanding.

The Big Picture

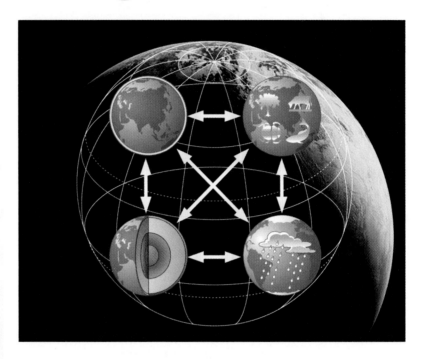

Key Concepts

Earth is a set of closely linked systems.

Earth's processes are powered by two sources: the Sun, and Earth's own inner heat.

The geology of Earth is dynamic, and has evolved over 4.6 billion years.

The geological evolution of Earth has left a record of its history that geoscientists interpret.

We depend upon Earth's resources—both mined and grown.

INVESTIGATING
FOSSILS

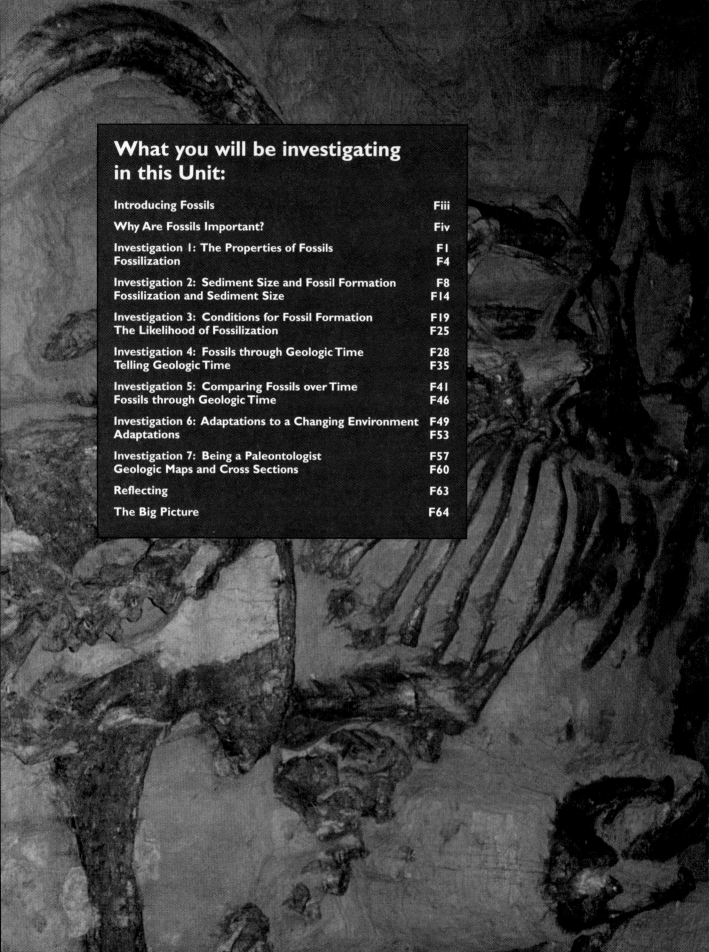

What you will be investigating in this Unit:

Introducing Fossils

Have you ever realized that algae can become fossilized?

Have you ever seen the remains of organisms in rocks?

Have you ever noticed how some rocks are arranged in layers?

Have you ever seen silt that has been washed from the land?

Why Are Fossils Important?

The word fossil comes from the Latin word *fossilis,* meaning "dug up." Today, the word generally refers to any evidence of past life, from insects preserved in amber to imprints of a dinosaur's foot.

To hold a fossil is to hold millions of years of history in the palm of your hand. The ridges, bumps, and curves of a fossilized clam are the same ridges, bumps, and curves that existed as it filtered water from the sea long ago. Studying fossils provides clues about the Earth's past, its climate, natural disasters, changing landforms, and changing oceans. Fossils tell about history and, like all good history, they help you to understand both the present and the future.

What Will You Investigate?

You and your group will be acting as detectives, trying to figure out how fossils form, where they form, and where they might be found today. In this way, you will be doing the work of a paleontologist, a geoscientist who studies life in prehistoric times by using fossil evidence.

Here are some of the things that you will investigate:

• why some things become fossils, but others do not;
• how the environment affects how fossils form;
• how fossils show the age of the Earth;
• how life has changed over time;
• what paleontologists do.

In the last investigation, you will have a chance to be a paleontologist and apply what you have learned about fossils. You will be given a fossil and a geological map. After completing the research, you will present a "portrait" of your fossil in an interesting and creative way.

Investigation I:

The Properties of Fossils

Key Question
Before you begin, first think about this key question.

Why does one animal or plant become fossilized, but millions of others do not?

Think about what you already know about fossils. What do you think leads to their formation? Why do some plants and animals decay, without forming a fossil?

Share your thinking with others in your group and with your class.

Materials Needed

For this investigation your group will need:

- fossil specimens

- four or five white index cards

- samples of fresh fruit

- samples of partially decomposed fruit in a tightly sealed, double-bagged, plastic bag

- a tightly sealed, double-bagged, plastic bag containing **one** of the following: peeled shrimp, unpeeled shrimp, clam-shell, chicken wing, leaf, small twig

Investigate

1. Your group will be given samples of different kinds of fossils. Study them closely.

    Make a small card to set beside each fossil type, and add any information about it that you can tell from your observations.

    a) What kinds of animals are represented (mammals, birds, reptiles, insects, shellfish)? What kinds of plants, if any, are represented?

Inquiry

Observations and Inferences

An observation is what you can see, smell, hear, touch, or in some way measure. An inference is what you believe to be true on the basis of your observations. An inference can lead to a prediction, especially if it can be proved or disproved.

Do not open any of the sealed bags. Do not eat any food in the lab.

2. Compare your fossils with those of other students.

   a) What do they all have in common?

   b) How are they different?

3. Discuss the following questions in your group. Record your answers in your journal.

   a) What kinds of things became fossilized (bones, skin, muscle, leaves, flowers, bark)?

   b) What kinds of living things seem to be missing from this collection?

   c) Do you think all living things can become fossils? Why or why not?

   d) List some questions of your own about the fossils.

4. Observe samples of fresh fruit and fruit that has been decomposing for several days. The decomposing fruit is contained in a sealed, double-bagged plastic bag. Handle the samples carefully, and do not open the bag.

   a) Describe the changes that seem to be happening to the decomposing fruit.

   b) What do you think caused these changes?

   c) What do you think is the likelihood of the fruit becoming a fossil, either wholly or in part? Be sure to explain your answer.

d) When would the fruit be more likely to become a fossil — if it decomposed quickly, decomposed slowly, or did not decompose at all? Explain your answer.

5. Examine one of the following items contained in a tightly sealed, double-bagged plastic bag: peeled shrimp, unpeeled shrimp, chicken wing, clamshell, green leaf, small twig.

   a) As you examine your item, carefully record your observations in a data table like the one shown.

   b) Think about its chance of becoming a fossil, either wholly or in part. From what you can infer from your observations, record a prediction in the table.

   c) Record a reason for your prediction.

Fossil Formation of Dead Organisms			
Item	Observations	Prediction (Can it become a fossil?)	Reason (Use an analogy if possible.)
unpeeled shrimp			
chicken wing			
clamshell			
green leaf			
small twig			
peeled shrimp			

6. As a class, discuss the following questions. Take notes during the class discussion, completing the chart and recording your answers. Be sure to ask for clarification if you are unsure of another group's observations, predictions, or reasons.

   a) In the right conditions, which of the items might become a fossil? Why is that?

   b) Which of the items might have only some of their parts become a fossil, and which parts?

   c) Which of the items would be very unlikely to have any of their parts become a fossil? Why is that?

   d) How do you think decomposition affects fossilization? Why do you think so?

Meat items should be fresh and kept refrigerated when not in use. Notify your teacher immediately of any leaking fluid, because it may carry disease. Wipe off desks and tables when you are done. Wash your hands after the activity.

Inquiry

Predictions

Keep in mind that predictions that you made do not need to be correct. Scientists often make many incorrect predictions or hypotheses before finding one that stands up to repeated testing.

Using Analogies

Predictions are often based on common experiences. You can compare your observations with previous experiences and base your prediction on what you are already familiar with. For example, in this investigation you might base your prediction on the fact that an unpeeled shrimp has a coating that looks like, and feels like, plastic.

As You Read...
Think about:

As You Read...
Think about:
1. What is a fossil?
2. Give two examples of a body fossil.
3. Can a plant yield a trace fossil? Why or why not?
4. What are organic compounds made up of?
5. Under what conditions is decomposition the fastest? Under what conditions is it the slowest?
6. What are some ways that animals become fossilized?

Digging Deeper

FOSSILIZATION

What is a Fossil?

A fossil is any evidence of past life. Fossils formed from animal bodies or their imprints are called body fossils. When people think about fossils, they usually think about body fossils. Trace fossils are another kind of fossil. A trace fossil is any evidence of the life activity of an animal that lived in the past. Burrows, tracks, trails, feeding marks, and resting marks are all examples of trace fossils. It is usually hard to figure out exactly which kind of animal made a particular trace fossil. Trace fossils are useful to paleontologists (scientists who study fossils), however, because they tell something about the environment where the animal lived and the animal's behavior.

Decomposition

Organisms are made up of chemical compounds, most of which are organic compounds. Organic compounds consist mainly of carbon, oxygen, and hydrogen. After a plant or animal dies, it decomposes. As organisms decompose, their organic compounds change into simpler compounds, mainly carbon dioxide and water. Decomposition is fastest when the organisms are in water that contains dissolved oxygen. Organisms can also decompose even without oxygen. Some kinds of bacteria feed on plant and animal tissues even though there is no oxygen. These are called anaerobic ("no air") bacteria. Sooner or later, almost all organic matter from plants and animals decays. Decay slows down only when the organic matter is buried in very fine mud. That seals the organic matter off from water with oxygen.

The soft parts of an organism decompose the fastest. You know how little time it takes for food to spoil and rot in warm weather when it is not in the refrigerator. Bones and shells decompose much more slowly. Over

long times their mineral materials dissolve. That can happen rapidly when the shells and bones lie on the ground surface or on the sea bottom. If the shell or bone is buried in sediment, it dissolves more slowly. Sometimes the shells are not dissolved before the rock becomes solid, so they are preserved. The woody parts of plants that consist mostly of cellulose and lignin decompose much more slowly than the softer parts.

Fossilization

Most animals become fossilized by being buried in sediment. For them to be fossilized, they have to be buried and leave an imprint before they decompose. Animals without skeletons are seldom fossilized, because they decompose so fast. Animals with hard skeletons are much easier to fossilize. The most common fossils are shells of marine animals like clams, snails, or corals. Insects, with thin outside skeletons of chitin, are not as easy to fossilize. Sometimes an insect is trapped in sticky material, called resin, that comes out of some kinds of trees. Then the resin hardens to a material called amber. The insect fossil is preserved in the amber, often perfectly.

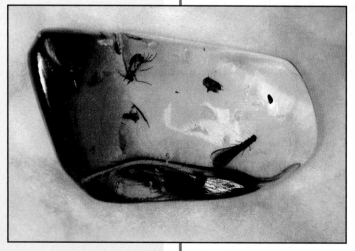

Sometimes the actual shell or bone is preserved. Usually, however, you see only its imprint. If the shell or bone resists being dissolved for a long enough time, the sediment around it turns into rock. Then, even though the shell or bone dissolves, the imprint is preserved. When a hammer splits the rock open, the fracture might pass through the imprint, and you see a fossil.

Review and Reflect

Review

1. What kinds of plant and animal materials decompose most quickly?

2. What kinds of plant and animal materials take the longest to decompose?

3. What is the difference between a body fossil and a trace fossil?

Reflect

4. What kinds of materials from organisms have the best chance of becoming a fossil? Explain.

5. Which of the following natural processes did you model in the investigation? Explain your reasoning.

   • decomposition at the Earth's surface;

   • scattering of organic matter by scavengers;

   • decomposition after an organism is buried by sediments.

6. Sediments can often accumulate very quickly in places where rivers flow into the open ocean. Would this be a likely or unlikely place for fossils to form? Explain your answer.

Thinking about the Earth System

7. From what you learned in this investigation, what connections can you make between the geosphere and the biosphere? Note any connections between these two spheres on your *Earth System Connection* sheet.

8. How are the atmosphere and hydrosphere involved in decomposition?

9. On your *Earth System Connection* sheet, note any roles that the atmosphere plays in the preservation of fossils.

Thinking about Scientific Inquiry

10. How is an observation different from an inference? Give an example of each from this investigation.

11. What is an analogy and why is it useful in scientific inquiry? Give an example.

Materials Needed

For this investigation your group will need:

- small amount of each sediment type: clay, fine sand, and coarse sand
- magnifier
- microscope (optional)
- sheet of white paper and black paper
- different-sized spherical objects (i.e., marbles, table-tennis balls, tennis balls, softballs, volleyballs, soccer balls, and basketballs—about three per group)
- metric measuring tape
- calculator (optional)
- newspapers to cover desk
- petroleum jelly
- small container
- plaster (molding plaster or plaster of Paris)
- water supply
- plastic spoon
- leaf, clamshell, and piece of dried fruit

Investigation 2:

Sediment Size and Fossil Formation

Key Question

Before you begin, first think about this key question.

Does sediment size affect how fossils form?

Think about what you know about how a fossil forms. If an animal dies and is buried by gravel, is it as likely to become a body fossil as when it is buried by mud? How might the size of grains of sediment affect whether or not a trace fossil can be formed?

Share your thinking with others in your group and with your class.

Investigate

Part A: Ranking Sediment According to Size

1. In your group, take a close look at samples of three different materials: clay, fine sand, and coarse sand.

Place a small amount of each of these particles on white paper and also on black paper.

Look at them first with the unaided eye, then with a magnifier, and, if possible, through a microscope. Compare the sizes of grains of sediment for the three samples.

a) Which grains are largest, which are medium-sized, and which are smallest?

b) If you were to compare the sizes of the grains quantitatively (using numbers rather than just ranking them), how many times larger do you think the largest grain is, compared to the medium grain? How many times larger do you think the medium grain is, compared to the smallest grain?

c) If you have access to a microscope with a scale, measure the size of the grains. You may have to measure several grains of each sediment and average the values. Record your results in your journal.

2. Sediment can range in size from large boulders to microscopic flakes of clay. Using a simple analogy, you can get a better idea of how the particle sizes compare with one another.

Obtain at least three different-sized spherical objects. Examples of some objects you can use are given on the following page.

Discuss how you could measure them.

Share your method with other groups and agree on a single method of measurement for the whole class. It is also important to use the same unit of measurement—metric units are highly recommended.

a) Record your method and the units you chose to use in your journal.

Inquiry

Using Measurements

Measurements are important when collecting data. In this investigation your group will need to agree on the measurement units you will use. Consider the United States system of measurement (inches) or metric measurement (millimeters, centimeters). Be sure to have good reasons for what you decide.

Wash your hands after the activity.

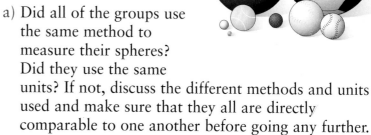

3. When your group has measured the spheres, share the results. Devise a good way to display the whole class's results, perhaps on a chalkboard, dry-erase board, or overhead transparency sheet.

a) Did all of the groups use the same method to measure their spheres? Did they use the same units? If not, discuss the different methods and units used and make sure that they all are directly comparable to one another before going any further.

b) When all groups have contributed their data, create a chart in your journal. Design it like the one shown below (for convenience later on, list the spherical objects in descending order of size). Calculate and record the class's average measurement for each item.

Class Results from Measurements for Sizes of Spheres		
Object	Class's Average Measurement (include units)	Comparison
basketball		
soccer ball		
volleyball		
softball		
tennis ball		
table-tennis ball		
marble		
other		

4. Choose a way of comparing the sizes (ratio, percent, or other method) and record this in your journal. For example, is a soccer ball 100 times larger than a tennis ball? Five times? Is a table-tennis ball twice the size of a marble? How can you calculate this?

Discuss the comparison method as a class.

a) When all groups are in agreement, record your comparison for each item. Include all calculations in your journal. If you use a calculator, include the setup for your calculations.

5. Copy the chart shown below into your journal:

Size of Different Sediment Types		
Sediment Type	Size Range (particle diameter)	Comparison
Very Coarse Sand	1.0–2.0 mm	
Coarse Sand	0.5–1.0 mm	
Medium Sand	0.25–0.50 mm	
Fine Sand	0.125–0.250 mm	
Very Fine Sand	0.0625–0.1250 mm	
Silt	0.0040–0.0625 mm	
Clay	< 0.004 mm	

Using the same comparison method, compare the sediment types in the chart. Because the values are given as a *range,* not an average, you may want to use the largest (or smallest) value in the range to compare.

a) Record your size comparisons in your journal.

b) Which four spherical objects best represent the relative sizes of the four sediment grains?

6. Discuss your group's results with the rest of the class.

a) Explain your comparisons mathematically. How did you arrive at your numbers?

b) Did your group do anything different, compared to other groups? Explain.

Part B: Sediment Grain Size and Fossilization

1. Suppose a group of marine snails is buried in sediment after dying. By chance, one snail gets buried by coarse sand, another by fine sand, and a third by clay. In your group, discuss the questions on the following page.

Inquiry
Using Mathematics

Using mathematics as a tool helps scientists to be more precise about the observations they make. Data often consists of numbers and calculations. In this investigation you used calculations to make size comparisons.

Inquiry

Hypothesis

A hypothesis is a testable statement or idea about how something works. It is based on what you think that you know or already understand. A hypothesis is never a guess. A hypothesis forms the basis for making a prediction and is used to design an experiment or observation. Guesses can be useful in science, but they are not hypotheses.

- Which sediment size do you think is likely to leave the most detailed impression of each of these items, and why?

- Which would make the least accurate impression, and why?

- Suppose that the snails were moving across the three kinds of sediment before their death. In which sediment is a trace fossil most likely to form? Why?

a) Record the results of your discussion in your journal. These are your predictions. Now you are going to have a chance to test them.

2. Your group will make an impression of a clamshell, a leaf, and a piece of dried fruit, using one of three sediments: coarse sand, fine sand, or clay. Then you will make an impression "fossil."

   To share the work, each group will be responsible for one sediment sample. However, each group will test the same items and follow the same procedure.

Here is the procedure for making impressions:

- Protect the surface of your desk by covering it with newspaper.

- Label a small container with the name of your group.

- Lubricate the insides of the container with petroleum jelly. (The container should be just big enough so that the leaf, the clamshell, and the fruit fit, with minimal extra space.)

- Add 1 cm of sediment (clay, fine sand, or coarse sand) to the container.

- Place each item on the bed of sediment.

- Gently push each item into the sediment. Hold it there for a moment, then carefully remove it and set it aside.

- Mix water with molding plaster or plaster of Paris. Stir and continue adding water until it has the consistency of thin pancake batter.

- Carefully spread an even layer of plaster on top of the imprint.

- Gently tap the sides of your container for one or two minutes. You should see tiny air bubbles come to the surface.

- Let the plaster harden overnight.

Wash your hands after the activity.

3. Carefully remove the plaster from the container, disposing of the sediment as directed by your teacher. Gently rinse and dry the plaster.

   Using a magnifying glass, observe the objects that were used to make the imprint.

   a) Can you see their features in the plaster?

   b) Is there any variation between the objects used to make the impression, and the quality of the impression? Explain.

4. Prepare a display of your impression fossils, labeling the type of sediment used.

5. Observe other groups' impression fossils.

   a) Which sediment type made the most detailed impression?

b) Which sediment type made the least detailed impression?

c) Give evidence to explain your answers.

d) Do you accept your original prediction or do you reject it?

6. Discuss the results with the rest of the class.

a) What generalization can you make about sediment size and its relationship to imprint fossils? Is there agreement among your classmates about this generalization?

b) What are other kinds of fossils that you know about?

Do you think that the same relationship between sediment type and fossilization would be seen with other kinds of fossils as well? Explain your answer.

As You Read...
Think about:
1. How are silt, clay, and mud related in terms of sediment size?
2. What are two ways that sediment is formed?
3. In what kind of sedimentary rock are fossils most common? Why?
4. Compare and contrast the formation of a mold fossil and a cast fossil.

Digging Deeper

FOSSILIZATION AND SEDIMENT SIZE
Sediments

Sediment ranges in size from large boulders to very fine mud. Sediments coarser than 2 mm (millimeters) are called gravel. Sand is defined as sediment with sizes between one-sixteenth of a millimeter and 2 mm. All sediment finer than sand is called mud. The coarser part of the mud is called silt, and the finer part is called clay.

Sediments are formed when rocks on the land surface are broken down by rain, wind, and sunlight. Sediments consist of particles of minerals, and also loose pieces of rock. Streams and rivers move the sediments downstream toward the ocean. Some of the sediment is stored in large river valleys, but most of it reaches the ocean. Some is deposited in shallow water near the shore, and some is carried far out into the deep

ocean. Most of the sediment deposited near the shore is coarse, and it gets finer farther away from the shore. Most of the sediment in the deep ocean is very fine mud.

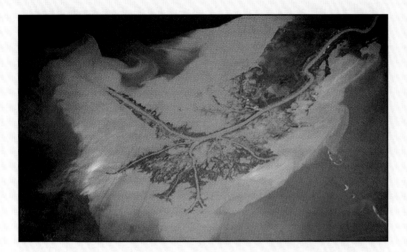

Sediments are also formed when calcium carbonate minerals are precipitated from warm, shallow waters in the ocean. Much of this is used by marine animals to make their skeletons. After the animals die, their skeletons become sediment. Where currents are weak, this sediment stays where the animals lived. Where currents are strong, the shells are moved along the bottom and are worn into rounded particles.

Fossils in Sedimentary Rocks

In certain conditions, and over a very long period of time, sediment becomes compacted and cemented into sedimentary rock. Fossils are more common in some kinds of sedimentary rocks than others. There are many factors that can contribute to the likelihood of an organism being preserved as a fossil. You investigated one of these, grain size, in this investigation. Fossils are most common in limestones. That is because most limestones consist partly or mostly of the shells of ➞

organisms. Sometimes, however, the shells are worn so much that they look like ocean sediment grains rather than "real" fossils. Fossils are also common in shales, which form from muds. As you have already learned, excellent imprint fossils can be formed in fine-grained sediments like muds. Only some shales contain fossils, however, because many areas of muddy ocean floor had conditions that were not suitable for animal life. In this case, only swimming or drifting organisms that die and fall into the mud have a chance to become fossilized. Although this does happen, it is a very rare occurrence. Some sandstones contain fossils as well. Most sandstones do not contain fossils, for various reasons. Water currents in the environment might have been too strong for animals to survive. Also, sands are very porous, so water seeping through the sand might have dissolved the shells away long before the sand was buried and changed into sandstone.

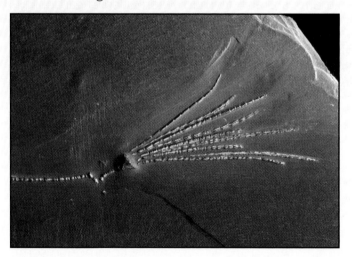

Kinds of Fossils

Sediments are home for many kinds of marine animals. Some animals live on the surface of the sediment, and some burrow into it. Some fossil shells are found mixed with the mud they lived in. Other fossil shells were

moved by strong currents and deposited along with sand or even gravel. If the shells are buried by more sediment before they are worn away or dissolved, they become fossilized.

Sometimes a fossil consists of original shell material. This is common in very young sediments that have not yet been turned into rock. Older sediments usually have been buried deeply by later sediments and turned into rock. Then it is more likely that the original shell has been dissolved away by water seeping through the pore spaces in the sediment. The fossil is left as an imprint of the original shell. An imprint like that is called a mold. Sometimes the space that was occupied by the shell is now empty. In other cases that space has been filled with later minerals that were precipitated by the flowing pore water. That material, which has the shape of the original shell, is called a cast.

Clams have shells that are in two parts, called valves. The valves are hinged along one edge. They are left and right, like your hands when you put them together along your little fingers. The clam can open its shell to feed and close its shell for protection. Think about what you might see when the clamshell is fossilized. Each valve has an outer surface and an inner surface. Depending on which valve you are seeing, and whether you are seeing the inside or the outside of it, and whether you are seeing its cast or its mold, eight different views are possible! Paleontologists have to be very careful to match up the fossils they see. Otherwise, they might think they are seeing fossils of several different kinds of animal rather than just one.

Review and Reflect

Review

1. Choose several objects from everyday life and compare them to the sizes of gravel, sand, and mud.

2. Give two reasons why fossils are relatively uncommon in sandstones.

Reflect

3. Think back to **Part B** of the investigation. Explain why you think that the clamshell made a better impression in fine-grained sediment than in the coarse-grained sediment.

4. From what you have learned in this investigation, do you think that a sandy beach is a good place for fossils to be preserved? Why or why not?

Thinking about the Earth System

5. Where do sediments come from? Describe any connections that you can make between the hydrosphere, the atmosphere, and the geosphere in the formation of sand and mud deposits. Note these on your *Earth System Connection* sheet.

6. How is the biosphere related to the formation of some sediments? Note any connections between the biosphere and sediment formation on your *Earth System Connection* sheet.

Thinking about Scientific Inquiry

7. How did you use mathematics in this investigation?

8. How did you support a prediction with evidence?

9. Describe how you modeled the process of fossilization in this investigation. In what ways was your model like the natural process of fossilization? In what ways was it different?

Investigation 3:

Conditions for Fossil Formation

Key Question

Before you begin, first think about this key question.

Where can fossils form?

In the last activity you discovered that sediment size affects fossilization. Think about what you know about fossil formation. What other factors affect whether or not an organism becomes a fossil?

Share your thinking with others in your group and with your class. Keep a record of the discussion in your journal.

Materials Needed

For this investigation your group will need:

- stream table, or similar setup
- wooden block (or books) to tilt stream table
- dry sand (as fine as possible)
- watering can
- water source
- two tree leaves, pre-soaked in water overnight
- two clamshells
- topographic map of your local area, or physical map of your region
- cardboard
- set of compasses
- scissors
- protractor
- sharpened pencil or dowel

Investigate

Part A: Location, Location

1. With your group, examine your school grounds and, if possible, wooded or moist areas like stream banks, gullies, and along the shores of lakes. You may need to complete this part of the activity on a weekend at home or at a local park, under adult supervision.

When examining the school grounds or other areas, you should be supervised by a teacher, parent, or other responsible adult.

Do not handle any living or dead organisms or other litter you find.

Look for living plants and animals like birds, small mammals, and insects. Also look for evidence of death or decay, like leaf litter, carcasses, feathers, and bones. If this is not available, look for human-made litter (i.e., trash).

a) In your journal, keep careful notes about what you observe, and where you observed it. Draw a map of the area and mark on the map where you found the objects.

2. Upon return to the classroom, talk over your observations with your group and with your class.

a) Describe what you observed that indicates decay.

b) Describe what you observed that indicates preservation.

c) Did you find any potential fossils? What were they and why do you think they could become fossils?

d) If most dead organisms can become fossils, would you have expected to find more evidence for this on your outdoor excursion? What does this tell you about the likelihood of something becoming a fossil?

e) What new questions arose from this discussion?

Together, make a class list of key points and questions.

3. You will now build a model that may help you find answers to some of the questions you have generated. In particular, you will model how remains of certain organisms are more likely to be protected from decay than others.

Use a stream table or a large, flat, plastic container about one meter long. Tilt the container by using a book or wooden block at one end.

Pour a little water into the lower end, and place a wet leaf and shell underwater on the container floor.

Put a pile of sand on the upper part of the container. Put a leaf and a shell on top of the sand.

4. Predict what will happen if you slowly add water to the upper end of the stream table, as if to model rain.

   a) Record your prediction. Include a reason for your prediction.

5. Slowly and carefully, model heavy rain falling on the land at the upper edge of your model. You may wish to use a watering can to apply the water to the sand.

6. When you have completed your test, observe where the leaves and shells have ended up. Review your predictions and the reasons for them.

   a) Were your predictions correct? Were the results surprising?

7. Think about the model and your trip outdoors.

   a) In nature, which of the two leaves would be more likely to become a fossil over time, and why?

   b) Which of the two shells would be more likely to become a fossil?

   c) Based on your model, what kind of places would fossils be more likely to form?

8. Look at the diagram and compare it to a topographic map of your local area.

Inquiry
Models

Scientists and engineers use models to help them think about processes that happen too slowly, too quickly, or which cannot be directly observed. Choosing a useful model is one of the instances in which intuition and creativity come into play in science and engineering. In this investigation, you will build a model that will help to identify locations in which an organism is more likely to become fossilized.

Keep in mind that models are imperfect representations of natural processes. They are both like and unlike what they represent, in a number of ways.

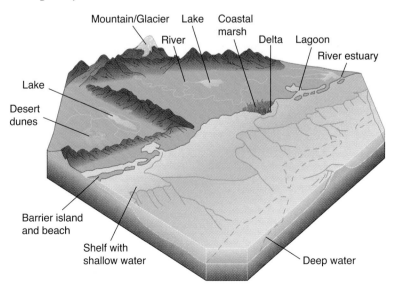

Mountain/Glacier Lake Coastal marsh
River   Delta   Lagoon
River estuary
Lake
Desert dunes
Barrier island and beach
Shelf with shallow water
Deep water

a) Looking at the diagram, where on the land and under water do you think fossils might have formed in the past? Why?

b) Where do you think there is a chance that fossils might begin to form now?

c) What conditions would be necessary for fossils to begin to form now? What would have to happen?

d) Where do you think you might find conditions that lead to fossil formation in your local area or region?

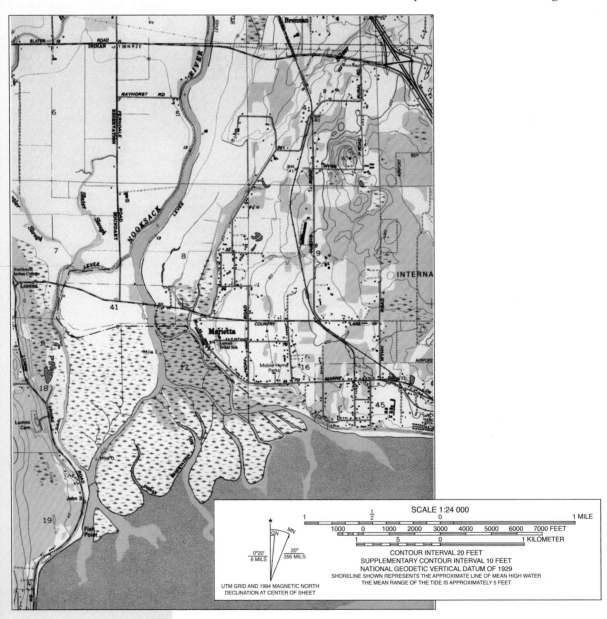

9. Test your ideas by conducting research on your local area and/or region.

   a) Did you find that there are fossils in your local area and/or region? Where were the fossils located? Were they abundant in the area that you thought they would be? If not, how do you explain this? Share your findings with your class.

Part B: "Wheel of Fossilization"

1. Imagine that you observe a recently living organism in the ocean.

   a) What might happen to the remains?

   b) Will it leave behind any fossil evidence? Explain why or why not.

2. To investigate the possible fates of different organisms, you will play a game using the "Wheel of Fossilization." First, your group will need to construct a "wheel," similar to the one shown in the diagrams.

   • Construct the wheel by cutting out a circle of cardboard.

   • Divide the circle into 12 roughly equal sections.

   • Number the sections 1-12.

   • Push a pencil through the center.

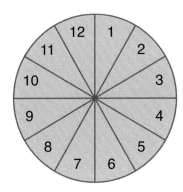

3. You will consider the position of a recently living organism, and the wheel will decide its fate. One of your group members will spin the wheel for you. The fate of the organism is determined by the number touching the desk when it stops spinning.

Possible Fates on the Wheel of Fossilization

1. You are a saber-toothed cat. Your body decomposes and your bones disintegrate in a field—NO FOSSIL
2. You are a shelled protozoan (a foraminiferan). Your body decomposes and your shell dissolves in the deep sea—NO FOSSIL
3. You are an oak tree. Your wood and leaves all decompose in a forest—NO FOSSIL
4. You are a snail. Your shell is preserved as a fossil, but rock erosion later destroys it—NO FOSSIL
5. You are a clam. Your shell is buried by mud in a quiet water setting—YOUR SHELL FOSSILIZES
6. You are a barnacle. Your body and shell are metamorphosed in an undersea lava flow—NO FOSSIL
7. You are a jellyfish. You have no hard skeleton, and your soft body decomposes —NO FOSSIL
8. You are a crab. You get eaten and your shell gets broken down into tiny bits in the process—NO FOSSIL
9. You are a tree fern. Your leaves are buried and preserved in swamp mud—YOUR TISSUES FOSSILIZE
10. You are a clamshell. Your body decomposes and your shell is broken to bits by waves—NO FOSSIL
11. You are a snail shell. Your body decomposes and your shell is recrystallized during mountain-building—NO FOSSIL
12. You are a *Tyrannosaurus rex*. Your footprint in mud is buried by sand along a river—YOUR TRACK FOSSILIZES.

4. Repeat so that each group member has three turns at the Wheel.

   a) How many members of your group ended up becoming fossils?

   b) Did any one person become a fossil more than once?

   c) What happened to you, according to the fates given by the Wheel?

   d) Do you think this is a realistic game? Why or why not?

   Share the results of your group's discussion with the rest of the class.

   e) Keep a record of the discussion in your journal.

THE LIKELIHOOD OF FOSSILIZATION

For a fossil to form, several conditions have to be met. First of all, the animal had to live in the given area! Animals live in many environments on Earth, but not everywhere. The water above many lake bottoms and some areas of the deep ocean bottom are stagnant. The bottom water is never exchanged with surface waters, so the water contains no dissolved oxygen. Animals cannot live without oxygen, so no animals live there. In these situations, the only possibility of fossilization is if a fish or other swimming or floating animal dies in oxygen-rich waters above, sinks down into the stagnant muddy bottom, and is buried by sediments.

Most environments on the land surface are populated with animals. Fossilization on land is very uncommon, however, because most areas of the land are being eroded. Unless there is deposition, fossils cannot be preserved. Deposition on land is common only in river valleys. Fossils are fairly common in sediments deposited on river floodplains.

Some ocean environments that support animal life are exposed to very strong currents and waves. After a shelled animal dies, the strong water motions cause the hard body parts to be broken and worn. Often the shells end up only as rounded grains of sand or gravel, which no longer look like fossils.

As You Read...
Think about:
1. *Why are very few fossils found in rocks made from sediments that are laid down in deep ocean waters? What fossils would you expect to find in these rocks?*
2. *How does erosion affect the likelihood of fossilization? How does deposition affect the likelihood of fossilization?*
3. *Under what conditions are soft-bodied animals fossilized?*

For animals without skeletons, like worms or jellyfish, fossilization is a very rare event. When paleontologists find a well-preserved fossil of a soft-bodied animal, it's an occasion for celebration. For a soft-bodied animal to be fossilized, its body must be protected from decomposition. The body is usually exposed to air and water with a lot of oxygen, so it decomposes rapidly. The animal is likely to be fossilized only if it is buried soon after it dies (or when it is buried alive!). Even then, it is likely to decompose, because water that seeps through the sediment around it is usually rich in oxygen. Sometimes, however, the body is buried rapidly by fine mud. Water seeps through mud much more slowly than through sand, so the body does not decompose as fast. Mud often contains a lot of other organic matter as well, and that uses up oxygen faster. Some animal bodies then escape decomposition. Under just the right conditions, a delicate impression of the animal might be preserved.

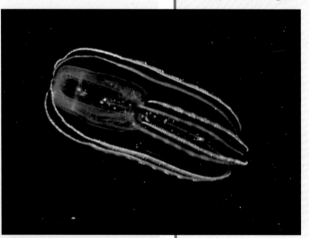

Paleontologists are sure that the fossil record is biased. That means that some kinds of organisms are much scarcer as fossils than they were when they were alive. Other kinds of organisms are much better represented by fossils. Animals with hard shells and skeletons are represented well in the fossil record. On the other hand, soft-bodied animals are probably represented very poorly. It's likely that most soft-bodied species that ever existed are gone forever without a trace. Land animals are probably very poorly represented as well. For example, most animals that are now alive, or have ever lived, are insects, but the fossil record of insects is poor.

Review and Reflect

Review

1. a) Why are low-lying areas more likely to accumulate fossils?

    b) Why is this not always true?

2. What are some factors that determine if a recently living organism ends up fossilized?

Reflect

3. Would you expect animals that lived in the oceans near a river delta to be better represented in the fossil record than animals that lived on land? Why or why not?

4. Would you be more likely to find a fossil of a freshwater fish or a hyena? Explain your reasoning.

5. Earth's earliest life was microscopic and soft-bodied. What challenges does this present for scientists who study early life on Earth?

6. What does it mean that the fossil record is biased? What causes it to be biased?

Thinking about the Earth System

7. On your *Earth System Connection* sheet, note how the things you learned in this investigation connect to the geosphere, hydrosphere, atmosphere, and biosphere.

8. What are some advantages and disadvantages of using the geosphere to understand the biosphere of the past?

Thinking about Scientific Inquiry

9. Scientists use evidence to develop ideas. What evidence do you have that becoming a fossil is rare?

10. How did you use a model in this investigation to investigate fossilization? How could you modify the model to make it more realistic?

Investigation 4:

Fossils through Geologic Time

Key Question

Before you begin, first think about this key question.

How can we determine the age of a fossil?

Think about what you know about the conditions under which fossils form. If different fossils are found in different layers of rock, could you tell which fossils are the oldest? The youngest?

Share your thinking with others in your class. Keep a record of the discussion in your journal.

Materials Needed

For this investigation your group will need:

- metric measuring tape (as long as possible)
- chalk
- chart paper
- calculator
- "stratigraphic" notebook with "fossils" (this can be made using the detailed instructions provided in the Teacher's Edition)

Investigate

Part A: Geologic Time

1. Geologists know that Earth is about 4.6 billion (4,600,000,000) years old. Primitive life evolved as much as 3.5 billion years ago, or more, but large and complicated life did not develop until much later. In terms of Earth's history, humans are very recent. Find them on the chart.

a) When did modern humans appear?

b) How does this compare to when life began on the planet?

2. To get a better sense of this kind of time scale, your group is going to think of time as if it were distance.

In a suitable place (a corridor or the schoolyard), mark a starting point with chalk. Next, each person should walk 10 normal paces, mark the distance with chalk, and put his or her name beside this point.

Major Divisions of Geologic Time
(boundaries in millions of years before present)

Era	Period	Event	
Cenozoic	Quaternary	modern humans	
			1.8
	Tertiary	abundant mammals	
			65
Mesozoic	Cretaceous	flowering plants; dinosaur and ammonoid extinctions	
			145
	Jurassic	first birds and mammals; abundant dinosaurs	
			213
	Triassic	abundant coniferous trees	
			248
Paleozoic	Permian	extinction of trilobites and other marine animals	
			286
	Pennsylvanian	fern forests; abundant insects; first reptiles	
			325
	Mississippian	sharks; large primitive trees	
			360
	Devonian	amphibians and ammonoids	
			410
	Silurian	early plants and animals on land	
			440
	Ordovician	first fish	505
	Cambrian	abundant marine invertebrates; trilobites dominant	
			544
Proterozoic		primitive aquatic plants	
			2500
Archean		oldest fossils; bacteria and algae	

⚠ Check for any hazards before pacing off your steps.

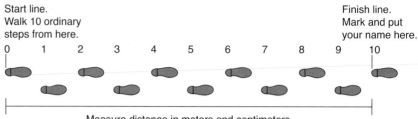

Start line.
Walk 10 ordinary
steps from here.

Finish line.
Mark and put
your name here.

0   1   2   3   4   5   6   7   8   9   10

Measure distance in meters and centimeters.
Divide by 10 to find each person's average step.

3. When everyone in your group has measured his or her 10-step distance, put the lengths on a chart like the one shown.

Names of Group Members	Distance of Steps (in meters and centimeters)	Average Step (total distance for each person divided by 10)
Total for Your Group (add each person's average)		T =
Average Group Step (divide total by number of persons in your group)		AGS =

4. Find the Average Class Step (ACS) by taking the Total (T) for each group, adding them all together, and dividing the total figure by the number of students participating. How does this number compare to the Average Group Step (AGS)?

   You may want to round the ACS figure up or down to make it into the nearest convenient number (for example, if it is 78 cm, round it up to 80 cm).

5. You will now apply your average distance to time.

   Think of one average step as representing 100 years of time. On this scale it means:

   • You have lived for about one-eighth of a step.

   • Your parents have probably lived for about one-third of a step.

   • Only someone at least 100 years old would have lived one step or more.

Look again at the Major Divisions of Geologic Time chart.

In your group, figure out how many steps would represent life through time for the beginning of each of the periods starting with the Cambrian Period, when a great many different kinds of animals become common in the fossil record. How many steps would be required to represent all of the time that life has been on Earth (about 3.5 billion years)?

6. To get another sense of the huge scale of geologic time, use some mathematical calculations. Imagine that you want to make a movie that will include life through time starting from the origin of the Earth to today. Suppose this movie is going to be 24 hours long!

a) How long would humans be on the screen?

Share your answer, and the calculations you used to get it, with the rest of the class.

Part B: Life through Geologic Time

1. On a long gymnasium floor, a corridor, or a parking lot, measure out a distance of at least 100 ft (about 30 m).

Use a 100-foot tape measure or lay out a 100-foot piece of rope between the beginning and end of that distance. This will represent all of geologic time.

2. Your teacher will give you a chart that shows the dates when various kinds of animals first appeared in the fossil record. Plot these dates along the line. To do that, you will have to form a ratio. For each kind of animal, divide the date of appearance by the total length of geologic time. Use that ratio to figure out where to put the point along your 100-foot line. If you are not sure how to do this, your teacher will help you.

a) Where would a point be that stands for your age?

b) Where would a point be that stands for your grandparent's age?

c) Where would a point be that stands for the beginning of recorded human history (about 4000 years)? How does that compare with the time since the dinosaurs became extinct?

Part C: Figuring out the Fossil Record

1. Your teacher will give each group a special notebook. Think of the notebook as a sequence of sedimentary rock layers. Geologists call this a stratigraphic section. You might see such a section in a highway cut, a river bank, or a sea cliff. Each page stands for a single layer in the sequence.

Each notebook comes from some place around the world. Each one is different. The number of layers is not the same from notebook to notebook, and the layers themselves are different.

Some of the layers contain fossils. Some do not. The names of the different fossils are shown by capital letters on the pages. These letters have nothing to do with the age of the fossils.

You need to keep three important things in mind.

- Sedimentary rock layers are originally deposited one on top of another in horizontal layers. The oldest layer is at the bottom of the stack, and the youngest is at the top.

  The first part of this statement (that sedimentary rock layers are deposited one on top of another) is called the "Law of Superposition."

  The second part of the statement (about originally being in horizontal layers) is called the "Law of Original Horizontality."

  Combined, these two ideas are very important, because they provide a means to tell which rock layers (and fossils in those rock layers) are older than others.

- Different kinds of plants and animals are called species. A species appears at a certain time and most become extinct at a later time. Once a species becomes extinct, it never appears again.

Inquiry

Laws in Science

In science and nature, the word "law" is given a very special status. A scientific law or a law of nature is generally accepted to be true and universal. Laws are accepted at face value because they have been so strongly tested, and yet have always been observed to be true. A law can begin as a hypothesis, but only after years and even decades of testing can a hypothesis become a law. It can become a law only if it has been shown to be true over and over again, without exception. A law can sometimes be expressed in terms of a single mathematical equation, but laws don't always need to have complex mathematical proofs.

- Geologists didn't know beforehand the succession of fossil species through geologic time. They had to figure that out from the succession of fossils in stratigraphic sections all around the world. You're going to do the same thing in this investigation.

2. You will use the data from each group's notebook to figure out the succession of fossil species. Each group has a sheet of poster board with blank columns (one for each group). On each sheet of poster board, plot your succession of layers in one of the columns. In the column, show the contacts between the layers with horizontal lines. If a layer contains one or more kinds of fossils, label them in the column.

Inquiry
Reporting Findings

In this investigation you are mirroring what paleontologists do. Findings are reported by many different paleontologists and are added to the fossil record.

Group 1   Group 2   Group 3   Group 4   Group 5   Group 6

F
33

3. The time interval when one or more species existed is called a zone. Your job is to figure out the "standard" succession of zones, worldwide. To help you do this, draw light pencil lines between the columns, to match up times when fossils A to Z lived. Erase lines and change them as needed.

4. When you are satisfied that you have figured out the succession, write it down in a vertical column on a blank sheet of paper, with the oldest at the bottom and the youngest at the top.

5. As a class, compare the succession of fossil zones from all of the groups.

   a) Are each group's results the same? If not, discuss the reasons why. Then agree on the single acceptable succession.

   b) Why do some layers contain fossils but other layers have no fossils?

   c) There are two basic reasons why a particular fossil zone might be missing from one or more of the columns. What are these reasons?

   d) How would you use the results of this investigation to tell the ages of the rock layers in a new stratigraphic section?

   e) Imagine that you are studying a newly discovered stratigraphic section somewhere in the world. You find an entirely new fossil species in one of the layers. Would that change your thinking about the standard succession of fossil zones? If not, why not? If so, how?

 Digging Deeper

TELLING GEOLOGIC TIME
Species

Every plant or animal belongs to a species. A species is a population of plants or animals that can breed to produce offspring that can then produce offspring themselves.

Biologists believe that new species evolve from existing species by a process called natural selection. Here's how it works. Genes are chemical structures in the cells of the organism. The nature of the organism is determined by its genes. The organism inherits the genes from its parents. Occasionally, a gene changes accidentally. That's called a mutation. The changed gene is passed on to the next generation. Most mutations are bad, some are neutral but some mutations make the organism more successful in its life. Organisms that inherit that favorable new gene are likely to become more abundant than others of the species.

Sometimes the population of a species becomes separated into two areas, by geography or by climate. Then the two groups no longer breed with each other. The two groups then slowly change by natural selection. Each group changes in different ways. Eventually, the two groups are so different that they can't breed to produce offspring any more. They have become two different species.

As You Read...
Think about:
1. *What is a species?*
2. *How do species change through time?*
3. *What are index fossils? How are they used in stratigraphic correlations?*
4. *How has radioactivity been used to refine the geologic time scale?*

Species eventually become extinct. That means that the population gets smaller and smaller, until no more organisms of that species are left alive. Species become extinct for various reasons. If the environment changes too fast, the species might not be able to adapt fast enough. Also, a new species might evolve to compete with an existing species. Biologists are sure that once a species becomes extinct it never appears again.

In the modern world, biologists can identify species by seeing whether the organisms can breed with one another. Paleontologists have much more trouble with fossil species, because the organisms are no longer around to breed! All that can be done is to match up shells or imprints that look almost identical and then assume that they represent a species. The features of an organism are controlled by its genetics. Thus, similar-looking fossil organisms had similar genetic composition.

The Fossil Record

Paleontologists want to know the history of evolution and extinction of fossil species through geologic time. To do that, they try to study all of the fossils that have been preserved in sedimentary rocks. That's called the fossil record. Paleontologists have been collecting fossils from sedimentary rock layers around the world for

over 200 years. Their goal is to figure out the succession of species through all of geologic time. Once that succession is known, it serves as a scale of geologic time. Then, if you find a particular fossil in a rock, you know where that rock fits into the geologic time scale.

Cambrian trilobites

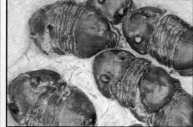

Ordovician trilobites

Devonian trilobites

There's a big problem in figuring out the succession of species through geologic time. You ran into this problem in the investigation. You don't know beforehand what the succession of species is! All you have are many stacks of sedimentary rocks (called stratigraphic sections) around the world to look at. No single stack spans all of geologic time, and no single stack has nearly all of the species that ever lived. You have to compare all of the stacks against one another to get the best approximation to the real succession. That's what you did in **Part C** of this investigation. You compared all of the stacks to one another and matched them up to figure out the succession of fossils. Paleontologists are still refining their ideas about the succession, as new fossils are found.

Stratigraphic Correlation

As you probably figured out already, matching up stratigraphic sections from around the world can be very difficult. If there were no fossils and you could only use the characteristics of the rock layers it would be even harder! This is because at any given time, very

different types of sediments can be deposited in different places. It is these sediments that will eventually become the sedimentary rock layers making up the stratigraphic sections. At any given time, mud may be slowly collecting in some places while in other places sand is piling up rapidly. In other places, maybe there is nothing collecting at all! So you see, very different looking rock layers may mark the same time interval in different stratigraphic sections. The process of matching up equivalent "time layers" of rocks in different places is called stratigraphic correlation. One of the best (and oldest) tools for correlating strata around the world is the use of special fossils called index fossils.

Index fossils have two important characteristics. First, they must have been widely distributed around the world. Second, they must have existed for only relatively short periods of geologic time before becoming extinct. Consider a fossil of an organism that lived only in one place, or that existed for very long periods of geologic time. It would be of little use in matching up layers of rock that were deposited far from one another over the same limited span of time.

Dating Rocks

Knowing the fossil record lets a geoscientist place a particular fossiliferous rock layer into the scale of geologic time. But the time scale given by fossils is only a relative scale, because it does not give the age of the rock in years, only its age relative to other layers. Long after the relative time scale was worked out from fossils, geologists developed methods for finding the absolute ages of rocks, in years before the present. These methods involve radioactivity. Here's how one of the important ones works:

Some minerals contain atoms of the radioactive chemical element uranium. Now and then, an atom of uranium self-destructs to form an atom of lead. Scientists know the rate of self-destruction. They grind up a rock to collect tiny grains of minerals that started out containing some uranium but no lead. Then they use a very sensitive instrument, called a mass spectrometer, to measure how much of the uranium has been changed to lead. Using some simple mathematics, they can figure out how long ago the mineral first formed. Rocks as old as four billion years can be dated this way.

Absolute dating of rocks has provided many "tie points" for the relative time scale developed from fossils. The result is an absolute time scale. When you collect a fossil from a rock, you can place it in the relative time scale. Then you also know about how old it is in years (or usually millions, or tens of millions, or hundreds of millions of years). Even though modern technology makes it possible to date some rocks, the relative time scale is still very important. This is because it takes a lot of time and money to obtain an absolute date, and most rocks cannot be dated using radioactivity.

Review and Reflect

Review

1. According to the chart in this investigation, how long have modern humans (*Homo sapiens*) been on Earth?

2. How are fossils used to match or correlate rock layers deposited in different places at the same time?

3. Why do geologists not use the characteristics of the rocks themselves to identify different rock layers that were deposited at the same time?

Reflect

4. In your own words, explain why you think that geologists still find the relative time scale to be a very useful tool.

5. Why is it that a scientist must look in many places to determine the succession of fossil species through geologic time?

Thinking about the Earth System

6. On your *Earth System Connection* sheet, note how the things you learned in this investigation connect to the geosphere, hydrosphere, atmosphere and biosphere.

Thinking about Scientific Inquiry

7. How did you model the fossil record?

Investigation 5:

Comparing Fossils over Time

Key Question
Before you begin, first think about this key question.

How are modern organisms different from ancient organisms?

Think about the age of the Earth. How has life changed since the first organisms appeared?

Share your thinking with others in your class. Keep a record of the discussion in your journal.

Materials Needed

For this investigation your group will need:

- fossil clamshell
- hand lens
- eight index cards
- metric ruler or tape measure
- pencil and other drawing implements
- paper clip or a stapler
- fresh clamshells (with clam removed)

Investigate

1. Each group will receive a fossil clamshell.

   Observe the fossil in detail, noting all its characteristics. Remember to observe it from all angles, both inside and out. Each group will have a fossil clamshell. At first glance, they all look very similar. If you look closely, however, you will see fine differences.

Think about any measurements you could make of the fossil clamshell.

Look for any distinguishing features.

Are there any parts or markings that you can use to help you recognize your fossil clamshell among other fossil clamshells?

Pay attention to size and shape. Take lots of measurements. Look for places where muscles might have been attached, where feeding organs may have protruded from the shell, how the animal moved, and any other aspects of "living" that you can suggest.

2. Obtain four index cards.

On one index card, describe the fossil as if you were sending the description to someone who had never seen it before. Include all the observations and any measurements you have made.

On the other three index cards, make as accurate drawings of the fossil as you can, from three different angles.

Outside view of clamshell fossil	Inside view of clamshell fossil	Side view of clamshell fossil

You will need to collaborate on this task. Share the work between your group members. Keep your index cards safe, because you will need them for the next step.

3. All the clam fossils will now be collected, mixed up, and then displayed for all to visit and study. They will be placed in a random order.

Using your index cards as a guide, try to find your fossil in the collection.

a) How difficult was it to find your fossil clam? What made it easy or difficult to find?

b) How accurate were your observations? How accurate is your record of those observations? Do you think that someone else could find your clamshell fossil from your recorded observations? Upon reflection, how would you change your observations and notes to improve them?

4. Fasten your index cards together. Use a paper clip or a staple. Write your names on the top of the first card.

All the sets of cards will be collected. They will be redistributed so that each group has another group's cards.

Once again, the clamshell fossils will be displayed, this time in a different order.

Using the data on the set of index cards you have been given, search and find the clamshell fossil it describes.

When you think you have identified the clam fossil correctly, check the names of the group members on the first card. Ask that group to verify that you have the correct one.

5. When each group has identified and verified the correct fossil, take time to discuss differences between the clam fossils.

Inquiry

Recording Observations

Scientists are very careful about recording observations. They try not to miss any detail that may turn out to be important later.

They also record their observations in a way that others can see and understand. This will also be important for you to do, because other groups are going to use your records later.

Record the results of your discussion in your journal.

a) How are all the clamshell fossils the same? How are they different?

b) What features can be measured, or counted?

c) What characteristics can help to sort one clamshell fossil from another?

d) Make a list of items that could be helpful for future study of clamshells.

This diagram will help you with your observations:

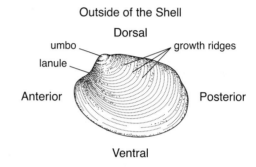

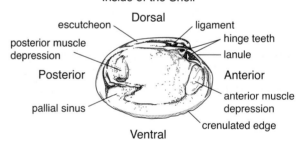

6. Your group will now be given a modern clamshell.

Once again, you will use four index cards to make a record of your observations.

You will also repeat the display-and-find process as before, using another group's index-card data to identify their clamshell and verify it.

7. Now, revisit your original fossilized clamshell, and the observations you made on index cards. Lay these alongside the modern clamshell and its set of observations.

Compare the two. Answer the following questions:

a) How are the two clamshells (ancient and modern) similar? How are they different?

b) Is there any way of telling that one is a fossil and the other is not? If so, how?

c) How can you tell that the fossilized clamshell may be a very ancient relative to the modern clamshell?

Discuss these questions, and any others you think important, first in your group, and then with all other groups. Try to reach an agreement about the similarities and differences between fossil clams and modern clams.

8. By now, you have discovered quite a lot about clams. Spend some time researching them. You will need to use all the resources available to do this.

The school library can be searched for reference books.

If you have access to computers, try CD-ROMs, encyclopedias, or log onto the Internet and search under "clams" (also try "pelecypods" and "bivalves," which are technical terms for clams) for further information.

a) When your group has completed its research, organize your information in a clear and understandable form. Try to be creative about this. Use any pictures you can find to make your presentation attractive and interesting to others.

Hold a whole-class session, in which each group shows what it has found out about clamshells.

9. When you have shared all the information you have collected about clams, think about other organisms that have existed through time. Review the Major Divisions of Geologic Time chart on page F29.

As you do so, discuss and answer these questions:

a) What other kinds of organisms besides clams have survived for millions of years?

b) What organisms have become extinct over time?

c) What might have given some organisms a better chance of survival than others?

Use any other resources you have available to help find answers to these questions.

Inquiry
Using References as Evidence

When you write a science report, the information you gather from books, magazines, and the Internet comes from scientific investigations. Just as in your investigations, the results can be used as evidence. Because evidence, like an idea, is important, you must always list the source of your evidence. This not only gives credit to the person who wrote the work, but it allows others to examine it and decide for themselves whether or not it makes sense.

As You Read...
Think about:

1. Why do paleontologists use geometric shapes to analyze a collection of fossils?

2. According to fossil records, how have organisms evolved during geologic time?

3. When did the first multicellular organisms appear in the fossil record?

Digging **Deeper**

FOSSILS THROUGH GEOLOGIC TIME

Identifying Fossils

When you sorted fossils by the features of their geometry, you were doing exactly what paleontologists do. A paleontologist collects as many fossils as possible from a rock or sediment. Once the fossils are prepared by scraping and cleaning, they are sorted by geometry. Fossils with very similar geometry are assumed to belong to a single species. That is because an organism's geometry is controlled by its genetics. Fossils with somewhat different geometry are assumed to belong to a different species. Usually, the fossil species has already been studied and named. Sometimes, however, the species is a new one. Then the paleontologist writes a detailed description of the new species, gives the new species a name, and publishes the description for others to read and use in their own work. Not much excites a paleontologist more than discovering a new species!

Sorting fossils is tricky business, for several reasons. Some organisms died when they were young and still developing, and some died when they were old. Some were male and some were female. Also, most species show a lot of natural variability. You know that from looking at other members of your own species! It's often impossible for paleontologists to

decide whether they are looking at a single species with a lot of variability, or two similar species.

Evolution in the Fossil Record

The oldest fossils are more than 3.5 billion years old. They are simple unicellular (single-celled) algae, very similar to algae that still exist today. Evolution was very slow until about 700 million

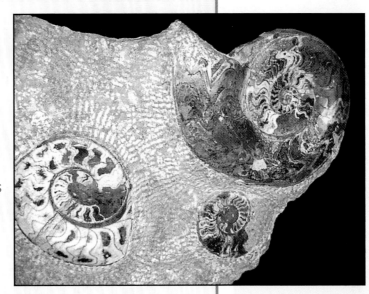

years ago, when unicellular organisms with larger and more complex cells evolved. Not long after that, a little more than half a billion years ago, multicellular (many-celled) organisms appeared. Instead of consisting of just a single cell, multicellular organisms have an enormous number of cells, grouped according to their function.

Several kinds of multicellular organisms evolved in a very short time, geologically. Paleontologists still do not understand very well how this happened. Many of these early kinds of multicellular organisms, like clams, snails, and corals, are still abundant today. More complex kind of animals, like reptiles, birds, and mammals, evolved even more recently in geologic time.

Review and Reflect

Review

1. What do fossil clams have in common with modern clams?

2. What kind of organism is the oldest found in the fossil record?

Reflect

3. How can you tell that the very ancient clam is related to the modern clam?

4. What are some of the difficulties in identifying fossils?

5. From what you've learned in this investigation, do you think that paleontologists have overestimated or underestimated the number of different species observed in the fossil record? Explain your answer.

Thinking about the Earth System

6. On your *Earth System Connection* sheet, note how the things you learned in this investigation connect to the geosphere, hydrosphere, atmosphere, and biosphere.

Thinking about Scientific Inquiry

7. Why is it important to take good observations?

8. Why is it important in a scientific investigation to record your observations and procedures carefully in a way that is easily understood by others?

Investigation 6:

Adaptations to a Changing Environment

Key Question

Before you begin, first think about this key question.

Why does any given plant or animal look the way it does, and has it always looked that way?

Think about a specific plant or animal and about what characteristics it may have that helps it to survive in this world.

Share your thinking with others in your class. Keep a record of the discussion in your journal.

Materials Needed

For this investigation your group will need:

• gaming die

• poster board

• colored pencils or markers

Investigate

Part A: Building a Better Beast

1. Look at the lists of different types of animal characteristics given on the next page. Each of these characteristics is an adaptation that can

help different animals to survive in the many different habitats on the Earth. For example, ducks have webbed feet to help them swim and dive for food, and they have a layer of down to keep them warm in the water. As a class, discuss some of these characteristics and how they are useful.

Now think about an animal that you may know of or perhaps may have even seen before.

a) What characteristics of that animal help it to adapt to its environment and thrive?

b) Look again at the list of different characteristics given below. Which of those characteristics does your animal have?

c) Share your thinking with your group. As a group, develop a list of animals and their characteristics or adaptations.

Animal Characteristics

Eyes	**Covering**	**Homes**
Forward in head	Fur	Trees
On sides of head	Feathers	Caves
	Scales	Underground
Feet	Skin	Water
Webbed	Shell	
Clawed		**When Animals Eat**
Padded	**Coloration**	Day
Hooved	Camouflage	Night
	Bright	Dawn or Dusk
Mouth		
Beak	**Movement**	**Dealing with Heat and Cold**
Tearing teeth	Running	Body Covering
Grinding teeth	Flying	Active/Feeding
Cutting teeth	Climbing	Times
	Swinging	Homes
	Leaping	
		Other Defenses
		Bad Smell or Taste
		Size

2. Look at the two possibilities listed for where the eyes of an animal are in its head. Hypothesize which adaptation you think would be better for a predator to have.

a) Propose an experiment or study that could test your hypothesis. Write the test in your journal.

b) Repeat this same thought process for another of the categories listed. Hypothesize what the advantage for a particular adaptation is and propose a means of testing your hypothesis.

3. It is now your group's job to "build a better beast." Using the table below, roll a die to see what environment your animal will live in.

Now, roll the die again to see if your animal will be a carnivore (meat eater), a herbivore (plant eater), or an omnivore (both a plant and meat eater).

No.	Habitat	No.	Animal Type
1	open grassland/savanna	1	herbivore
2	tropical rainforest	2	herbivore
3	temperate forest	3	carnivore
4	mountains	4	carnivore
5	desert	5	omnivore
6	wetlands	6	omnivore

4. Work together with your group to design an animal that would have the adaptations necessary to survive given the conditions dictated by your rolls of the dice. To do this, you should first make a list of some of the characteristics of the habitat in which your animal lives.

You can pick adaptations from the categories listed below. You can also invent your own adaptation.

a) Draw a picture of your creature and give it a name. Also list each adaptation, and describe how each adaptation will be of benefit to your creature.

5. Participate in a class discussion about each group's animals and adaptations.

 Digging **Deeper**

ADAPTATIONS

Living organisms are adapted to their environment. This means that the way they look, the way they behave, how they are built, or their way of life makes them suited to survive and reproduce in their habitats. For example, giraffes have very long necks so that they can eat tall vegetation, which other animals cannot reach. The eyes of cats are like slits. That makes it possible for the cat's eyes to adjust to both bright light, when the slits are narrow, and to very dim light, when the slits are wide open.

Behavior is also an important adaptation. Animals inherit many kinds of adaptive behavior. In southern Africa there are small animals called meerkats, which live in large colonies. The meerkats take turns standing on their hind legs, looking up at the sky to spot birds of prey. Meanwhile, the meerkats in the rest of the colony go about their lives. You can probably think of many other features of body or behavior that help animals to lead a successful life.

As You Read...
Think about:
1. *Describe in your own words what it means that an organism is adapted to its environment.*
2. *What is an ecological niche?*
3. *What is a vestigial structure? Provide an example.*

→

In biology, an ecological niche refers to the overall role of a species in its environment. Most environments have many niches. If a niche is "empty" (no organisms are occupying it), new species are likely to evolve to occupy it. This happens by the process of natural selection, which you learned about in **Investigation 4.** By natural selection, the nature of the species gradually changes to become adapted to the niche. If a species becomes very well adapted to its environment, and if the environment does not change, species can exist for a very long time before they become extinct.

The Modern Horse and Some of Its Ancestors

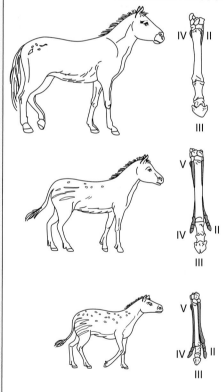

Equus
- Lived from about 5 million years ago to the present
- Lives in areas of the grassy plains
- Eats grasses and is classified as a grazer
- Is about 1.6 m tall at the shoulder
- Has 1 hoofed toe on each of its front and rear limbs.

Merychippus
- Lived from about 17 to 11 million years ago
- Lived in areas with shrubs and on the grassy plains
- Ate leafy vegetation and grasses and is classified as a grazer (the first in the line of horses)
- Was about 1.0 m tall at the shoulder and had a long face and legs making it appear much like a modern horse
- Had 3 hoofed toes on each of its front and rear limbs. The central toe was much larger than the others.

Miohippus
- Lived from about 32 to 25 million years ago
- Lived in less thickly wooded areas
- Ate leafy vegetation and is classified as a browser
- Was about 0.6 m tall at the shoulder (about the size of a German shepherd dog) and had padded feet
- Had 3 toes on each of its front and rear limbs.

Hyracotherium (Oldest known horse)
- Lived from about 55 to 45 million years ago
- Lived in thickly wooded areas
- Ate leafy vegetation and is classified as a browser
- Was about 0.4 m tall at the shoulder (about the size of a small dog) and had padded feet
- Had 4 toes on each of its front limbs and three on each of its rear limbs.

Horses are an excellent example of an animal evolving to fill a niche. Many fossils of different kinds of horses have been discovered, and paleontologists think that the earliest ancestor of the modern horse lived in North America more than 50 million years ago. This animal was a small padded-foot forest animal about the size of a dog. If you saw one next to a modern horse, you might not even think the two were related! As time passed, the climate of North America became drier, and the vast forests started to shrink. Grasses were evolving, and the area of grassland was increasing. Horses adapted to fill this new grassland niche. They grew taller, and their legs and feet became better adapted to sprinting in the open grasslands. Their eyes also adapted to be farther back on their heads to help them to see more of the area around them. Each of these adaptations helped the evolving grassland horses to avoid predators. Their teeth also changed to be better adapted to grinding tough grassland vegetation.

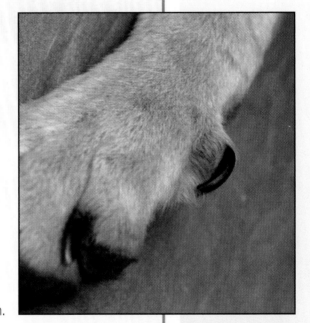

Have you ever wondered what purpose the "dew" claw on the inside of a dog's paw serves? The claw is the dog's thumb. Because a dog runs on the balls of its feet and four digits, the claw no longer serves a purpose. Organs or parts of the body that no longer serve a function are called vestigial structures. They provide evidence that the species is still changing. Even humans have vestigial structures. The human appendix is one such example. It used to store microbes that helped to digest plant matter, but it is no longer needed in the human.

Review and Reflect

Review

1. Are all animal adaptations physical adaptations? Explain your answer.

2. Pick an animal living today and describe two adaptations that help it to survive in its environment.

3. Describe three ways that horses have changed over the past 50 million years.

Reflect

4. Describe how adaptation relates to the process of natural selection that was described in the **Digging Deeper** reading section of **Investigation 4.**

5. What advantage might there be in a predator having soft, padded feet?

6. Examine the diagram on page F29 showing the Major Divisions of Geologic Time. How can the concept of ecological niches explain the rapid increase in the number of mammals since the end of the Cretaceous Period?

Thinking about the Earth System

7. What correlation did you make in this investigation between changes in the atmosphere/climate system and changes in the biosphere?

Thinking about Scientific Inquiry

8. How did you use the processes of scientific inquiry in this investigation?

Investigation 7:

Being a Paleontologist

Key Question

Before you begin, first think about this key question.

What can fossils tell you about life through time?

Think about what you have learned so far. What kinds of clues can fossils give about Earth history and changing life?

Share your thinking with others in your class. Keep a record of the discussion in your journal.

Materials Needed

For this investigation you will need:

- unknown fossil
- metric ruler and measuring tape
- fossil record charts
- set of known fossil samples
- state or regional geologic map
- access to research material
- materials to create a display

Investigate

1. You will be given an unknown fossil and a geologic map from its state of origin. Examine the fossil carefully.

   a) Write down your first thoughts about it in your journal. Think about these things:

   - What could have made this fossil?

- What kind of rock is it in?
- How old might it be?

Inquiry

Using Maps as Scientific Tools

Scientists collect and review data using tools. You may think of tools as only physical objects like shovels and hand lenses. However, forms in which information is gathered and stored are also tools. In this investigation you are using a geologic map as a scientific tool.

You will have the opportunity to conduct research on your fossil, so that you can compare what you think about it now, to what you think about it later on.

2. Using all of your knowledge and resources about fossils, including your geologic map, find out as much as you can about your fossil.

   Later, you can summarize this to give a "portrait" of your fossil sample. This can be in the form of: a model, a poster, a web page, a magazine article, a newspaper article, a brochure, a diorama, a free-standing display, or any other method that you choose.

3. Information that you may be able to find out about your fossil should include:

   - what kind of organism it represents;
   - what the organism looked like when it was alive;
   - what parts of the organism were fossilized and what were not (and why);
   - where the organism might have come from originally;
   - what kind of rock the fossil is in;
   - during what time period the fossil organism lived;

- detailed description of the fossil itself (dimensions, visual description, texture).

Review the resources that you have in your classroom, in your school, and in your community. Decide what would be the most useful ones, and collect these as you need them.

4. Do your research on your fossil, carefully recording what you find out in your journal, as well as the resources you have used.

5. When you have finished your research, construct your fossil portrait, using one of the methods listed in **Step 2**, or a presentation method of your own.

Be sure that your portrait covers as many of the questions in **Step 3** as possible.

Using both pictures and words, make the portrait appealing to your target audience.

6. When all of the fossil portraits are completed, you will have the opportunity to present your work.

Be prepared to answer questions about your research, the sources of your information, how recent they are, and how reliable they are. Be prepared, also, to ask other students in your class questions about their fossil portraits when they present.

Inquiry

Presenting Information

Scientists are often asked to provide information to the public. In doing so, they need to consider both the information they wish to present and the best method of presenting the information. In this investigation you will need to choose the method of presentation that you think will be the most effective.

Be sure your teacher approves your plan before you begin.

GEOLOGIC MAPS AND CROSS SECTIONS

Geologic maps show the distribution of the solid rock (bedrock) at the Earth's surface. In some places this rock is exposed and in other areas it is buried beneath a thin layer of surface soil or sediment. The number of different kinds of rock in the Earth's crust is enormous. However, the bedrock over a large area is usually the same type. That is because rocks are originally formed in large volumes by a specific process. The rock bodies formed during the same process are called rock units.

A geologic map is more than just a map of rock types. Most geologic maps show the locations and relationships of different rock units. Each rock unit is identified on the map by a symbol of some kind. The symbol is explained in a legend or key, and is often given a distinctive color as well. Part of the legend of a geologic map consists of one or more columns of little rectangles, with appropriate colors and symbols. The rectangles identify the various rock units shown on the map. There is often a very brief description of the units in this part of the legend. The rectangles for the units are arranged in order of decreasing age upward.

Geologic maps show other information as well. They show the symbols that are used to represent such features as folds or faults. They have information about latitude and longitude. They always have a scale, expressed both as a labeled scale bar and as a ratio— 1:25,000, for example. The first number is a unit of distance on the map and the second number, after the colon, is the corresponding distance on the actual land surface.

Geologic maps present a general picture of the rock units present. Such generalization is the responsibility of

As You Read...
Think about:

1. What kind of information does a geological map contain?
2. What is a rock unit?
3. Look at the map and cross section on page F61.
   a) What rock layer is the youngest? Explain your answer.
   b) What rock layer is the oldest? Explain.
   c) How do you know the layers were deformed by pressure?

the geologist doing the mapping. The amount of generalization increases as the area covered by the map increases.

Most geologic maps are accompanied by one or more vertical cross sections. These are views of what the geology would look like in an imaginary vertical plane downward from some line on the land surface. The geologist constructs these cross sections after the map is completed. Their locations are selected so as to best reveal the three-dimensional nature of the geology. The degree of certainty about the geology shown on the cross section decreases downward with depth below the surface.

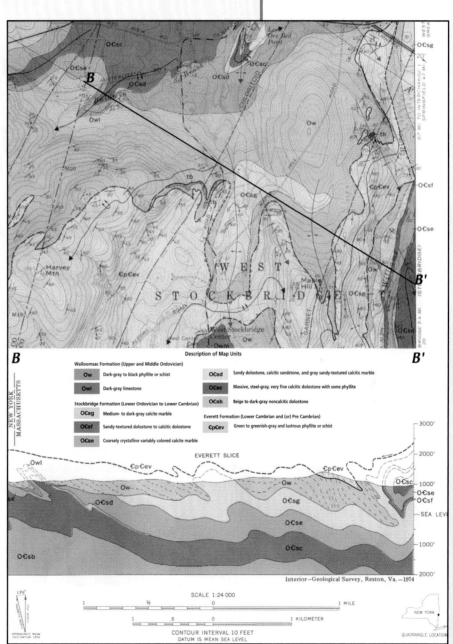

Review and Reflect

Review

1. What were the names of the fossils in your classmates' fossil portraits?

Reflect

2. What useful information about fossils could be found on a geologic map?

3. What information on a geologic map could be verified using the fossil record?

4. What have you discovered from this investigation to add to your understanding of life through time?

5. How does the study of fossils help geologists understand life through time?

6. How might understanding Earth's history be useful to humans now and in the future?

7. Think back on the entire research experience with your unknown fossil.

   a) How difficult was it to find the information you wanted?

   b) What resource was most helpful in finding out about your fossil? Why was that?

Thinking about the Earth System

8. How can you use the type of rock that your fossil was in along with information about the fossil animal itself to interpret the environment in which it lived?

Thinking about Scientific Inquiry

9. How did you collect evidence in this investigation?

10. How did you present your findings to others? Why was this important?

Reflecting

Back to the Beginning

You have been studying fossils in many ways. How have your ideas changed since the beginning of the investigation? Look at the following questions and write down your ideas in your journal:

- What is a fossil?
- How are fossils are formed?
- How can we find out how old a fossil is?
- What can fossils tell you about how life changed through time?
- What are some things that you want to understand better about fossils and changes in life through time?

How has your thinking about fossils changed?

Thinking about the Earth System

Consider what you have learned about the Earth system. Refer to the *Earth System Connection* sheet that you have been building up throughout this module.

- What connections between *Fossils* and the Earth system have you been able to find?

Thinking about Scientific Inquiry

You have used inquiry processes throughout the Unit. Review the investigations you have done and the inquiry processes you have used.

- What scientific inquiry processes did you use?
- How did scientific inquiry processes help you learn about fossils?

A New Beginning!

Not so much an ending as a new beginning!

This investigation into *Fossils* is now completed. However, this is not the end of the story. You will see the importance of fossils where you live, and everywhere you travel. Be alert for opportunities to observe the importance of fossils and add to your understanding.

The Big Picture

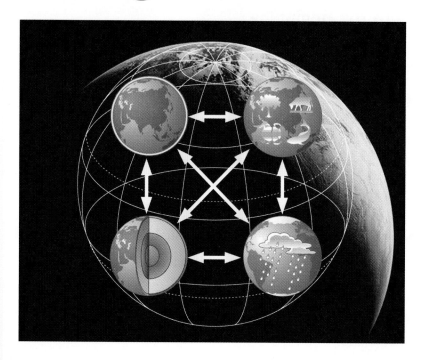

Key Concepts

Earth is a set of closely linked systems.

Earth's processes are powered by two sources: the Sun, and Earth's own inner heat.

The geology of Earth is dynamic, and has evolved over 4.6 billion years.

The geological evolution of Earth has left a record of its history that geoscientists interpret.

We depend upon Earth's resources—both mined and grown.

INVESTIGATING
CLIMATE AND WEATHER

Unit 4

What you will be investigating in this Unit:

Introducing Climate and Weather

Have you ever been in the middle of a powerful storm?

Have you ever wondered where the information for weather reports comes from and why weather forecasts are important?

Have you ever seen the effects of a serious lack of rain?

Have you ever seen clouds forming over a body of water?

Why Are Climate and Weather Important?

"What's the weather going to be like today?" That is often the first question on your mind when you wake up in the morning. What you wear, and sometimes even what you do on any given day depends on the weather. Weather can change very quickly. It could be sunny and warm in the morning, and in the afternoon you could be faced with dangerous thunderstorms and even tornadoes. You count on meteorologists (scientists who study the weather) to provide you with daily weather information.

On the other hand, you depend on the climate to give you fairly similar weather conditions year after year. Farmers expect the same length of growing season each year. Ski-resort operators anticipate a reasonable snowfall each year. They rely on the climate in the area to remain the same. Yet over very long periods of time, climate can change. Climatologists (scientists who study the climate) have evidence that the climate has changed many times in the past.

What Will You Investigate?

These investigations will put you in the roles of weather reporter, fact finder, and inquiring student. You will be using weather instruments and observations to make weather maps, weather reports, and weather forecasts. You will look for patterns in your weather data and explore reasons for those patterns. You will explore how climate has changed over time, the effects of climate on your life now, and what might happen if the climate changes in the future.

Here are some of the things that you will investigate:

• how weather instruments work;
• what is contained in a weather report and map;
• how weather observations are made;
• the underlying causes of weather patterns;
• the difference between climate and weather;
• how scientists know that the climate has changed in the past;
• how climate is changing now.

In the last investigation, you will have a chance to apply all that you have learned about climate and weather. You will make a prediction about what the climate where you live will be like 100 years from now. Then, you will gather and present evidence for or against your prediction.

Investigation 1:

Observing Weather

Key Question

Before you begin, first think about this key question.

How is weather observed?

Think about what you know about weather reports and weather maps. What sort of information goes into one? How is this information obtained? Make a list that combines what you know about obtaining weather information with questions that you might be able to answer in this investigation. Keep your list for review later.

Share your thinking with others in your group and with your class.

Materials Needed

For this investigation your group will need:

- reference resources about weather (books, CD-ROMs, access to the Internet)

- weather instruments (thermometer, wind vane, anemometer, rain gauge)

- instructions for using each weather instrument

- graph paper for making charts

- large flat-bottomed plastic pail or metal can

- street map of town, city, county, or school district

- white, self-adhesive labels, about 2.5 cm × 2.5 cm

Investigate

Part A: Kinds of Weather Observations

1. Your group members are going to become specialists in making a weather measurement or observation.

Your job will be to:

- research the science behind your weather observation;
- learn about the techniques for making your observation;
- study any instrument that is needed for your observation;
- practice making your weather observation;
- write a protocol for making your weather observation;
- set up a center for your classmates to learn how to make your weather observation correctly.

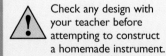

Check any design with your teacher before attempting to construct a homemade instrument.

2. Your group may be assigned one or more of the following weather observations: temperature, wind speed, wind direction, cloud types, cloud cover, precipitation type, or precipitation amount.

Research your weather observation.

a) Describe the science behind the weather observation in your journal.

b) What instrument, if any, is used to make your weather observation?

c) If you did not have a commercial version of your weather instrument, how could you make a homemade version? Draw a sketch of a homemade version in your journal.

3. You will be provided with information on how to make your weather observation properly so that your data are dependable.

Read the information carefully.

a) Write this information in the form of a protocol that others can easily understand and follow. Begin by writing a draft protocol for your weather observation. Remember to include the following in your protocol:

- the technique for taking the data;

- how to locate and set up your instrument properly, if your observation relies upon an instrument;

- how to read your instrument;

- how to record your data;

- the units of measurement to be recorded.

4. Exchange your draft protocol with one from another group in your class.

Read the other group's protocol.

a) Make comments on the other group's protocol. Your comments should be consistent with the criteria for a protocol outlined in Step 3 (a).

5. When you get your protocol back, revise it.

Practice making your weather observation using your protocol. Let each member of your group try this and compare the data you get from each person.

a) Does data vary between group members? If yes, how can the variation be reduced?

Inquiry

Writing a Protocol

A protocol is a procedure for a scientific investigation. It is a set of directions that someone else can read and follow. An important quality that your protocol should have is the ability to be replicated. In other words, your protocol should give consistent and reliable results, for anybody who uses it.

 Check your protocol with your teacher before proceeding to make observations.

6. Design a center to teach others about your weather observation.

a) Make a sketch in your journal of how your center will look, and what questions your center will address. Some suggested questions are:

- What does this weather observation tell you about the weather picture for a particular day?

- What ideas do you have about how this weather measurement helps in predicting the weather?

- In thinking about the protocol, what sorts of things could affect the accuracy of the weather data?

Address any additional questions that you think will help others to understand your center.

7. Construct your center. Set it up where it will work best for visitors to make weather measurements or observations.

8. Work through the centers according to a schedule set by your teacher. Be sure that you are clear on how to follow each protocol. Also, be sure that you understand what you are observing.

a) Record your measurements in your journal.

b) Write any questions that come to mind as you work through the center.

Part B: Making Observations for a Weather Map

1. Each student in the class will make weather observations at home for a week. The goal is to make a daily weather map of the local region.

As a class, decide on a protocol for your observations. Here are some of the things you need to think about for the protocol:

- An ideal weather map shows weather observations from many stations that are uniformly spaced.

- Observations need to be made at exactly the same time of day.

- Each observer needs to make exactly the same kinds of observations. On the next page is a list of these observations, with some helpful comments.

Temperature: Your thermometer needs to be mounted in a shady place one to two meters above the ground. Make sure that it will not be blown away by a strong wind. Also, make sure it is a shady spot. If you decide not to leave it outside the whole time, give it a few minutes to reach the outdoor temperature after taking it outside. Record temperatures in degrees Fahrenheit and degrees Celsius.

Wind direction: Record the wind direction as north, northeast, east, southeast, south, southwest, west, or northwest. Important: meteorologists record the direction the wind is blowing *from*, not the direction the wind is blowing to. For example, a northeast wind blows from the northeast toward the southwest.

Wind speed: You may not have an anemometer (an instrument that measures the speed of the wind), so you can use the Beaufort scale of wind speed. The Beaufort wind scale provides an estimate of wind speed based on observed effects of the wind. It is only approximate, but it is useful.

The Beaufort Wind Scale

Beaufort number	Kilometers per hour	Miles per hour	Wind Name	Land Indication
0	<1	<1	calm	smoke rises vertically
1	1–5	1–3	light air	smoke drifts
2	6–11	4–7	light breeze	leaves rustle
3	12–19	8–12	gentle breeze	small twigs move
4	20–29	13–18	moderate breeze	small branches move
5	30–38	19–24	fresh breeze	small trees sway
6	39–50	25–31	strong breeze	large branches move
7	51–61	32–38	moderate gale	whole trees move
8	62–74	39–46	fresh gale	twigs break off trees
9	75–86	47–54	strong gale	branches break
10	87–101	55–63	whole gale	some trees uprooted
11	102–119	64–73	storm	widespread damage
12	>120	>74	hurricane	severe destruction

Clouds: Important types of clouds are pictured below. Observe which type or types of clouds are in the sky, and estimate how much of the sky is covered by clouds (zero-tenths, one-tenth, two-tenths, etc., up to complete cloud cover). If you are not sure about the types of clouds, write one or two sentences in your notebook to describe how they look.

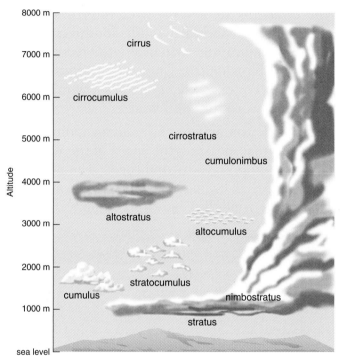

Precipitation: Is rain, drizzle, snow, or sleet falling? If so, is it light, moderate, or heavy? If it has rained since your last observation, how much rain has fallen? If it has snowed since your last observation, what is the depth of the new snow? Record rainfall or snowfall in inches and centimeters.

- You need to decide upon a set of symbols for representing your weather observations on the map. The diagram on the following page shows the standard way of doing this on weather maps. Once you get used to this system, the data will show you at a glance what the weather was like at the station.

a) Once everyone has agreed on the protocol, write it down and make copies of it for each student.

b) Make your daily observations, and record them in your journal.

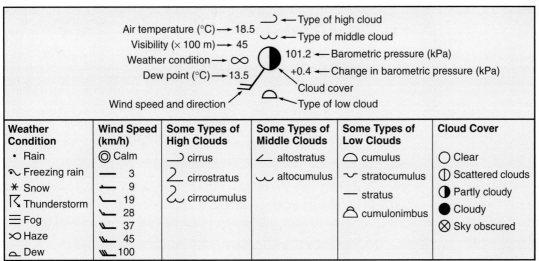

Weather Condition	Wind Speed (km/h)	Some Types of High Clouds	Some Types of Middle Clouds	Some Types of Low Clouds	Cloud Cover
• Rain	◎ Calm	⌐ cirrus	∠ altostratus	⌒ cumulus	○ Clear
⌐ Freezing rain	— 3	2 cirrostratus	∽ altocumulus	⌄ stratocumulus	◐ Scattered clouds
✳ Snow	— 9	2 cirrocumulus	— stratus	◑ Partly cloudy
⍗ Thunderstorm	— 19			● Cloudy
≡ Fog	— 28		△ cumulonimbus	
✕ Haze	— 37			⊗ Sky obscured
⌒ Dew	— 45			
	— 100			

2. Your teacher will supply a base map for making each day's weather map. As a class, mark the locations on the map of all the "stations" that have been decided upon.

   After each day's observations, plot all of the data on the weather map for that day.

3. After all five daily weather maps have been plotted, have a class discussion that deals with the following questions.

   Record the results of your discussion in your journal.

   a) How much did the weather vary from place to place at the same time over the local region?

   b) Do you think that the variation seen on the maps reflects real variations in the weather, or were they caused by differences in the way observations were made? Explain.

   c) Give reasons for the changes you observed from day-to-day on your weather maps.

   d) Are there regions of the United States where typical day-to-day variations in the weather are greater than in your local region? Where they are less? What do you think might be the causes for these differences?

Inquiry

Making Observations

Every field of science depends upon observations. Meteorology starts with observations of the weather. It is important that all observations be made carefully and recorded clearly. In this investigation others in your class will be relying on the accuracy of your observations to draw a weather map.

 Digging Deeper

ELEMENTS OF WEATHER

All sciences begin with observations. Without observations, scientists have no way to develop new theories and to test existing theories. The weather is no exception. Meteorologists (scientists who study the weather) observe many elements of the weather. This takes place both at the Earth's surface and at high altitudes. The observations you made in this investigation include many of the most important elements of the weather. Weather observations are needed both for predicting the weather and for developing and testing new theories about how the weather works.

Air Temperature

Air consists of gas molecules, mostly nitrogen (N_2) and oxygen (O_2). Although you cannot see them with your eyes, the molecules are constantly moving this way and that way at very high speeds. As they move, they collide with one another and with solid and liquid surfaces. The temperature of air is a measure of the average motion of the molecules. The more energy of motion the molecules have, the higher the air temperature.

Air temperature is measured with thermometers. Common thermometers consist of a liquid-in-glass tube attached to a scale. The scale can be marked (graduated) in degrees Celsius or degrees Fahrenheit. The tube contains a liquid that is supplied from a reservoir, or "bulb," at the base of the thermometer. Sometimes the liquid is mercury and sometimes it is red-colored alcohol. As the liquid in the bulb is heated, the liquid expands and rises up in the tube. Conversely, as the liquid in the bulb is cooled, the liquid contracts and falls in the tube.

As You Read...
Think about:
1. *What does air temperature measure?*
2. *Why and how does wind blow?*
3. *How are clouds formed?*
4. *How is rain formed?*

When you are measuring the air temperature, be sure to mount the thermometer in the shade. If the Sun shines on the thermometer, it heats the liquid, and the reading is higher than the true air temperature. Also, when you take the thermometer outside, give it enough time to adjust to the outdoor air temperature. That might take several minutes.

Wind

The wind blows because air pressure is higher in one place than in another place. The air moves from areas of higher pressure to areas of lower pressure. Also, the greater the difference in air pressure from one place to another, the stronger the wind. Objects like buildings, trees, and hills affect both the direction and speed of the wind near the surface. To get the best idea of the wind direction, try to stand far away from such objects. A park or a playing field is the best place to observe the wind.

Wind speed is measured with an anemometer. Most anemometers have horizontal shafts arranged like the spokes of a wheel. A cup is attached to the end of each shaft. The wind pushes the concave side of the cup more than the convex side, so the anemometer spins in the wind. The stronger the wind, the faster the cups spin. The cup spin rate is calibrated in terms of wind speed (e.g., miles or kilometers per hour).

You do not need an anemometer to estimate the wind speed. You can use a verbal scale, called the Beaufort wind scale (page C5). It describes the effect of the wind on everyday objects like trees.

Wind direction is measured with a wind vane. You can also estimate the wind direction by yourself just by using your face as a "sensor." Face into the wind, and then record the direction you are facing.

Clouds

Clouds are formed when humid air rises upward. As the air rises, it expands and becomes colder. With enough cooling, water vapor condenses into tiny water droplets (or deposits into tiny ice crystals). The droplets or crystals are visible as clouds. Condensation is the change from water vapor to liquid water. Deposition is the change from water vapor directly to ice crystals. Condensation or deposition takes place when air is cooled to its dew-point temperature. When humid air is cooled at the ground (that is, when air reaches the dew point at ground level), fog is formed. You will learn more about clouds later in this Unit.

Clouds form at a wide range of altitudes, from near the ground to very high in the atmosphere. The appearance of clouds varies a lot, depending on the motions of the air as the clouds are formed. Other important things to observe about clouds are the percentage of the sky they cover, where they are located in the sky, how much of the sky they cover, and their direction of movement. A good way to find their direction of movement is to stand under a tree branch or an overhang of a building and watch the clouds move relative to that stationary object. Clouds move with the wind, so observing cloud motion provides information on the wind direction high in the atmosphere.

Cirrus

Altostratus

Altocumulus

Nimbostratus

Cumulonimbus

Cumulus

Stratocumulus

Stratus

Precipitation

Raindrops are formed when the cloud droplets grow large enough to fall out of the clouds. Most of the rain that falls in the winter, and even much of what falls in the summer, is from melting of snowflakes as they fall through warmer air.

Rainfall is measured by the depth of water that falls on a level surface without soaking into the ground. Rainfall is measured with a rain gauge. A basic rain gauge is nothing more than a cylindrical container, like a metal can with a flat bottom, that is open to the sky. The only problem is to get an accurate measurement of the depth of water that has fallen. Accurate rain gauges are designed so that the water that falls into the container is funneled into a much narrower cylinder inside. In that way, the depth of the water is magnified, and is easier to read.

If you live in a part of the United States where it snows in winter, you can easily measure the snow depth with a ruler graduated in either centimeters or inches. The best time to make the measurement is right after the snow stops falling. The measurement can be tricky, because wind can cause snow to drift. The best place to measure snow depth is on level ground far away from buildings and trees. Take measurements at several spots and compute an average.

Review and Reflect

Review

1. List the weather instruments you studied in this investigation and describe what each measures.

2. What factors do you need to consider to get an accurate reading of each of the following:

   a) Air temperature?

   b) Wind speed and direction?

   c) Rainfall? Snowfall?

Reflect

3. What are some drawbacks to relying on weather measurements taken by your class, as opposed to following the reports issued by professionals?

4. Most of the weather observations you made can be made and recorded automatically by instruments. Using one kind of observation as an example, describe an advantage and disadvantage of using technology to record weather information versus people recording the information.

Thinking about the Earth System

5. How do seasonal changes in air temperature affect plants and animals?

6. How does the wind interact with the surface waters of the ocean or large lake?

7. How does the wind affect trees, bushes, and other vegetation?

8. How does air temperature and wind speed influence how comfortable you are when outside?

Thinking about Scientific Inquiry

9. How is writing and following a protocol important to the inquiry process?

10. How did you use mathematics in this investigation?

11. Describe an example of how you collected and reviewed data using tools.

Investigation 2:

Comparing Weather Reports

Key Question

Before you begin, first think about this key question.

What does a weather report contain?

Think about what you already know about weather reports. What information is contained in one? What do you need to know to interpret a weather report?

Share your thinking with others in your group and with your class.

Materials Needed

For this investigation, your group will need:

- sample weather report

- weather reports or forecasts for three consecutive days, from one of the following media: television, national newspaper, local newspaper, commercial or public radio, the NOAA weather radio, Internet, telephone

- weather data for each of the three days following the reports (temperature, wind speed, precipitation, cloud cover, humidity, etc.)

- reference resources about weather

Investigate

1. A *weather report* tells you what the weather conditions are at the time. A *weather forecast* tells you what the weather is likely to be in the future. Your group will receive one of several different kinds of weather reports.

   a) Make a list of all the weather words in the report.

b) Turn the list into a table like the one below. If someone in your group knows some of the other information for the table, fill in that part. If not, leave it blank for later. If you find a term that you do not understand, write it down as a question to answer later.

Weather Word	Descriptors Used	Definition	Instrument Used for Measuring	Unit of Measurement
Wind Speed				
Wind Direction				
Clouds				
Kind of Precipitation				
Amount of Precipitation				
Temperature				
Pressure				
Other				

2. Study your group's report a second time.

a) This time, make a table that shows what kind of weather information your report includes.

The table should clearly show the kinds of weather reports your class is studying (newspaper, radio, and so on),

the categories of weather information the report includes (temperature, wind speed, etc.), and the date and time the report was produced.

b) Share your findings with other groups, in order to fill in your table completely.

Weather Report Source	Date & Time of Report	Temperature	Wind Speed	Humidity	Cloud Cover	Other
Local paper						
National newspaper						
Radio						
Internet						
Television						
Phone						

Inquiry

Collect and Review Data Using Tools

One important science inquiry skill is the collecting and reviewing of data using tools. In this inquiry you are using tables as data management tools. You could also use a computer as a tool to make your table.

3. Obtain the weather forecasts (temperature, wind speed, precipitation, etc.) from your weather source during a three-day period.

a) Record the forecasts in the form of a table.

b) Also record the actual weather data.

c) Share your findings with other groups, in order to fill in your table completely.

The following is an example of a table that you can use:

Source	Day 1 Forecast	Day 1 Actual Data	Day 2 Forecast	Day 2 Actual Data	Day 3 Forecast	Day 3 Actual Data
Local paper						
National newspaper						
Radio						
Internet						
Television						
Phone						

d) Compare the predicted weather with the actual weather, to judge the accuracy of each of the weather forecasts. Look over the information in your table carefully. Rank the weather-forecast sources from most accurate to least accurate. You can do this by giving the number 1 to the most accurate report, 2 to the second, and so on.

e) What evidence do you have to support your rankings?

4. Discuss the following questions within your group. Record the results of your discussion in your journal. (Report in these questions means report or forecast.)

a) Which kind of weather report has the most information?

b) How does the format of the report make that possible?

c) Which kind of weather report has the least information? Explain.

d) What information do all of the weather reports include?

e) Why do you think that this information is included in every weather report?

f) Which kind of weather report best helps you to understand patterns in the weather? Why?

g) Which weather report would be most helpful for planning an outdoor event three days in the future? Why?

h) Which weather report would be most helpful if you were traveling to another part of the country? Why?

5. After discussing the weather report questions, share your ideas with the whole class.

a) What kinds of information need to be included in an accurate and useful weather report?

b) How do you think you would obtain the information that you need to make a more complete and accurate weather report?

6. Go back to your table of weather terms from the beginning of the investigation.

Divide up the terms in the table equally among your group members. Use the resources in your classroom, library, and at home to complete the information in the table.

a) Complete the table in your journal.

b) Write down any questions you think of as you do your research.

Inquiry

Predictions in Science

Scientists make predictions and justify these with reasons. A meteorologist uses all the data available to make a complete picture of the present and future weather. By using these data, and his or her knowledge of how weather systems form and move, the meteorologist can predict or forecast the weather.

c) Make a class table of information about weather words by having each group contribute the words it has found. Keep this table posted as a reference for the rest of the investigations in this module. Keep a copy in your journal

As you work through the other investigations in this module, you will probably find other words related to weather and climate. Add these to the table as you accumulate them.

As You Read...
Think about:

1. *What is the difference between a weather report and a weather forecast?*

2. *What information is contained in a detailed weather report?*

3 *What does normal average temperature mean?*

4. *How has weather forecasting changed during the past 200 years?*

Digging   Deeper

WEATHER REPORTS AND FORECASTS

Weather Reports

Different weather reports contain different amounts of information. The simplest and shortest weather report contains only one piece of information, the present temperature. This is the kind of report you often hear on the radio. More detailed weather reports contain information about precipitation, wind speed and direction, relative humidity, atmospheric pressure, and so on.

1 TODAY MONDAY, JUNE 11

Chicago: A good deal of sunshine, breezy and warm. Humidity continues slowly upward, and a passing late-afternoon or evening thunderstorm cannot be ruled out. Partly cloudy and mild overnight.

HIGH | **LOW**
84 | **64**

A typical weather report tells you the highest and lowest temperatures for the past day. The day's lowest temperature usually occurs just after sunrise. The day's highest temperature is usually reached during early to mid-afternoon. A weather report also tells you the present temperature. It may also give you the average temperature for the day. The average daily temperature lies halfway between the highest temperature and the lowest

temperature. The weather report might also tell you how many degrees the average temperature is above or below the normal temperature for that day. The normal temperature is found by averaging the average temperatures for the calendar day for the past 30 years.

Most weather reports give the amount of precipitation (rain or melted snow), if any, that fell during the past day. They also tell you the totals for the current month and the current year. Reports also indicate how much the monthly and annual precipitation totals are above or below normal (the long-term average).

Weather Forecasts

Most people are interested in what the weather will be tomorrow or in the next few days. Predictions of the weather for up to a week in the future are called short-term forecasts. Meteorologists also try to make long-term forecasts (called "outlooks") of the weather for a month, a season, or a whole year. Long-range outlooks are different from short-term forecasts in that they specify expected departures of temperature and precipitation from long-term averages (e.g., colder or warmer than normal, wetter or drier than normal).

In earlier times, before invention of the telegraph and the telephone, weather observations from faraway places could not be collected in one place soon after they were made. In those times, the only way of predicting the weather was to use your local experience. Given the weather on a particular day, what kind of weather usually follows during the next day or two? As you can imagine, the success of such forecasting was not much better than making a random guess.

Beginning in the 1870s, a national weather service used the telegraph to gather weather observations from weather stations located over large areas of the

country. Simultaneous weather observations allowed meteorologists to plot weather maps and follow weather systems as they moved from place to place, greatly improving the accuracy of weather forecasts.

Through the 20th century, meteorologists developed even better tools for observing and predicting the weather. As you will learn in the following investigations, special instruments measure weather in the atmosphere far above the ground. Satellites orbiting the Earth send back images of the weather over broad areas of the planet. In addition, computer models were developed for weather forecasting. The important processes operating in the Earth system that govern weather are built into a computer model. The model starts with the present weather and tries to simulate how the weather will evolve in the future. These computer models are run on supercomputers. They can handle enormous amounts of observational data and make billions of computations quickly. Today's computer models do a very good job of predicting the weather for the next few days. You know, however, that sometimes the forecast is wrong! The science of weather forecasting is still developing.

Weather prediction will never be perfect. One reason is the absence of reliable weather observations from large areas of the globe (especially the oceans). These observations are needed for computer models to accurately represent the present state of the atmosphere. A second reason is that even small changes in the weather in one place can cause much larger changes in weather elsewhere. The effects are small at first, but they become much greater. It's very difficult for computers to simulate these interactions. Although forecasts will never be perfect, they will continue to improve in the years ahead. Through research, meteorologists learn more and more about the details of how weather in the Earth system works.

Review and Reflect

Review

1. What was the most accurate weather forecast that your class studied? Explain.

2. Where do the weather reports and forecasts that your class studied come from?

3. Why does the accuracy of weather forecasts usually decrease as the number of days ahead increases?

Reflect

4. If you were to write your own weather report, what would you include and how would you get your information?

5. Why do you think weather reports vary over a given area?

6. Which kind of weather report is most useful to you on a daily basis? Why is that?

Thinking about the Earth System

7. How has communication technology helped to develop a better understanding of the Earth system? Give an example.

8. Write down all the connections you can think of in this investigation that show a relationship between weather and the Earth's systems. Keep this record on your *Earth System Connection* sheet.

Thinking about Scientific Inquiry

9. What question did you explore in this investigation? Can you answer the question now? Explain.

10. What tools did you use to collect and review data in this investigation?

Investigation 3:

Weather Maps

Materials Needed

For this part of the investigation your group will need:

- three weather maps from different newspapers

- information on weather-map symbols

- weather map with symbols for clear skies, cloudy skies, partly cloudy skies, and rain

- weather map with symbols for high pressure and low pressure

- overhead transparency sheet

- two or three colors of overhead transparency markers

- weather map with temperatures only

- weather map showing 10° isotherms

- colored pencils

Key Question

Before you begin, first think about this key question.

What can weather maps tell you about weather?

In a previous investigation you learned about some of the techniques used to measure elements of weather. You have already learned some of the ways this information is displayed on maps. What are some of the other ways this is done?

Share your thinking with others in your group and with your class. Keep a record of the discussion in your journal.

Investigate

Part A: Working with Weather Maps

1. Obtain copies of three newspaper weather maps from different sources.

In your group, look for at least five things that the maps have in common.

a) Write these down. Share your list with another group.

b) What kinds of information are included in all three weather maps?

c) Make a list of what you already know about the information on weather maps.

d) Write down what you would like to know.

2. Read any information you have available on weather-map symbols.

Share your information about weather-map symbols with the rest of the class.

a) Make up a class chart of weather symbols to use for reference. Include a copy in your journal.

b) How many of your weather-map questions above can you now answer with this information? Record the answers in your journal.

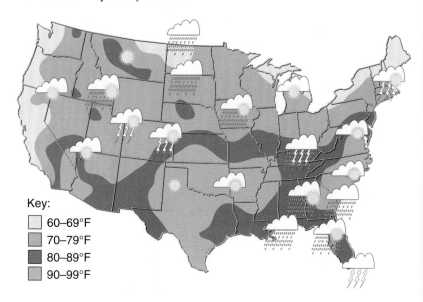

Key:
- 60–69°F
- 70–79°F
- 80–89°F
- 90–99°F

3. Obtain a weather map that has symbols for sky conditions on it.

Place an overhead transparency sheet on top of the map and copy the outline of the map.

Inquiry

Consider Evidence

Scientists look for likely explanations by studying patterns and relationships within evidence. By circling similar types of weather, you developed groupings that reveal patterns. Meteorologists also group different types of weather to reveal patterns that help them correlate factors like high-pressure systems and fair weather.

On the transparency, circle all the areas that have a sunny symbol. Shade these areas with one color of overhead transparency marker.

Make a key showing which color you are using for sunny areas on the map.

4. Repeat this process using another color for precipitation areas. By convention, green is usually used to indicate precipitation on weather maps. Remember that precipitation includes rain, drizzle, snow, sleet, and hail.

Add this color to your key.

All the uncolored areas will be cloudy or partly cloudy. You can leave these uncolored or use a new color to show them.

5. Put your transparency sheet on a map that shows high-pressure areas, low-pressure areas, and fronts.

a) What relationships can you see between the first map, showing the sky conditions and the second map, showing the pressure systems and fronts? Be sure that you are comfortable with the relationships between sky conditions and pressure systems before you move on. Ask for help as you need it.

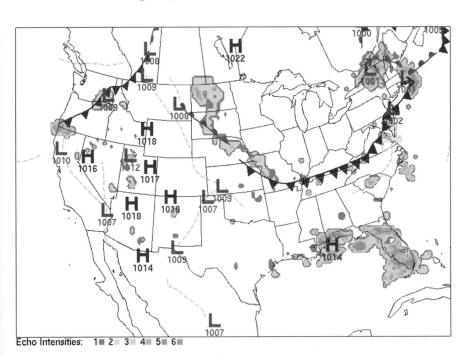

Echo Intensities: 1 ■ 2 ■ 3 ■ 4 ■ 5 ■ 6 ■

6. Obtain a weather map showing temperatures only.

With different colored pencils, draw smoothly curving lines to connect points on the map where temperatures are the same. These curves are called isotherms (*iso* means same, and *therm* stands for temperature). Use a contour interval of 10°F.

For example, your map might show an isotherm for 50°F. The curve would pass through points where the temperature was 50°F. Drawing contours is not easy, because most of the temperatures shown on the map are different from the ones you selected for the isotherms. You have to interpolate. To interpolate means to find a value that falls in between two other values. For example, suppose that one point on your map has a temperature of 47°F and a nearby point has a temperature of 55°F. You know that the 50°F isotherm has to run somewhere between those two points. Also, it has to be closer to the 47°F point than the 55°F point. That's because 50° is closer to 47° than to 55°. An example has been provided.

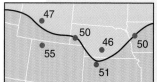

Draw your isotherms at first with light pencil lines, and use an eraser to adjust them if necessary. Once you feel comfortable with your isotherms, draw them permanently with the colored pencils.

7. Now look at a new weather map that just shows bands of temperature readings. The boundaries between these bands are isotherms.

Study the temperature bands on your map carefully. Discuss and answer the following questions:

a) How do the temperature bands help you to understand what weather is like in different parts of the country?

b) How might this be useful in forecasting the weather conditions for a particular area?

c) What patterns can you see in temperatures? (Where is it typically warmer, for example? Where are the temperatures typically cooler?)

d) What reasons can you think of to explain the temperature patterns you notice?

Inquiry

Hypothesis

When you make a prediction and give your reasons for that prediction, you are forming a hypothesis. A hypothesis is a statement of the expected outcome of an experiment or observation, along with an explanation of why this will happen.

A hypothesis is never a guess. It is based on what the scientist already knows about something. A hypothesis is used to design an experiment or observation to find out more about a scientific idea or question.

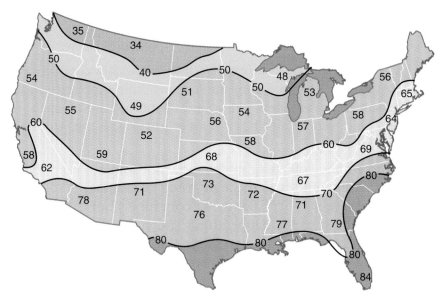

8. Test your knowledge of what a weather map tells you by using a weather map (past or current) to write a weather report for your part of the country.

a) In your journal write the report so that it is easily understandable by others.

Part B: The Movement of Air Masses

1. Read the steps for **Part B** of the investigation. Although you will use water instead of air, the investigation is a model of what happens when two air masses of different temperature meet.

   a) Before you conduct the investigation, make and record your prediction about what will happen when the card is removed between the two bottles. Also record your reason for your prediction. This is your hypothesis.

2. Fill a 500-mL bottle with cold water and add a few drops of blue food coloring to it.

3. Fill another 500-mL bottle with hot water and add a few drops of red food coloring to it.

   Cap this bottle and shake gently to mix.

   Uncap both bottles.

4. Place a piece of poster board card on top of the cold water bottle.

   Hold the bottle over the sink or the large pan.

   Hold the card tightly to the neck of the bottle, and quickly invert it over the hot water bottle.

   Put the bottles together at their necks. Make sure they match exactly.

5. While holding both bottle necks together (cold on top), have someone in your group quickly pull the card out from between the bottles.

   Keep the two necks together and observe what happens to the red and blue water.

   a) Record what you observe.

6. When all water motions seem to be completed in the bottles, empty out the colored water and rinse the bottles for the next group.

Materials Needed

For this part of the investigation your group will need:

- two identical, clear, heavy plastic, 500-mL bottles with medium-size necks

- caps for the two bottles

- one piece of poster board, 10 cm × 10 cm

- supply of hot water and cold water

- blue and red food coloring

- sink or large pan over which the bottles can be inverted

⚠️

The water should not be so hot that it can cause burns. Clean up spills.

Answer the following questions in your journal:

a) What happened when the two bottles were put together? How could you explain this?

b) Air is a fluid, just like water. How does what you observed with the two bottles explain what happens when cold air masses and warm air masses meet?

c) When cold and warm air masses meet, what do you expect to happen? Why is that?

d) How did your results compare with your hypothesis?

Part C: Atmospheric Pressure

1. Your teacher will arrange a field trip to a nearby building that is at least four stories tall and has an elevator.

   At the lowest floor, before you get in the elevator, read the pressure with the barometer. To do that, tap the glass front very gently with your fingernail several times and watch the position of the needle on the dial.

   a) Record the average position of the needle as you tap the glass.

Materials Needed

For this part of the investigation your group will need:

- aneroid barometer, with scale marked in inches of mercury

 Stay with an adult supervisor at all times.

2. Take the elevator to the top floor, carrying the barometer with you.

   While the elevator is going up, watch the needle. To help the needle adjust its position, you can tap the glass front gently with your fingernail now and then.

3. When the elevator has reached the top floor, step out of the elevator and read the barometer again.

   a) Record how barometric pressure changed as you were riding up the elevator.

   b) Record the barometer reading on the highest floor.

4. Ride the elevator back down to the lowest floor.

   Read the barometer again.

   a) Record this reading, and any relationships between the top and bottom floor readings.

   b) Explain what you think caused the change in the reading of the barometer as you rode up in the elevator.

5. Most barometers record the atmospheric pressure in "inches of mercury." The average atmospheric pressure at sea level (zero elevation of the land surface) is about 30 in.

   Calculate the percentage change in the atmospheric pressure as you went up in your elevator ride.

   a) Find the difference in pressure between the lowest floor and the highest floor.

   b) Divide the difference in pressure by the value for the reading at the bottom floor.

   c) Then multiply the result by 100 to convert your answer to a percentage. This is approximately the percentage of the Earth's atmosphere you went up through on your elevator ride!

6. Look at a weather map that shows barometric pressure across the United States.

   a) Where is the air pressure the lowest? Where is it highest?

   b) What do the H (or High) and L (or Low) symbols indicate on the map?

   c) How does the pressure change moving away from the H? How does the pressure change moving toward the L?

Inquiry
Using Mathematics

In this investigation you made measurements using inches of mercury as a unit to collect data. (In the International System of Units, pressure is measured in pascals, symbol Pa.) Calculations were then used to interpret the data you collected. Scientists also use mathematics in their investigations.

d) What is the general relationship between air pressure (high or low) and the type of weather (storms, sunny, etc.) in a region?

e) In a rapidly ascending elevator or an airplane taking off, you may feel a popping sensation in your ears. What do you suppose causes this, and how might it be related to the drop of air pressure with increasing altitude?

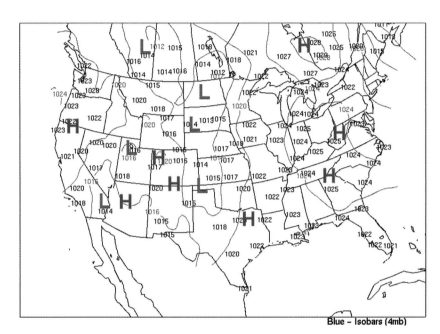

Blue – Isobars (4mb)

As You Read...

Think about:

1. Who drew the first weather map, and how was the information obtained?

2. What is an isotherm? What is an isobar?

3. Why does air pressure always decrease upward in the atmosphere?

4. Why is the weather in high-pressure areas usually fair? Why is the weather in low-pressure areas usually cloudy and stormy?

5. What is the difference between a cold front and a warm front?

Digging Deeper

WEATHER MAPS

A weather map is a graphical model of the state of the atmosphere over a broad region at a specific time. Meteorologists call these synoptic maps (*syn-* means at the same time, and *-optic* stands for seeing). In the late 1700s, Benjamin Franklin drew the first synoptic weather map. He asked a number of friends living in eastern North America to record the weather each day for several days and then mail their journals to him. He then drew weather maps for each day. The mails were very

slow then, so that Franklin was not able to draw the maps until long after the observations were made. Nonetheless, the maps were useful because they revealed, for the first time, that winds blow around the centers of storm systems that move day by day.

Weather maps that are available to the public vary a lot in how much information they show. Most weather maps in newspapers and on television show only temperature bands that are defined by isotherms, areas of precipitation, the location of high-pressure systems and low-pressure systems, and weather fronts. More specialized weather maps show air pressure, wind speed and direction, cloud cover, and precipitation. The maps you created in Investigation 1 were a simplified version of this kind of weather map.

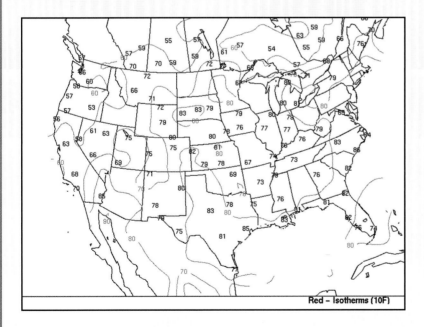

Red – Isotherms (10F)

Atmospheric Pressure

Air has weight. That idea might seem strange to you, because air seems very thin, even at sea level. Remember, however, that the atmosphere extends to great ➡

altitudes. You can think of air pressure as the weight of a column of air above a unit area on the Earth's surface. The column of air above a square area that is one inch on a side averages about 14.7 lb at sea level. In the metric system, that's about 1.0 kg/cm^2 (centimeter squared). If you try to pump the air out of a closed container, the outside air pressure will cause the container to collapse unless the container is very strong. The reason you don't feel air pressure is that the pressure inside your body is equal to the air pressure acting on the outside of your body!

You saw from your elevator ride with the barometer that the air pressure decreases upward in the atmosphere. That's because at higher levels in the atmosphere there is less air above to cause the pressure.

Detailed weather maps show the atmospheric pressure by means of curved lines called isobars. As with an isotherm for temperature, an isobar connects all points with the same atmospheric pressure. Air pressure always decreases with altitude so that the pressure at the land surface is less where the elevation of the surface is high. To remove the effect of elevation on air pressure readings, meteorologists adjust the readings to what they would be if the weather station were at sea level. The adjusted pressure is what you would measure if you could dig a very deep shaft all the way down to sea level and put your barometer at the bottom of the shaft. The adjusted pressure is plotted on weather maps.

High-Pressure Areas and Low-Pressure Areas

Most weather maps show areas, labeled with an **H** (or **High**), where the atmospheric pressure is relatively high, and areas labeled with an **L** (or **Low**) where the atmospheric pressure is relatively low. The isobars around such areas are usually closed curves with the approximate shape of circles. Viewed from above, surface winds blow clockwise (in the Northern Hemisphere) and outward

about the center of a high as shown in the diagram. As air leaves the high-pressure area, the remaining air sinks slowly downward to take its place. That makes clouds and precipitation scarce, because clouds depend on rising air for condensation of water vapor. High-pressure areas usually are areas of fair, settled weather. Viewed from above, surface winds blow counterclockwise (in the Northern Hemisphere) and inward about the center of a low as shown in the diagram. Converging surface winds cause air to rise, producing clouds. Low-pressure areas tend to be stormy weather systems.

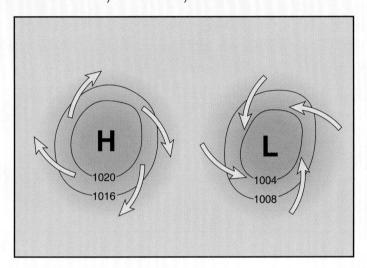

Air Masses and Fronts

Large masses of air, as much as 1000 km across, take on certain weather characteristics when they stay at high latitudes (near the poles) or at low latitudes (near the Equator) for weeks at a time. They may be very cold or very warm, or they may be very humid or very dry. Then, as they move into other areas, they can cause changes in the weather. The coldest winter weather in much of the United States occurs when a bitter cold air mass from the high arctic regions of northeastern Asia, Alaska, or northern Canada sweeps down into the southern parts of North America. At other times, a flow of warm ➤

and humid air from the tropics causes uncomfortably muggy weather over the eastern United States.

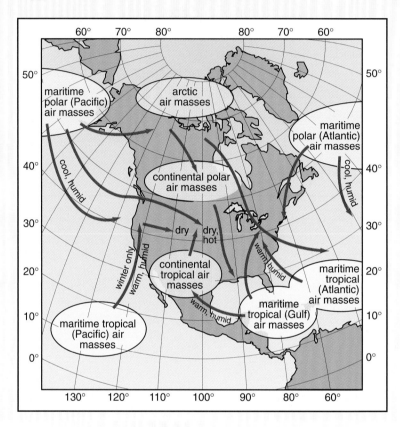

The boundaries between air masses are often zones of very rapid changes in temperature and humidity. Storms (low-pressure systems) tend to develop along these zones of rapid change. The line with the triangular teeth, called a cold front, shows where the cold air mass is wedging under the warm air mass. (See the cross-sectional diagram on the following page.) As the warm air is lifted along the front, thunderstorms may develop. The line in the diagram with the circular teeth, called a warm front, shows where the warm air mass is moving up over the cold air mass. Broad areas of light to moderate rain or snow are often associated with the warm front.

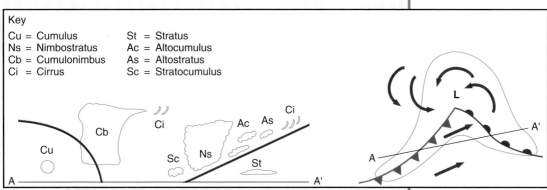

Key

Cu = Cumulus   St = Stratus
Ns = Nimbostratus   Ac = Altocumulus
Cb = Cumulonimbus   As = Altostratus
Ci = Cirrus   Sc = Stratocumulus

A typical large rainstorm along a zone of rapid change.

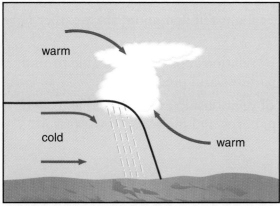

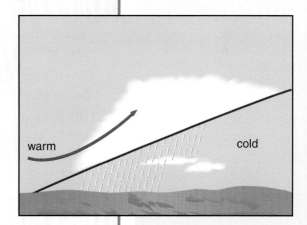

Cross-sections through warm fronts and cold fronts.

If the pattern of the fronts in the diagram looks to you a bit like a wave, you are right. A low-pressure system is developing like a wave along the boundary between the two air masses! You can see that the pattern of surface winds, shown by the arrows, is developing a counterclockwise and inward pattern. After a storm like this develops, the swirling pattern of winds continues for many days, until it finally dies out. A storm of this kind can move hundreds of kilometers in a day, or it can remain in almost the same position for a day or even longer. Much like a flying disk, the storm combines rotational and translational motion as it travels across the nation.

Review and Reflect

Review

1. What kinds of information were plotted on the weather maps that you investigated?

2. Use your observations of the two bottles of water in Part B of this investigation to explain what happens when a cold air mass meets a warm air mass. Which air mass is likely to rise? Which air mass is likely to stay near Earth's surface?

3. What evidence did you obtain from your investigation that shows that air pressure decreases with altitude?

Reflect

4. What do weather maps tell you about the weather now and in the future?

5. What evidence of relationships were you able to find between cloud patterns and precipitation?

6. What evidence of relationships were you able to find between cloud patterns and high- and low-pressure systems?

Thinking about the Earth System

7. On your *Earth System Connection* sheet, note how the things you learned in this investigation connect to the different Earth systems.

   a) Describe how air pressure (atmosphere) is related to elevation (geosphere).

   b) Describe how air masses (atmosphere) are related to the regions over which they form (geosphere or hydrosphere).

Thinking about Scientific Inquiry

8. What weather data did you use to look for relationships in this investigation?

9. How did you use mathematics in this investigation?

10. Give an example of how you used evidence to develop ideas in your investigations into weather.

Investigation 4:

Weather Radiosondes, Satellites, and Radar

Key Question

Before you begin, first think about this key question.

In addition to weather observations on the Earth's surface, how else is weather data collected?

In the previous investigation, you studied weather maps. Some of the information used to make the maps is obtained at weather stations at the surface. Much of the information, however, is obtained from other sources. How else can weather observations be made?

Share your thinking with others in your group and with your class. Keep a record of the discussion in your journal.

Materials Needed

For this investigation your group will need:

• two pieces of graph paper

Investigate

Part A: Data from Radiosondes

1. The tables on the following pages gives data on how temperature changes with altitude.

Radiosonde Data June 26, 2001			
Jacksonville, Florida		Fairbanks, Alaska	
Temperature (°C)	Altitude (m)	Temperature (°C)	Altitude (m)
20.6	9	17	138
24.2	88	16.4	197
24.6	203	14.1	610
24.8	327	12.8	842
23.2	610	9.7	1219
21.6	884	7	1545
18.4	1219	3	2164
13.2	1829	−2.5	2923
11.2	2134	−6.4	3658
5	3224	−11.4	4540
−0.3	4267	−16.3	5180
−4.3	4997	−22.1	5970
−12.7	6096	−27.7	6746
−23.7	7570	−32.7	7620
−28.3	8230	−38.7	8469
−39.1	9610	−44.9	9300
−43.7	10830	−54.7	10668
−56.7	11983	−57.7	11900
−59.7	13766	−51.7	12719
−64.1	15240	−50.3	15240
−64.9	16540	−49.3	16619
−67.7	17692	−50.1	18601
−64.9	18700	−48.1	20950
−59.7	20780	−48.6	22555
−54.2	22555	−46.6	23774
−49.8	26518	−43.6	25603
−50.7	27432	−40	27432
−42.1	30480	−36.3	29403
−39.9	31270	−33.3	31840
−39	33223	−28.1	33528

A radiosonde is an instrument package that is carried upward by a balloon. As it rises to great altitudes it makes weather observations.

2. For each data set, use a sheet of graph paper to plot how temperature changes with altitude.

   a) Use the vertical axis for altitude above sea level. Use the horizontal axis for temperature. See the sample shown.

   b) Plot the temperature at each altitude.

   c) Then connect the points (which scientists call "data points") with a continuous line. A line like this is called a sounding.

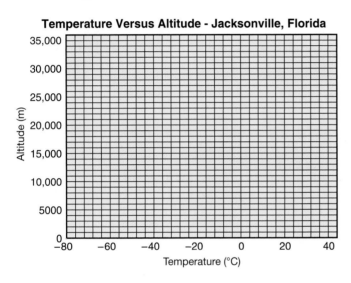

3. Use your graph to answer the following questions:

   a) Does the air temperature generally increase or decrease with altitude?

   b) What do you think is the cause of the increase or decrease?

   c) The "cruising altitude" of commercial jetliners is usually in the range of 10,000 m (about 30,000 ft) to 13,000 m (about 40,000 ft). Judging from the two temperature profiles you plotted, what is the typical air temperature in that range of altitudes?

   d) In the Jacksonville sounding, the temperature shows an increase with altitude in the lower part of the atmosphere. What do you think is the cause of that increase? (Hint: the lower atmosphere is heated and cooled from below.)

Inquiry

Mathematical Relationships

In the previous investigation you discovered that the higher the altitude, the lower the air pressure. This is an example of an inverse relationship. In this investigation you are studying another inverse relationship.

Part B: Satellite Images

1. Look carefully at the satellite image.

   a) What do you think it shows? How can you check your ideas?

   b) How might satellite images be helpful in forecasting or understanding weather? What do you think?

   c) Compare your ideas with those from another group. How do they compare?

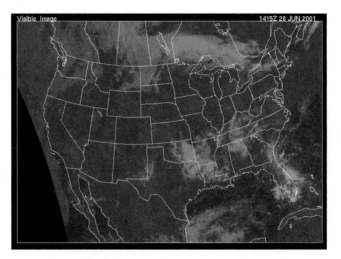

2. Compare the satellite image to the sky conditions shown on a weather map for the same time period.

   a) List and describe as many relationships as you can between the satellite image and the weather elements on your map. Discuss the relationships you discovered with another group.

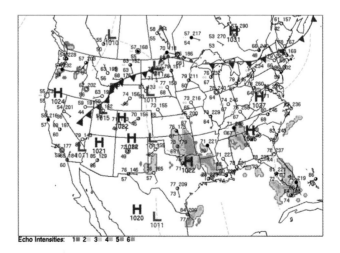

3. Over the next few days, visit a web site that has both satellite images and weather maps. You might also watch television weather reports that show both weather maps and satellite images.

a) Do you see any pattern in the way weather systems move? Explain.

b) Compare the movement of weather systems and the map of the movement of air masses (page C34). What relationships can you see?

Inquiry

Using Evidence Collected by Others

In this investigation you used evidence that you were provided to formulate your ideas about weather systems. Meteorologists must also consider the evidence provided by others to develop their ideas about weather patterns.

Part C: Radar Images

1. Compare the radar and satellite images shown on the following page.

a) What do you notice about the relationship between the clouds and radar echoes?

b) Are all the clouds producing precipitation? How can you tell?

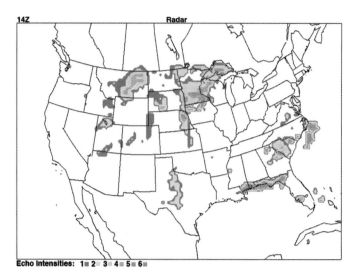

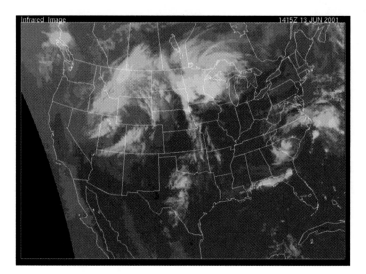

2. Look at the radar image at the top of the next page. It was taken four hours later.

a) What has happened to the area coverage and intensity of the precipitation over Minnesota and Wisconsin?

b) What has happened to the area coverage and intensity of the precipitation over North and South Carolina?

3. Look at the infrared satellite image on the next page taken four hours later.

a) What has happened to the clouds along the border between West Virginia and Virginia?

b) What do you think is responsible for this change?

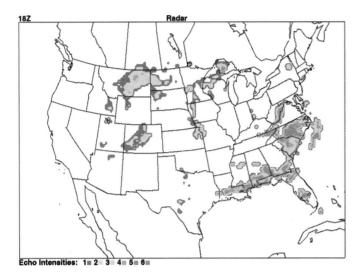

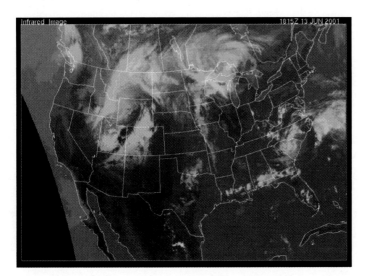

4. Note that on the infrared satellite image, temperature is given on a gray scale—ranging from bright white for lowest temperatures (high clouds) to black for highest temperatures (land). The temperature decreases with altitude, so that high clouds are cold and appear brighter than warmer low clouds.

a) What do the bright white in the clouds over West Virginia and Virginia indicate?

b) Thunderstorm cloud tops rise to great heights. What kind of weather do you think that this area of West Virginia and Virginia was having at the time?

THE WEATHER HIGH IN THE ATMOSPHERE

Radiosondes

You experience weather at the Earth's surface, but there is weather high in the atmosphere also. What is the weather like at high altitudes? Have you ever taken a ride in a hot-air balloon or climbed a mountain? You would know that the air temperature usually decreases with altitude. The basic reason has to do with how the atmosphere receives and loses its heat energy. The Earth's surface is heated by the Sun at some times and places, that is, when and where it is daylight. It loses heat to outer space at all times (day and night) everywhere. On a global and average annual basis, however, the Earth's surface gains more heat than it loses. The atmosphere near the ground is then heated by the ground. High up in the atmosphere, however, the air loses more heat to space than it absorbs from sunlight. Hence, air usually gets colder with increasing altitude—at least up to an altitude of about 10,000 m (33,000 ft).

As You Read...
Think about:

1. *Why does temperature usually decrease with altitude in the lower portion of the atmosphere?*

2. *What weather observations are typically made by radiosondes?*

3. *What piece of weather information are satellites especially good at showing?*

4. *How is information from radiosondes and satellites transmitted to the Earth?*

How is the weather in the upper atmosphere measured? It is difficult and expensive to measure the weather in the upper atmosphere. But knowing what conditions are like in the upper atmosphere is important for modern weather forecasting. Since the late 1930s, meteorologists have relied mainly on radiosondes for profiles of temperature, pressure, and humidity from Earth's surface to the upper atmosphere (to altitudes of 30,000 m or 100,000 ft). Balloons carry radiosondes up through the atmosphere. As they rise, they send back measurements by radio. Tracking of radiosonde movements from the ground shows wind speed and direction in the upper atmosphere. Eventually the balloon bursts, and the instruments fall back to Earth by parachute. (Some radiosondes are recovered and reused.) Their fall is not dangerous to humans, because the instruments are very small and light. Radiosondes are launched at the same time every 12 hours at hundreds of weather stations around the world. A similar instrument, called a dropwindsonde, is released from an aircraft to determine atmospheric conditions in areas where radiosonde data is absent (e.g., in a hurricane over the ocean).

Weather Radar

Radar (**RA**dio **D**etection **A**nd **R**anging) has become an essential tool for observing and predicting weather. Radar was invented and developed in Britain and the United States at the beginning of World War II. It was used to detect the approach of enemy airplanes. An antenna

sends out pulses of microwave energy. These waves are reflected from solid or liquid precipitation particles in the air and received back by the antenna. The radar equipment shows the position and distance of the particles. The results (the radar echoes) are shown as blotches on a screen, similar to a television or computer monitor. Radar echoes are electronically superimposed on a map of the area to show the location of areas of precipitation. The strength of the echoes is used to find the intensity of precipitation and to tell frozen forms (e.g., hail) from unfrozen forms of precipitation (e.g., rain). Meteorologists use radar to track the movement and follow the development of storm systems, especially small-scale systems like thunderstorms.

Weather Satellites

The first weather satellite was launched into orbit on April 1, 1960, when the United States orbited TIROS-I. Today, satellites are a routine and valuable tool in monitoring the Earth system. Satellite sensors obtain images of the Earth's weather from space. They are especially good at showing cloud cover and the temperatures of clouds and other surfaces in the sensors' field of view. A visible satellite image is like a black-and-white photograph of the planet and is available only for the areas of the planet that are in sunlight. An infrared satellite image shows the temperature of surfaces based on the invisible infrared (heat) radiation emitted by objects. Infrared satellite imagery is available both day and night and is the usual satellite picture shown on televised weathercasts. The most useful satellites are ones in a geostationary orbit. That is an orbit adjusted so that the speed and direction of the satellite matches the Earth's rotation. Then the satellite is always above the same point on Earth's surface and views the same area of the planet.

Review and Reflect

Review

1. How do meteorologists make observations of the weather at high altitudes without going there in airplanes?

2. How are radiosondes and weather satellites similar? How are they different?

3. How is radar used to track thunderstorms?

Reflect

4. What advantages are there in looking at the world from space to observe weather?

5. In what ways, other than those you investigated, can meteorologists obtain weather data from the upper atmosphere?

Thinking about the Earth System

6. How might remote sensing by satellite be used to monitor the geosphere and hydrosphere?

7. How might satellites be used to observe features of the landscape like the distribution of vegetation and ice and snow cover?

Thinking about Scientific Inquiry

8. Give three examples of inverse relationships related to weather that you have discovered in your investigations.

9. How did you use evidence to develop ideas in this investigation?

Investigation 5:

The Causes of Weather

Key Question

Before you begin, first think about this key question.

What causes weather?

Materials Needed

For each station in this investigation you will need:

- paper towels
- student journal

Think about what you know about weather patterns and weather reports from previous investigations. How does weather originate?

Share your thinking with others in your class. Keep a record of the discussion in your journal.

Investigate

Part A: Visiting the Stations

1. There will be a series of stations for you to visit. The investigations at the stations will allow you to ask and answer questions about:

Station 1: The Effects of the Wind

Station 2: Cloud Formation

Station 3: Temperature and Air Pressure

Keep a record of what you do and discover at each of the stations. At the end of your "station journey," you will be looking for common threads that seem to be a part of all aspects of weather.

Station 1: The Effects of the Wind

1. Wet the back of one of your hands with room-temperature water. Leave the other hand dry.

2. Have someone turn on the fan and direct the wind toward the backs of both your hands at the same time.

   a) Observe and record any differences in how your hands feel.

   b) Explain any differences you feel.

   c) How does this experience help to explain why winds help to cool you down on a hot day? Why a cold day feels even colder when the wind is blowing?

Materials Needed

For this station your group will need:

- water supply
- battery-powered fan
- alcohol thermometers
- tape
- cotton batting

Wash your hands after the activity.

Inquiry

Models in Scientific Inquiry

In this investigation you are using models. A model is the approximate representation (or simulation) of a real system. For example, a weather map is a graphical model of the state of the atmosphere over a given area. Models are used by scientists to study processes that happen too slow, too quick, or on too small a scale to be observed; that are too vast to be changed deliberately; or that might be dangerous. Models are also used to organize your thinking on some complex process. These are called conceptual models.

Be careful that the fan does not touch the thermometers.

Wash your hands after the activity.

3. Using your results, develop a hypothesis related to the rest of this investigation.

a) What do you predict will happen? Why?

4. Two thermometers are taped to a cardboard stand about 50 cm apart.

5. Read the temperatures on both thermometers

a) Record these temperatures.

6. Hold a fan about 10 cm away from the bulb of one thermometer and turn on the blades. Observe what happens to both thermometers.

a) Record your observations.

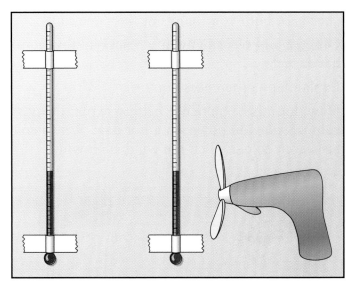

7. Next, dampen a small amount of cotton batting and tape it to one of the thermometer bulbs, so that it is exposed to the air.

Direct a fan at the bulb of both the wrapped and the unwrapped thermometers.

Observe what happens to the temperature readings on both thermometers.

a) Record your observations.

b) Compare your observations when the thermometer bulb was not dampened and when the bulb was dampened.

c) Review your hypothesis. Explain why you think there was a difference in the temperatures of the two thermometers.

Station 2: Cloud Formation

1. Place a metal container in a cooler.

   Put a brick in the bottom of the metal container to weigh it down.

   Place the lid on the metal container.

   Pack ice around the metal container in the cooler.

   Put the lid on the cooler.

2. After fifteen minutes or so the air in the metal container has been chilled. Carefully remove the lid of the cooler.

   Slowly raise the lid of the metal container a few centimeters above its rim.

   Shine a beam from a flashlight into the metal container.

   Take a deep breath; hold it for a few seconds.

   Put your mouth close to the top of the container. Very slowly and gently breathe some air out through your mouth down into the container.

   a) Record your observations.

   b) Describe how what you observed relates to the formation of clouds.

   c) Explain how you think clouds are formed.

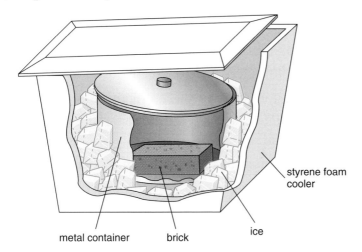

metal container   brick   ice

styrene foam cooler

3. Using the flashlight beam, try especially to observe the size of the particles in the cloud.

   a) Record your observations.

Materials Needed

For this station your group will need:

- styrene foam picnic cooler

- brick or other heavy mass

- metal container, with lid, small enough to fit in the cooler but large enough to contain the brick

- bag of ice cubes

- flashlight

Clean up spills immediately. Wash your hands after the activity.

Station 3: Temperature and Air Pressure

Materials Needed

For this station your group will need:

- two large round balloons (same size)
- metric measuring tape (or string and meter stick)
- two thermometers
- ice bath

1. Blow up two balloons to the same size and tie them shut.

   a) What do you think will happen when one balloon is cooled and the other is not? Why?

2. Measure the circumference (distance around the center) of both balloons.

   a) Record your measurements.

3. Read the temperature of two thermometers. They should both be at the same room temperature.

   a) Record this temperature.

4. Put one balloon and one thermometer into an ice bath for 10 min. Let the other balloon and thermometer stay at room temperature.

5. After 10 min, read the temperature of the thermometer in the ice bath and the temperature of the room.

   Take the balloon and thermometer out of the ice bath.

   Immediately measure the circumference of each balloon.

   a) Record the temperatures and the circumferences in your journal.

   b) What happened to the balloon in the ice bath?

   c) Did any air escape from the balloon in the ice bath?

   d) Did the density of the balloon increase or decrease because of cooling?

   e) What do you think was happening to the air inside the balloon?

Clean up spills immediately. Dry the thermometer so it is not slippery.

Wash your hands after the activity.

6. Let both balloons stay at room temperature for five minutes.

   Observe both balloons over that time.

   Measure the circumference of each balloon again after five minutes.

   a) Record your observations and your measurements.

   b) What can this investigation tell you about warm and cold air masses? Which air mass would you expect to be denser: warm or cool? Which type of air mass might take up more space: warm or cool?

   c) If a warm and a cool air mass were to meet, what do you think would happen, and why?

   d) How is air pressure involved?

Wash your hands after the activity.

Part B: Sharing and Discussing Your Findings

1. When your group has completed all of the stations, share your findings with one other group in the class.

   Help each other to answer questions you might have about the science behind the weather. Look for areas that are common across the stations.

   a) In your journal record anything new that you discover during your discussion.

2. When you have finished, hold a class discussion about the science behind the weather.

   Make one large list of the common science elements for the whole class.

   a) Keep a record of the list in your student journal.

Inquiry

Sharing Findings

An important part of a scientific experiment is sharing the results with others. Scientists do this whenever they think that they have discovered scientifically interesting and important information that other scientists might want to know about. This is called disseminating research findings. In this investigation you are sharing your findings with other groups.

As You Read...

Think about:

1. What is the water cycle?

2. What is the difference between evaporation and condensation?

3. On the Earth's surface, where would you likely find more evaporation than condensation occurring? Where would you likely find more condensation than evaporation?

4. How are clouds formed?

5. How is rain formed?

6. How does temperature affect air pressure?

Digging Deeper

THE WATER CYCLE

The Main Loop of the Water Cycle

A "closed system" consists of a container that allows energy, but not matter, to pass back and forth across the walls of the container. The Earth's atmosphere, ocean, and land surface act as an almost closed system. Water moves along a variety of pathways in this closed system. This system of movement is the global water cycle.

There is one main loop in the water cycle. Water evaporates at the Earth's surface and then moves as water vapor into the atmosphere. The water vapor condenses into clouds and falls from clouds as precipitation back to Earth's surface. Water that falls onto the continent can follow a number of pathways: some water evaporates back into the atmosphere, some is temporarily stored in lakes, reservoirs, and glaciers, some seeps into the ground as soil moisture and groundwater, and some runs off into rivers and streams. Ultimately, all the water on land drains into the ocean.

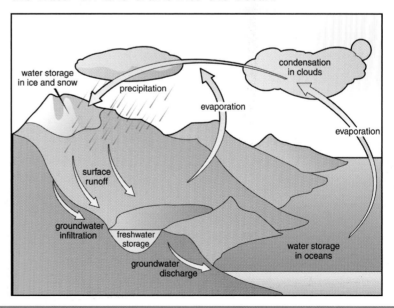

Each year, there is an excess of evaporation over precipitation on the oceans, and an excess of precipitation over evaporation on the continents. The net gain of water on the continents equals the net loss of water from the ocean. Under the influence of gravity, the excess water on land flows to the sea.

Evaporation and Condensation

With the range of temperature and pressure conditions in the Earth system, water coexists in all three phases (solid, liquid, vapor). It is continually changing from one phase to another. In the solid phase, water molecules vibrate about fixed locations, so an ice cube is crystalline and retains its shape (as long as its temperature is below freezing). In the liquid phase, water molecules have considerably more energy. The molecules are free to move around one another. For this reason, water takes the shape of its container. In the vapor phase, water molecules have the most energy. Even a small amount of water vapor spreads evenly throughout the volume of any container.

At the interface between water and air (e.g., the surface of the ocean or lake), water molecules move in two directions. Some molecules leave the water surface to become vapor, and some molecules leave the vapor phase to become liquid. Evaporation occurs if the flux of water molecules becoming vapor exceeds the flux of water molecules becoming liquid. Condensation occurs if the flux of water molecules becoming liquid exceeds the flux of water molecules becoming vapor. Surface water temperature largely controls the rate of evaporation, because more energetic water molecules (in warmer water) escape a water surface more readily than less energetic water molecules (in colder water).

A similar type of two-way exchange of water molecules takes place at the interface between ice (or snow) and air. Sublimation occurs when more water molecules

become vapor than solid, and deposition occurs when more water molecules become ice than vapor.

Water vapor enters the atmosphere mostly by evaporation and sublimation of water at the Earth's surface along with transpiration of water by plants. There is an upper limit to the water-vapor component of air. This limit depends largely on temperature. Air is saturated when the water vapor component of air is at its upper limit. The saturation concentration of air increases with temperature, so that warm saturated air has more water vapor than cold saturated air. It follows that sufficient cooling of unsaturated air causes it to become saturated. When air is saturated, excess water vapor condenses (or deposits) into clouds. This happened when you breathed into the cold metal container in the cooler at Station 2.

The relative humidity is defined as the ratio of the actual amount of water vapor to the amount of water vapor at saturation. It is always expressed as a percentage. Suppose that a 1-kg sample of air at 20°C (68°F) has 7.5 g of water vapor. At that temperature a 1-kg sample of air would be saturated if it had about 15 g of water vapor. Hence, the relative humidity of the sample is (7.5 g/15 g) × 100% = 50%. When air is saturated, its relative humidity is 100%. As unsaturated air is cooled, its relative humidity increases. At a relative humidity of 100% water vapor condenses into liquid water droplets or deposits into ice crystals.

If you fill a glass with ice water on a warm and humid day, small drops of water soon appear on the outside surface of the glass. That water did not leak through the glass. It condensed from the air. The relatively cold surface of the glass chilled the air in contact with the glass causing its relative humidity to increase to 100%. At saturation, water vapor condensed to the small liquid drops. Dew or frost on the grass on a chilly morning forms in the same way, when the ground surface is chilled by radiating its heat out to space on a clear night.

Clouds and Precipitation

When air is heated in a rigid closed container, it tries to expand, because air molecules move faster when the air is warmer. The molecules collide more and more strongly with the walls of the container. This increases the pressure on the inside surfaces of the container. The atmosphere has no walls (except the Earth's surface) and is free to expand when heated. For this reason, at constant pressure (at the Earth's surface, for example) the density of air increases with falling temperature. The density of air decreases with rising temperature. The balloons at Station 3 are flexible, so that the air inside was free to expand and contract in response to changes in temperature.

If air is heated near the ground, it expands. It is then less dense than the air nearby. The cooler, denser air nearby ➡

pushes under the warmer, less dense air, causing it to rise in the atmosphere. Earlier in this module you learned that the air pressure decreases upward in the atmosphere. As the air rises, it expands in response to the falling pressure. As the air expands, it cools. The reason for the cooling is that the air uses some of its thermal energy doing the work of pushing on the surrounding air. That leaves the air with less thermal energy; in other words, its temperature falls.

Most clouds consist of water droplets that have condensed from water vapor in the air. The droplets fall very slowly toward the Earth. Larger droplets fall faster than smaller droplets. When a larger droplet catches up with a smaller droplet on the way down, the two combine to form an even larger droplet. That one then falls even faster, and sweeps up even more small droplets. Soon a large drop is formed, which falls to Earth' surface as rain.

Raindrops that fall through very cold air near the Earth's surface can freeze to form little grains of ice called ice pellets or sleet. Snowflakes, however, are not frozen raindrops. Snowflakes grow in clouds by addition of water molecules onto their crystal surfaces, directly from the water vapor of the surrounding air—a process called deposition.

Review and Reflect

Review

1. Describe briefly what you discovered at each station.

Reflect

2. Explain why the global water cycle is called a cycle. You may wish to use a diagram to illustrate your answer.

3. What is the role of heat energy in weather? Give some examples.

4. Make a list of all of the different kinds of pathways you can think of that a water molecule might follow as it goes through the global water cycle. Remember that the water molecule can exist as water vapor, liquid water, or ice, and that it can occur at or near the Earth's surface.

Thinking about the Earth System

5. What role do plants play in the global water cycle?

6. What controls the part of precipitation that runs off into river and stream channels versus the part that infiltrates into the ground?

7. In what sense does the global water cycle involve the flow of energy as well as water?

Thinking about Scientific Inquiry

8. How did you use modeling in this investigation?

9. Why do you think sharing findings is an important process in scientific inquiry?

Investigation 6:

Climates

Key Question

Before you begin, first think about this key question.

What is the difference between weather and climate?

Think about what you have learned about the nature of weather and how it is reported. How does it differ from climate?

Share your thinking with others in your class. Keep a record of the discussion in your journal.

Materials Needed

For this investigation, all groups will need:

- a blank global map
- colored pencils or markers
- three heat-resistant containers with a pencil-size hole punched in the center of each lid (three per group)
- water supply
- sand
- three thermometers
- heat lamp
- graph paper
- climate resources (books, CD-ROMs, Internet access, etc.)
- poster board and presentation supplies

Investigate

Part A: Climatic Regions of the World

1. Look at the map on the following page showing the various climatic regions of the world. Read over the names of the types of climate.

   a) What weather elements do the name of the climates imply?

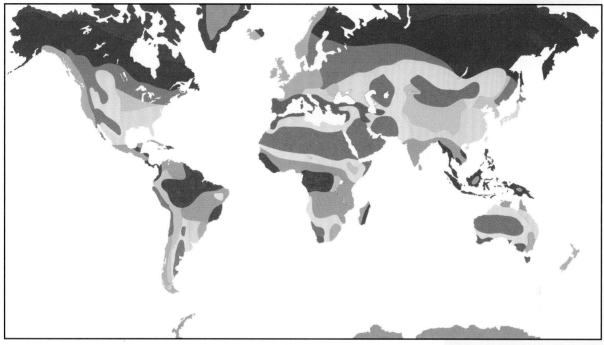

■ Tropical Rain forest, Monsoon (wet)
■ Tropical Savanna (wet summer, dry winter)
■ Steppe (semi arid)
■ Desert (dry)
■ Mediterranean (dry summer)
■ Humid Subtropical

■ Marine West Coast (no dry season)
■ Humid Continental, Warm Summer
■ Humid Continental, Cool Summer
■ Subarctic (snow climate)
■ Tundra (cold ice climate)
■ Ice Cap

b) What does this tell you about how climate is defined?

c) Write down any other questions you may have about the map, its legend, and the climatic regions of the world.

2. Find the area on the map where you live.

   With your group, discuss any ideas that you might have about the weather where you live. Write down your ideas.

   a) What is it usually like in the summer? (Mostly high temperatures or mostly low? Mostly wet or mostly dry?)

   b) What is it usually like in the winter?

   c) What kinds of plants and animals live in your area?

   d) How do people adapt to changes in the seasons?

3. Make a class profile of your ideas about your local climate. Think carefully and record your answers to the questions on the following page.

Inquiry
Scientific Questions

Scientific inquiry starts with a question. Scientists take what they already know about a topic, then form a question to investigate further. The question and its investigation are designed to expand their understanding of the topic. You are doing the same.

a) What is it about your area that helps vegetation or crops to grow well, or not well?

b) What is it about your area that makes it suitable for the animals that live there?

c) What kind of clothing do people wear in winter in your area? In the summer?

d) At what latitude do you live?

e) Are you close to a large body of water (e.g., ocean, Great Lakes), or are you landlocked?

f) What is your elevation above sea level?

4. Find other parts of the world that have the same climate as your area.

a) Shade these regions in on a blank copy of the map of the world.

b) What do all of the areas have in common?

c) What other factors might affect areas that have your climate?

d) Would you expect to find the same climate as yours in the polar regions? Why or why not?

5. As you saw from your climate map, the two main weather elements that are used to describe climate are air temperature and precipitation.

a) Why do you think it is that some areas of the world are typically hot and others are typically cold?

b) Why are some areas typically dry and others typically moist?

Part B: Ability of Different Materials to Hold Heat

1. One factor related to weather and climate is how different forms of matter that make up the Earth (solids, like soil; liquids, like water; and gases, like air) hold the heat from the Sun.

Work together in your group to design an experiment to investigate what happens when these three kinds of matter are heated and left to cool.

Be sure that your teacher checks your procedure before you begin.

You will be using the following materials:

- heat-resistant containers with lids that have a thermometer-size hole in the center;

- sand, water, and air;

- thermometers;

- heat lamp.

Make sure that the experiment you design is "fair" (objective and systematic).

Complete your design. Decide on the steps you will take from start to finish. Be sure to include any safety precautions you will take.

As a group, decide what you think will happen.

a) Record your group's prediction and the reason for the prediction. This is your hypothesis.

b) Include your procedure in your journal.

c) In your journal create a table for recording your data.

2. With the approval of your teacher conduct your experiment.

a) Record all your observations.

b) Graph your data and look for any patterns that emerge.

c) Which substance had the highest beginning temperature? Why do you think that was?

d) Which substance cooled most slowly? most quickly? What ideas do you have about that?

e) How can what you just observed about land, water, and air help you to understand some of the factors that affect climate?

Inquiry

Hypothesis

When you make a prediction and give your reasons for that prediction, you are forming a hypothesis. A hypothesis is a statement of the expected outcome of an experiment or observation, along with an explanation of why this will happen.

A hypothesis is never a guess. It is based on what the scientist already knows about something. A hypothesis is used to design an experiment or observation to find out more about a scientific idea or question. Guesses can be useful in science, but they are not hypotheses.

Dependent and Independent Variables

In all experiments, there are things that can change (vary). These are called variables. In a "fair" test, scientists must decide which things will be varied in the experiment and which things must remain the same. In this investigation you will make measurements to determine how well each kind of matter holds heat. This is the dependent variable. The kind of matter that you are testing is called the independent variable. All other variables must be controlled; that is, nothing else should change.

Wash your hands after the activity.

Part C: Creating Climate Clues

1. To help you learn about climates, each group in your class will specialize in researching a particular climate type.

   Choose a particular climatic zone on the map.

   You are going to prepare a set of six clues that your classmates will need to use to guess your climate type.

   Clues that you can give about your climate can include:

   • graphs of monthly temperature and precipitation for the climate;

   • descriptions of what people are wearing on a typical day;

   • nearby bodies of water;

   • well-known landforms;

   • typical animals that live there;

   • crops that are grown in the area.

2. Use all the resources you have available to conduct your research and make up your clues.

3. When all the clues are ready, each group in the class gets the chance to present its clues to the other groups.

4. To participate, someone from another group must raise his or her hand. That person then gets a chance to guess what the climate is. The person trying to guess must also give a good reason why he or she thinks your clue fits with a certain climate.

5. Continue until all groups have a chance to present their climate clues.

   a) Which clues were the most useful in guessing the climates, and why?

   b) Which resources were most useful, and why?

 Digging Deeper

WEATHER AND CLIMATE
The Difference between Weather and Climate

Weather is the state of the atmosphere at a particular place and time described in terms of temperature, air pressure, clouds, wind, and precipitation. Climate is the long-term average of weather. It is observed over periods of many years, decades, and centuries. In many areas of the United States, the daily high temperature or the daily low temperature can vary by as much as 30°F from one day to the next. In contrast, the average temperature for a whole year seldom varies by more than 1°F.

Factors That Determine the Climate

The two most important factors in describing the climate of an area are temperature and precipitation. The yearly average temperature of the area is obviously important, but the yearly range in temperature is also important. Some areas have a much larger range between highest and lowest temperature than other areas. Likewise, average precipitation is important, but the yearly variation in rainfall is also important. Some areas have about the same rainfall throughout the year. Other areas have very little rainfall for part of the year (the dry season) and a lot of rainfall for the other part of the year (the wet season).

As You Read...
Think about:
1. What is the difference between weather and climate?
2. What factors determine the climate?
3. How does average yearly temperature vary with latitude?
4. How does precipitation affect vegetation?
5. Why can local climate vary over very short distances?

The average temperature in an area depends mainly on the latitude. Generally, areas near the Equator have high average temperatures, and areas nearer the North and South Poles have lower average temperatures. The range of temperature, however, depends more on where the area is located in relation to the ocean. Areas where winds usually blow from the ocean have a smaller range of temperature than areas far away from the ocean, in the interior of a continent. That is because water has a much greater heat capacity than rock and soil, as you saw in your investigation. It takes much more heat from the Sun to warm up water than it takes to warm up rock and soil. Likewise, water cools off much more slowly than rock and soil on cold, clear nights and in the winter.

Climate and Vegetation

The plant community in an area is the most sensitive indicator of climate. Areas with moderate to high temperatures and abundant rainfall throughout the year are heavily forested (unless humans have cleared the land for agriculture). Areas with somewhat less rainfall are mainly grasslands, which are called prairies in North America. Humans have converted grasslands into rich agricultural areas around the world. Even in areas with high yearly rainfall, trees are scarce if there is not much rainfall during the warm growing season. As you know, regions with not much rainfall and scarce vegetation are called deserts, or arid regions. Areas with somewhat greater rainfall are called semiarid regions. The major problem with using semiarid or arid regions for agriculture is that ground water is removed to irrigate crops. In many cases, the removal of

ground water exceeds the rate at which it is naturally replaced (by precipitation that reenters the ground water system). As a result, water resources are lost, water levels in wells fall, and less ground water flows to recharge streams and rivers, which has other impacts on the Earth system. Another problem with semiarid regions is that when humans use them for agriculture, the loss of natural vegetation can cause the areas to become deserts.

Microclimate

It is easy to understand how climate can vary over very large areas, because of slight changes in temperature or rainfall. Climates can also vary over very short distances. Local differences in climate are described by the term "microclimate." Differences in microclimate might explain some of the differences in weather from place to place you likely observed in the first investigation in this module.

Sometimes, low-lying areas are colder at night than higher ground nearby. On clear nights, the ground is chilled as its heat is radiated out to space. The cold ground then chills the air near the ground. The chilled air is slightly denser than the overlying air, so it tends to flow slowly downhill, in the same way that water flows downhill. The cold air "ponds" in low areas. These are places where the first frosts of autumn are earliest and where the last frosts of spring are latest. If you ever have a chance to plant fruit trees, plant them on the highest ground around!

In hilly areas, north-facing slopes get less sunshine than south-facing slopes. Local temperatures on the north-facing slopes are colder than on south-facing slopes in both summer and winter. In areas with winter snows, the snow melts much later on north-facing slopes.

Review and Reflect

Review

1. Which climate type has the most rainfall? Which has the least?

2. Which climate type has the shortest growing season? Which has the longest?

3. How and why do oceans and continents affect climate?

Reflect

4. Does climate influence human population size in an area? If so, how?

5. Imagine that the climate in your area changed suddenly.

    a) What would have to be done to homes and other buildings?

    b) How would this affect what you wear?

    c) How would this affect what you eat?

    d) How would it affect what you could grow in a garden?

    e) How would it affect transportation?

    f) How would it affect the work people do?

    g) How would it affect what you do for recreation?

Thinking about the Earth System

6. On your *Earth System Connection* sheet, note how the things you learned in this investigation connect to the geosphere, hydrosphere, atmosphere and biosphere.

7. Global warming would cause sea level to rise. How would this affect other Earth systems? What would be the effect? Higher sea level means a higher base level for rivers. How might this affect erosion by rivers?

Thinking about Scientific Inquiry

8. How did you use questions to answer by inquiry in this investigation?

9. How is a hypothesis different from a guess?

10. What factors must be considered when designing a "fair" experiment?

Investigation 7:

Exploring Climate Change

Key Question
Before you begin, first think about this key question.

What evidence suggests that climate has changed in the past?

Think about what you have learned so far. Is global climate changing? How do you think scientists learn about what the global climate was like before weather data were recorded? What "climate clues" are out there?

Share your thinking with others in your class. Keep a record of the discussion in your journal.

Materials Needed
For this investigation your group will need:

- resources on global-climate change (books, CD-ROMs, Internet access, etc.)

Investigate

1. Studying weather data is only one way of learning about climate and how it changes. Paleoclimatologists are climatologists who study evidence from the past (ice cores, ocean bottom cores, tree rings, rocks, and fossils, among others) to find out more about climate in the past.

Look at the climate evidence that follows.

Also look at the climate map of the world in the previous investigation.

Read the information about the items in the pictures (fossils, tree rings, etc.) to find out more about climate in the past.

Discuss the questions with your group.

Keep a record of your group's discussion in your journal.

Climate Evidence 1

Fossil shells, found on the coast of Greenland, show that certain species of warm-water mollusks lived there about 8500 years ago.

a) What is the climate like in Greenland today?

b) What clues do you think these fossils give about climate changes in Greenland?

c) What ideas do you have about what might have caused climate changes in Greenland?

Climate Evidence 2

A fossilized impression of a banana, 43 million years old, was found in the state of Oregon. Find some of the places on the world climate map where bananas grow in the world today.

a) What is the climate like in Oregon today?

b) What clues can the fossil give you about climate changes in Oregon?

c) What ideas do you have about what might have caused climate changes in Oregon?

Inquiry

Considering Evidence

Scientific judgments depend on solid, verifiable evidence. Claims by scientists that the global climate is changing must be supported by evidence. You must be certain about the reliability of any evidence that you use. You must also know how the accuracy of the evidence can be checked.

Climate Evidence 3

Fossils found near Antarctica include a meat-eating dinosaur that lived 200 million years ago. The dinosaur preyed on small animals that, in turn, fed on lush plants.

a) What is the climate like in Antarctica today?

b) What did the climate need to be like for the dinosaur to survive?

c) What clues can the fossils give about climatic changes in the area around Antarctica?

Climate Evidence 4

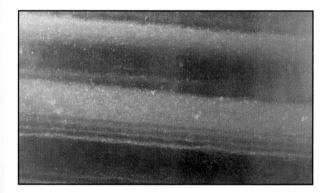

Ice cores can be taken wherever very deep ice exists. Some of these ice cores have sampled ice that is more than 400,000 years old. Ice traps air and dust in tiny bubbles in the ice. Climatologists can study these materials to find out about past climates.

a) How many darker layers and how many lighter layers can you see in this example?

b) What do the layers suggest about the climate during the time period that was sampled?

Climate Evidence 5

Cave paintings like this have been found in the Sahara Desert. They have been dated as far back as 4000 B.C. Observe the kinds of animal it shows.

a) What is the climate like in the Sahara today?

b) What did the climate need to be like for the animal in the painting to live in the Sahara?

Climate Evidence 6

This picture shows the tree growth rings from a bristlecone pine tree. Some of these trees live to be as old as 4000 years. A wide ring means warm, humid weather; a narrow ring means cold, dry weather.

a) Count the number of growth rings on this example (approximately the number of years the tree has lived).

b) What evidence do you have about past climate, on the basis of the tree rings pictured?

2. When you have finished working with all of the evidence, look over what you have written about climate in the past.

Consult any resources you have available about climate in the past to add more information to what you already know.

a) Write down any new ideas you discover.

3. As a class, pull all your investigations together. Discuss your answers and come to a consensus as a class.

a) List all the evidence you have been able to find that shows how climates have changed over time. Wherever possible, include the time scales involved.

b) What evidence do you now have that shows that climate change happens slowly? What evidence do you now have that climate change can happen rapidly?

As You Read...
Think about:
1. *What is a climate proxy?*
2. *How are ice cores used to determine past climates?*
3. *In your own words, explain the astronomical theory of the ice age.*
4. *What are two events that can affect worldwide climate over a period of a few years?*

Digging Deeper

MEASURING CLIMATE CHANGE
Climate Proxies

The Earth's climate has changed greatly through the billions of years that constitute geologic time, and even in recent centuries. The study of past climates is called paleoclimatology (*paleo-* means early or past).

Something that represents something else indirectly is called a proxy. There are many proxies for past climate. They provide a lot of information, although none is perfect. Some, like kinds of past plants and animals, are easy to understand. Some important proxies, involving the chemical element oxygen, are more difficult to understand.

Ice Cores

Thin cores of ice, thousands of meters deep, have been drilled in the ice sheets of Greenland and Antarctica. They are preserved in special cold-storage rooms for study.

Glacier ice is formed as each year's snow is compacted under the weight of the snows of later years. A slightly darker layer that contains dust blown onto the ice sheet during summer, when not much new snow falls, marks each year's new ice. The winter layer consists of cleaner and lighter-colored ice. The layers are only millimeters to centimeters thick. They can be dated by counting the yearly layers. The oxygen in the water molecules also holds a key to past climate. Scientists are able to use the oxygen atoms in the glacier ice as a proxy for air temperature above the glacier.

Past Glaciations

Ice sheets on the continents have grown and then shrunk again at least a dozen times over the past 1.7 million years. Many climate proxies make that very clear. Deposits of sediment and distinctive landforms left by these glaciers are present over large areas of North America and Eurasia. Proxies for global temperature show gradual cooling as the ice sheets form. They also then show very rapid warming as the ice sheets melt back. Intervals of relatively high temperature between glaciations are called interglacials. Past interglacials have lasted about 10,000 years. Civilization developed only within the last interglacial—and you are still in it! The graph shows the estimated global surface temperature for the last 420,000 years.

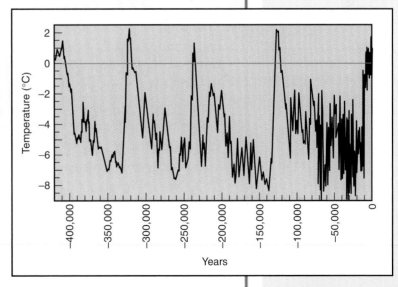

This was obtained from the longest and most informative ice core. This core was taken at the Vostok station in Antarctica by a team of Russian, American, and French scientists.

Causes of Climate Change

Probably the two most important factors that determine Earth's climate are the amount of heat the Sun delivers to the planet, and also where the continents are located relative to the Equator. Continental ice sheets cannot develop unless plate tectonics cause one or more continents to be at high latitudes.

The Earth revolves around the Sun once a year. Its orbit is in the shape of an ellipse. If the Earth were the only planet, its orbit around the Sun would be almost unchanging. The pull of the other planets on the Earth causes the Earth's orbit to be much more complicated. The orbit changes slightly in several different ways. These changes occur over periods that range from about 20,000 years to about 100,000 years. They cause slight differences in how much of the Sun's heat the Earth receives in winter versus summer and at high latitudes versus low latitudes.

One theory holds that the small changes in the Earth's orbit trigger the advance and retreat of ice sheets. This

theory is known as the astronomical theory of the ice ages. It was first developed in the 1920s and 1930s by the Serbian astrophysicist Milutin Milankovitch (1879–1958). It was not widely accepted by the scientific community until the 1970s. Although most scientists today accept this theory, details of how the changes govern the volume of ice sheets are still only partly understood. For example, the extremely fast melting of the ice sheets, compared to the long times needed for them to form, is still a mystery.

The astronomical theory is only part of the story. Climate is known to change on time scales as short as a century or even a few years, and the cause (or causes) of these changes are still not clear.

Some violent volcanic eruptions are known to influence climate on a scale of one to two years. Substances from the volcano are blasted into the air. Some are so small that they can remain in the atmosphere for many months to a few years. While there they both absorb and reflect solar radiation. This reduces the amount of sunlight that reaches Earth's surface. A cooling of up to 1°C at Earth's surface may be observed.

El Niño and La Niña are large-scale air—sea interactions in the tropical Pacific. They can also affect the climate in many regions of the world over periods of one to two years. Changes occur in the sea-surface temperature. This affects the air pressure patterns in the tropical Pacific. As a result, storm tracks at middle and high latitudes are altered. Some regions that are usually wet have droughts. Other regions that are arid or semiarid have heavy rains.

Review and Reflect

Review

1. Describe at least three ways that scientists can detect or measure climate change.

2. What are some of the possible causes of climate change?

Reflect

3. What kinds of evidence suggest that climates have changed over time?

4. How convincing does this evidence seem to be?

5. What further evidence is needed to answer some of the questions about climate change?

Thinking about the Earth System

6. On your *Earth System Connection* sheet, note how the things you learned in this investigation connect to the geosphere, hydrosphere, atmosphere, and biosphere.

Thinking about Scientific Inquiry

7. What are some sources of error associated with the ways of detecting climate change that are described in this investigation?

Investigation 8:
Climate Change Today

Putting It All Together

Key Question

Before you begin, first think about this key question.

How is the global climate changing?

Think about what you have learned about climate change. Do you think that the world's climate is changing? If so, what are the prospects for the future? What will the climate be like for you, your children, and your grandchildren?

Share your ideas with your classmates. Record your thoughts in your journal.

Materials Needed

For this investigation, your group will need:

- your weather data

- weather data for your area for the past 30 years

- resources on global-climate change (books, CD-ROMs, Internet access, etc.)

- presentation materials (poster board, markers, etc.)

Investigate

1. Pull together all the weather data and climate information that you have collected over the course of the Unit.

Examine the climate of your area and compare it to the weather data you have collected.

Also compare the climate with the weather data from your area for the past 30 years.

Discuss what patterns and relationships you notice in your climate and weather data with your group.

a) What trends, if any, do you notice in the weather data over the past 30 years?

b) Do the temperatures appear to be increasing, decreasing, or staying about the same? How can you tell?

c) What is the average yearly rainfall in your area?

d) On the average, have you had more or less rainfall than one would predict for your climate over the past 10 years?

e) How could you explain what you observe?

2. Now think about what the future climate might be like in the region where you live.

Think about these questions:

• Will it be much warmer or much cooler than it is now? If so, how much warmer or cooler? Or, will the climate be about the same as now?

• Do you think there will be much more rainfall per year, much less, or about the same? Why do you think that?

a) Write down a prediction for what you think the climate will be like where you live 100 years from now. Also include the reasons for your prediction.

3. Discuss your predictions with other people in your class.

a) List the predictions and reasons that others have.

4. For this investigation you may decide to stay in your normal groups or to work with people who have ideas similar to yours. Whichever you decide, your next task is to look at the individual predictions and the reasons you gave for them.

In your group, develop a final prediction, with reasons, that you all agree on.

a) Write this down clearly. It will be the key starting point for your research.

5. Begin by assessing what information you already have available, then discuss what additional information sources you need to consult.

Keep in mind that you need to look for data that both do and do not support your predictions, and the reasons you gave for them.

In your search for new information, you might want to divide the tasks. For example, one person could be responsible for exploring the Internet, another for locating and investigating text books, another looking at trade books, and so on. Also, do not forget to consult each group member's journal for information.

When you have a plan, make a schedule for the information-gathering part of your research project.

a) Record your schedule in your journal.

6. Once you have gathered all the information you can, look at what you have. In your group discuss these questions:

• What evidence is there from all of this information that is relevant to the research prediction, and the reasons you gave for it?

• Which parts of the evidence support the prediction, which do not support it, and which do neither but are still important?

It may be helpful to construct a chart within which to put these various pieces of evidence. You may find an alternative way to do this. By now you have enough experience of dealing with data to decide.

As well as using this way of sorting your information, keep in mind that you might later want to include data charts, or other forms of representation, in your final report. If one person in your group has special talents in designing these things, give this job to him or her.

7. When you have fully reviewed all your collected evidence and information, you need to analyze it against your prediction.

This is a very important step. Here you need to decide whether your prediction is supported by the evidence, not supported, or supported somewhat but not enough to be conclusive.

Together, work on this analysis and then reach agreement on how both your prediction and the reasoning behind it are reflected by the evidence. When this is complete, and all are agreed, your research phase is complete.

8. Decide on a way of presenting the results of your research for others to see and understand. This is going to be your research report. This must include:

   • your predictions and the reasons for them;

   • your evidence for or against your predictions;

   • your conclusions about whether the global climate is changing or not, based upon the evidence you have found and analyzed;

   • what inquiry processes you used in your research and how you used them;

   • how your research relates to the Earth system.

   Together, discuss how you will do this in your report. Decide what sections your report will contain, where illustrations and data representations will be included, and how you will present the written information.

9. Create your research report and share it with the class.

   Be sure to study carefully each other group's research reports.

   a) What did you learn from the other reports?

   b) How much agreement is there between the various reports on global change? Explain.

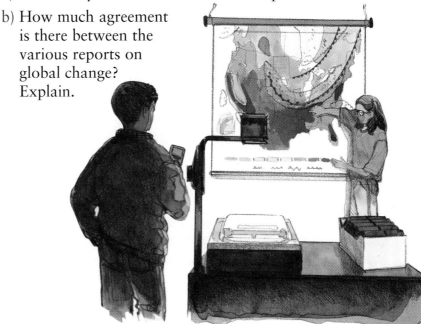

 Digging Deeper

GLOBAL CLIMATE CHANGE

The Earth seems to be getting warmer. *Graph 1* shows how yearly average temperature has changed since 1880. This is about the time when temperatures first began to be recorded in an organized way at weather stations around the world. The curve on the graph has lots of ups and downs, but there is a clear upward trend. Graphs like this have some uncertainties, however. For example, there is a problem about how to adjust the curve to take into account the growth of large cities, where so many of the weather stations are located. Urbanization causes temperature readings in large cities to be somewhat higher than in surrounding rural areas. The upward trend shown is almost certainly real, though. Other evidence, like the general shrinking of glaciers all around the world and the thinning of the Arctic ice pack, tell the same story.

As You Read...
Think about:
1. *How has yearly average temperature changed since 1880?*
2. *How has global average temperature changed during the past 2400 years?*
3. *What is Earth's principal greenhouse gas?*
4. *Why has carbon dioxide increased over the past decades?*
5. *Why are computer models limited in their predictions of Earth's future climate?*

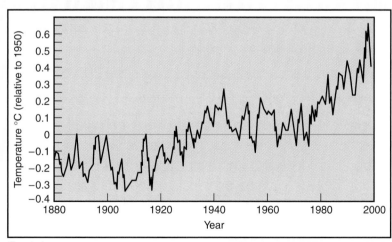

Graph 1

Graph 2 is similar to *Graph 1*. It shows global average temperature for the past 2,400 years. The curve is less certain than the one in *Graph 1,* because it is based on various proxies for temperature. You learned

about these in the previous investigation. The highest temperatures are about 1°C above 20th century mean temperatures. The lowest temperatures are about 1°C below 20th century mean temperatures.

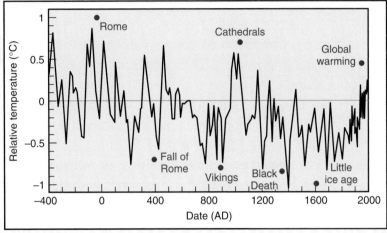

Graph 2

Here's a big question, and an important one. Has the increase in temperature since the beginning of the 20th century been caused by human activity, or is it just another natural upward "spike" like several during the past two millennia, shown in *Graph 2*? Most climatologists think that the upward trend in temperature during the 20th century is at least partly caused by human activity.

Several gases in the Earth's atmosphere are called greenhouse gases. The most important is water vapor, but carbon dioxide is also important. Early on in Earth's history, carbon dioxide was the principal greenhouse gas. Carbon dioxide has always been part of the Earth's atmosphere, but has been increasing more and more rapidly in recent times (*Graph 3*). Coal, oil, and natural gas are called fossil fuels, because they come from plant and animal material that was buried in the Earth's sediments. When they are burned, they add carbon dioxide gas to the atmosphere. Along with the other greenhouse gases, carbon dioxide absorbs some of the heat that the Earth's surface sends

out to space and radiates heat back to the surface. That increases the Earth's average surface temperature. The effect is the same as with the glass of a greenhouse, although the process itself is not exactly the same.

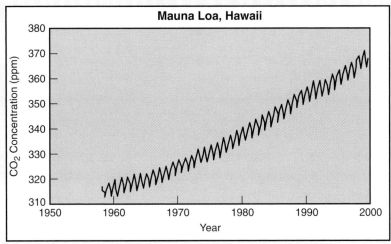

Mauna Loa, Hawaii

Graph 3

Several groups of climatologists have been developing computer models of the Earth's climate. They try to build in all of the important controls of climate into the model. Then they start the model with the present climate and let it run to see what the future climate will be. The models are not perfect, because it is very difficult to simulate some of the most important influences on climate. The behavior of clouds is especially tricky to model. The models have one thing in common, though. They predict that the Earth's surface temperature is likely to increase by as much as 2°C between 2000 and 2050 if the upward trend in

atmospheric carbon dioxide continues. A look back at *Graph 2* shows that a rise of 2°C would make the Earth's temperature much higher than during even the warmest periods in human history.

If the predictions about global warming come true, many things about the Earth's climate, aside from just temperature, are likely to change. Some regions will get more rainfall, and other regions will get less. The frequency and intensity of severe storms are likely to increase. As the world's glaciers continue to melt, sea level around the world will rise, by as much as half a meter or so. That might not sound like a lot to you, but think of the flooding that it would cause in coastal cities and islands around the world!

Will the predictions of the computer models come true? That is likely, although not certain. All that science can do is try to make likely predictions. How to act upon the predictions is for human society to decide.

Review and Reflect

Reflect

1. How did your ideas about how global climate will change in the future differ from those of other groups? Explain why there might be differences of opinion.

Thinking about the Earth System

2. Add any new connections that you have found between climate change and the Earth system (biosphere, atmosphere, hydrosphere, and geosphere) to your *Earth System Connection* sheet.

Thinking about Scientific Inquiry

3. What evidence did you find for future climate change?

Reflecting

Back to the Beginning

You have been investigating climate and weather in many ways. How have your ideas changed since the beginning of the investigation? Look at the following questions and write down your ideas in your journal.

- What information is contained in a weather report and how is this information obtained?
- What is the difference between climate and weather?
- What evidence is there that climate change has happened?
- What evidence is there that climate change is happening?

Thinking about the Earth System

At the end of each investigation, you thought about how your findings connected with the Earth system. Consider what you have learned about the Earth system. Refer to the *Earth System Connection* sheet that you have been building up throughout this module. What connections between climate and weather and the Earth system have you been able to find?

Thinking about Scientific Inquiry

You have used inquiry processes throughout the Unit. Review the investigations you have done and the inquiry processes you have used.

- What scientific inquiry processes did you use?
- How did scientific inquiry processes help you learn about climate and weather?

A New Beginning!

Not so much an ending as a new beginning!

This investigation into *Climate and Weather* is now completed. However, this is not the end of the story. You will see the importance of climate and weather where you live, and everywhere you travel. Be alert for opportunities to observe the importance of climate and weather, and add to your understanding.

The Big Picture

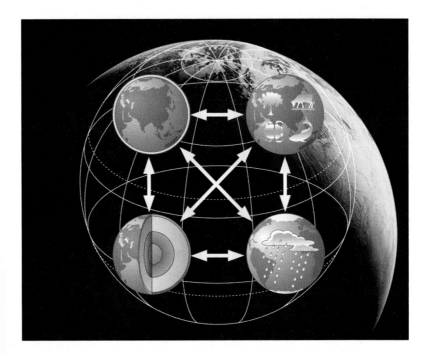

Key Concepts

Earth is a set of closely linked systems.

Earth's processes are powered by two sources: the Sun, and Earth's own inner heat.

The geology of Earth is dynamic, and has evolved over 4.6 billion years.

The geological evolution of Earth has left a record of its history that geoscientists interpret.

We depend upon Earth's resources—both mined and grown.

INVESTIGATING
EARTH IN SPACE: ASTRONOMY

Unit 5

What you will be investigating in this Unit:

Introducing Earth in Space: Astronomy

Have you ever looked at the stars and wondered how far away they were?

Have you noticed changes in the way the Moon looks?

Did you ever wonder what it would be like to travel in space?

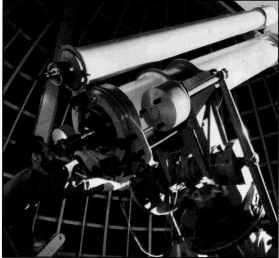

Have you ever looked through a telescope?

Why is Astronomy Important?

Astronomy is the study of the Moon, stars, and other objects in space. It is important because it helps you understand how the Earth system works within the Solar System and beyond. It is an amazing science because it explores space from its tiny specks of dust to its huge clusters of stars. From the beginning, humans have been fascinated by the objects in the night sky. At first, it seemed like there was just the Moon and stars, but early astronomers began to notice other objects, too. They noticed comets and meteors (called "falling stars" by early observers) moving across the skies. They also discovered that the planets were brighter and moved differently than the stars. One of the most important advances in the history of astronomy was the invention of the telescope in the 1600s. A telescope could magnify the objects in the sky. The more complex telescopes became, the more discoveries astronomers were able to make. The planet Mars looked red. Saturn had rings around it, but why? The telescope created even more questions than it answered, but astronomers kept seeking the answers. Astronomy is important because it helps you understand the universe within which Earth exists.

What Will You Investigate?

To help you understand more about the science of astronomy, you will be conducting research. Your research will include hands-on investigations. You will also make and study models. Here are some of the things you will investigate:

- what characteristics the planet Earth has;
- where Earth is in our Solar System;
- what other planets and objects are in the Solar System;
- what the similarities and differences are between the planets;
- the role of the Sun in the Solar System;
- how the different parts of the Solar System relate to one another;
- the objects outside our Solar System;
- the life cycle of stars;
- how people have studied the universe over time;
- the latest theories about how our universe formed.

You will need to practice your problem-solving skills and become an accurate observer and recorder. You will also need to be creative in researching information about the universe.

In the last investigation you will have a chance to apply all that you learned about Earth and space. You will create an exciting piece of communication on an astronomy topic you have learned about in this Unit.

Investigation 1:

There's No Place Like Home

Key Question

Before you begin, first think about this key question.

What characteristics does the planet Earth have and how do scientists know this?

A look at Earth from space.

Think about what you already know about the Earth. Write down two things that you feel confident you know about the Earth as a planet. You may want to draw a picture as well. Then, write down how you think scientists have discovered these things about the Earth. What tools or methods do you think they have used?

Materials Needed

For this investigation your group will need:

- colored pencils or markers and blank paper

- diagram of the Earth, showing the different layers

- relief map or globe of the Earth

- 5" x 8" index cards

- computer with Internet access, if possible

When you finish, share your ideas with other students in your group. Make a group list of what you know and what questions you would like to investigate about the Earth and how scientists study the Earth. Keep this list for later in your investigation.

Investigate

1. Use the ideas and drawings about the Earth that your group members have already finished. Work together to draw two sketches.

   a) One sketch should show the Earth as if you were looking down on it from space. Try to show as many features of the planet as you can. Label any features (continents, oceans, mountains, etc.) that you know.

Inquiry

Making Diagrams

Sometimes the best way to show the results of a scientific investigation is by drawing a diagram. Complicated concepts can often be illustrated more easily than they can be explained in words. The diagram should be labeled.

b) The second sketch should show what you and your other group members think that the inside of the Earth looks like. Imagine that you could cut the Earth in half. Do your best to show what it might look like beneath the surface. Label your sketch with descriptions of the different parts you have drawn. If you know the names of any of the Earth's layers, label these, but don't worry if you don't know this yet.

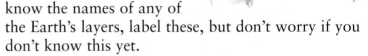

2. Label your drawings with your group's initials. Then post them up in a gallery around the room. Taking your journals, go on a "tour" around the gallery.

   a) Write down ideas that other groups have about the outside and inside of the planet.

3. When you finish the tour, talk about these ideas in your group. What ideas did you get from the other groups?

4. Now, look at the world map or globe your teacher will provide. Also look at the diagram of the inside of the Earth in the **Digging Deeper** section.

   a) How are your drawings (and those of your classmates) similar to or different from these maps and diagrams?

   b) What surprised you about the maps and diagrams?

   c) Use this new information to make your drawings as accurate as possible.

5. Next make a "Planet Card" (like a baseball card) about the Earth. Draw a picture of the Earth on one side of a 5" × 8" card and put important information that you have learned about the Earth on the back. You might include information on the following topics:

   • What the surface of the Earth is like.

   • What the interior of the Earth is like.

As you continue reading this Unit and learn more about the Earth, you can add to the Planet Card. You can also make other Planet Cards as you learn about the other planets in the Solar System. These cards can be used as a review tool later.

6. At the beginning of this investigation, you also wrote down your thoughts about how scientists found out about the characteristics of the Earth. Share your thoughts with your group. Then, as a group, choose one question that you wish to investigate further. Possible topics may include, but are not limited to, the following:

   • How did scientists discover the composition of Earth's atmosphere?

   • How do scientists know what the inside of Earth is like?

   • How deep are the oceans and how can you be sure about this?

   • How high are the highest mountain ranges on Earth?

   • What is the deepest spot in the ocean?

   • Where is the highest mountain?

7. Your class will go to the library or computer center in your school to research these topics. Be sure to ask for help from your teacher if you are having difficulty finding the information you are looking for.

8. When you finish your research, think of a way that you can present your information so that your classmates find it interesting and informative. You might want to use a PowerPoint™ presentation, an overhead transparency, a poster, photographs, or even some tools.

   a) Prepare your group's presentation.

9. Make your presentation, being sure to answer any questions from your classmates.

   a) As other people are presenting, refer to your original ideas about the Earth. Add information as you discover it. Save all this information for later investigations.

Inquiry
Scientific Questions

Science inquiry starts with a question. Scientists take what they already know about a topic, then form a question to investigate further. The question and its investigation are designed to expand their understanding of the topic. You are doing the same in this investigation.

Digging Deeper

EARTH, A CONSTANTLY CHANGING PLANET

Earth Systems

As You Read...
Think about:
1. *What are the layers of the Earth?*
2. *What are the Earth's systems?*

The Earth has many features and parts that work together in important ways. One way to study the Earth is to look at its different parts and understand how they are connected. With this information, you can begin to understand how the planet works and how it is always changing. Parts of the Earth that work together are known as systems. Planet Earth has four main systems: the atmosphere, the biosphere, the hydrosphere, and the geosphere.

Atmosphere

Earth as viewed from space. Which parts of the Earth systems can you see in this photo?

The picture shows Earth as viewed from space. Notice the clouds that surround the planet. They are part of an envelope of gases, called the atmosphere, that surround the Earth. When you look up into the sky from the Earth's surface, you are looking into the Earth's *atmosphere*. The gases in the atmosphere play an important role in all the Earth systems. For example, 21% of the Earth's atmosphere is oxygen. Many organisms (living things) need the oxygen in the air to live. Another important gas in the atmosphere, carbon dioxide, is used by plants to make food. Ozone is a naturally occurring gas found in a layer of the atmosphere called the stratosphere. At this level, ozone protects life on Earth from harmful energy given off by the Sun. Finally, the swirling cloud layer that you see in the photograph is condensed water vapor. This water vapor plays an important role in Earth's weather systems.

Biosphere

The Earth supports millions of different types of living organisms that make up part of the Earth's *biosphere*. Organisms survive in many places, from high atop mountains to the extreme environments of the deep ocean floor. Some live on land surfaces, while others live below thousands of meters of glacial ice. Many organisms that once lived on the Earth no longer exist. They could not adjust when conditions such as climate and food supplies changed drastically. Fossils in ancient rocks are evidence that these organisms once did live on the Earth.

Hydrosphere

Water covers nearly 71% of the Earth's surface. The part of the Earth that contains water is known as the *hydrosphere*. Most of the water on the Earth's surface is in the oceans. Oceans are found in basins that are huge depressions in the Earth's surface. Water can be found on the Earth's land surface as streams, rivers, ponds, and lakes. Water exists underground in soil and rocks. Water in the form of vapor (gas) is an important part of the Earth's atmosphere. Water is also in the cells of every living thing on the Earth.

This image shows a massive phytoplankton bloom off the coast of Tasmania. Phytoplankton are part of the Earth's biosphere.

Geosphere

The Earth is made of layers of rock, which together make up the *geosphere*. A relatively thin layer of solid rock called the crust covers the Earth's surface. The crust has a wide variety of shapes. In some places it takes the shape of hills, mountains, slopes, or canyons. In other places it takes the shape of flatlands, shorelines, or even meteorite craters. The shape of the land is always changing. One reason for these changes is that the

The shape of Earth's crust is always changing. This image shows the mountains and valleys of the Himalaya Mountains.

Earth's massive continents are constantly being moved by processes deep within the Earth. Many of these processes occur in the part of the geosphere that lies beneath the crust. This part is called the mantle. The rocks in the mantle are continuously being squeezed, deformed, and moved in different directions. Sometimes the rocks of the crust move upward to form mountain ranges. Mountain ranges can even be found beneath the oceans and are called mid-ocean ridges.

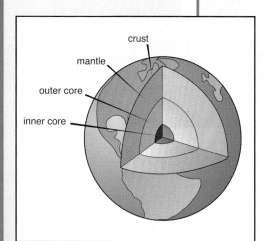

Processes deep within the Earth's interior change the shape of the landscape.

Deep beneath the Earth's mantle are two other layers: the outer core and the inner core. Both the inner and outer cores of the Earth are made mostly of iron. The inner core is solid and the outer core is liquid. These four layers – the crust, mantle, outer core, and inner core – make up Earth's geosphere.

Examining the Earth's systems provides an explanation for many of the most important features of how planet Earth works. Scientists use this knowledge when they study other planets. They compare the Earth's systems to the systems of other planets to understand how those planets work. The more they know about the Earth, the more they can learn about the other planets in the Solar System.

Review and Reflect

Review

1. What questions about the inside and outside of the Earth were you able to answer through this investigation?

2. What questions about how scientists know about the Earth were you able to answer?

Reflect

3. What ideas about the inside and outside of the Earth surprised you the most?

4. What ideas about how scientists learn about the Earth were most interesting to you? Why were they interesting?

Thinking about the Earth System

5. What are the four main systems of Earth?

6. Describe two ways that the atmosphere and biosphere are connected. Remember to write any connections you find on the *Earth System Connection* sheet.

7. How do Earth's systems help scientists study other planets?

Thinking about Scientific Inquiry

8. In which parts of the investigation did you:

   a) Ask your own questions?

   b) Record your own ideas?

   c) Revise your ideas?

   d) Use your imagination?

   e) Share ideas with others?

   f) Find information from different sources?

   g) Pull your information together to make a presentation?

Investigation 2:

The Earth's Moon

Key Question

Before you begin, first think about this key question.

What are the features of the Moon?

Share what you know about what the Moon looks like. Keep a record of your ideas in your journal.

Share your group's ideas with the rest of the class.

The universe is so vast that it is a very difficult job to study all its parts in depth. Scientists can start with the Earth, as you did in this Unit. From there, one method of learning more about the universe might be to investigate Earth's nearest neighbor, the Moon. Another method might be to study the object on which we depend the most for energy, the Sun. Scientists also study the relationships among Earth, Moon, and Sun.

Investigation 2 will get you started by focusing on the Moon.

Materials Needed

For Station 1 your group will need:

• Moon map

• tape (optional)

• Learning Station materials (poster board, markers, blank paper, tape, stapler)

Investigate

Your class will work in specialist groups to study the Moon. Your group will then set up Learning Stations for other class members.

Moon Station 1: Moon's Features

1. Spread out the Moon map (or tape it up) so that you can see all the information on the map. Observe the main types of features on the Moon.

2. Try to answer all the following questions about the Moon map. You can use this information in your Learning Station.

a) What differences do you observe between how the two sides of the Moon look on the map? How could you explain these differences?

b) What are the Moon's maria? How might they have formed?

c) How do you think the craters formed on the Moon?

d) Do you see any evidence that there once might have been water on the Moon? Do you see evidence that there once might have been life on the Moon? Explain your answer.

e) How does the Moon's surface compare to the Earth's? (Look at a relief map of the Earth, or a globe.)

3. When you have finished studying the Moon map and answering the questions, think about how you could build a Learning Station to help others in your class learn more about the Moon's features.

a) Record your plan and show it to your teacher.

Moon Station 2: Moon Phases

1. Study the Moon-phase diagram carefully. How does the Moon appear to change, as you observe it from the Earth, over the course of a month? How could you explain this, thinking about the relationships among the Moon, the Earth, and the Sun? (You might want to look at a diagram of the Solar System.)

2. Now, look over the materials you can use to make a model of how the Moon appears to change shape. Think about these questions before you make your model:

a) What object(s) do you have in your materials set that could represent the Sun? The Earth? The Moon?

Materials Needed

For Station 2 your group will need:

• Moon-phase diagram

• strong lamps or flashlights

• table-tennis ball

• pencil

• tape

• overhead projector (optional)

• Learning Station materials (poster board, colored pencils, blank paper, tape, stapler)

• tennis ball

Phases of the Moon

b) Which objects would you have to move and which will you keep still?

c) How might you move those objects to show how the Earth and the Moon move?

3. You might find it useful to draw a diagram of the Sun/Earth/Moon system before building your model.

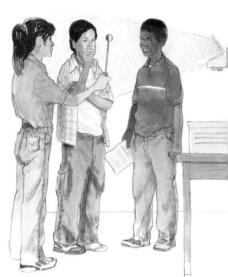

a) Draw a diagram of your model and submit it to your teacher for approval. Use the model in your Learning Station.

Materials Needed

For Station 3 your group will need:

- Moon map
- deep metal or plastic container (such as a rectangular cake pan or storage bin)
- flour
- index card
- metric ruler
- meter stick
- small objects of various sizes and shapes (golf ball, wooden block, rock, etc.)
- Learning Station materials (poster board, colored pencils, blank paper, tape, stapler)

Moon Station 3: Moon Craters (optional)

1. Study the Moon map carefully. Note its features, particularly the craters (depressions).

a) What are the characteristics of the craters (shape, depth, special features)?

b) How do you think they formed?

c) What shape and type of object most likely formed the craters?

2. Make a model of how craters formed. Fill the pan to a depth of 2.5 cm (1") with flour. This will represent the Moon's surface before it was cratered. Now, think about how you can use the collection of objects (ball, block, etc.) to make similar craters in the flour.

a) When you have a plan, write it down and submit it to your teacher for approval.

3. Test your plan.

a) Be sure to record what happens and what the craters look like. You might also want to measure both the objects and the craters they form.

b) How do the craters you made in the flour compare to the Moon's craters on the Moon map? How are they different?

c) What object was the most likely shape to have made the craters? What evidence do you have for that?

4. When you have finished working with your crater model, figure out how you can design and build a Learning Station to help others understand how the Moon's craters were formed.

Building and Visiting the Learning Stations

1. After your teacher has approved your plans, prepare your Learning Station. Make sure it includes the following:

   - name of your station (Example: Moon Phases.)

   - objective(s) for the station (Example: This station is designed to help visitors understand how the phases of the Moon change.)

   - materials for other groups to do part of the investigation at the station (Example: maps, models, diagrams.)

   - procedure for the investigation (guidelines for how to do the investigation).

   - two questions for groups to answer or two tasks to perform to check their understanding (Example: Draw and label three phases of the Moon.)

   - scientific explanation of the important concepts for the station. (Example: A new moon occurs when . . .)

   You might find it useful to have explanation handouts to give to visitors to your center.

2. When all the Learning Stations are set up, your teacher will work with you to organize group visits to all stations. You will need to take your journals with you to record your answers to the questions at each station. Your journal will also help organize any handouts other groups may have prepared for you to take away. When you finish each station, be sure to set it back up the way you found it so that other groups have the same experience you did.

   a) Answer the questions for each station in your journal.

3. When everyone finishes all the Learning Stations, have a whole-class discussion about what you learned from each station. Check your understanding of the key ideas from each station with other groups and with your teacher. Write down other questions about the Moon that you can investigate on your own later on.

Inquiry
Sharing Findings

An important part of science inquiry is sharing the results with others. Scientists do this whenever they think that they have discovered interesting and important information. This is called disseminating research findings. In this investigation you are sharing your findings with other groups.

Digging Deeper

As You Read...
Think about:

1. Why does the Moon look different from Earth during the lunar cycle?
2. When does the new Moon occur?
3. When does the full Moon occur?

THE LUNAR CYCLE

As you discovered in this investigation, the Moon's appearance changes during its orbit around the Earth. This series of phases is called the *lunar cycle*. You can only see the Moon when sunlight is reflected from its surface. The same side of the Moon always faces the Earth. As the Moon orbits the Earth, the angle between the Sun, the Earth, and the Moon changes. As this angle increases, you can see more of the Moon. Scientists can predict lunar cycles because the directions and speeds of the orbits of the Earth and Moon are very well understood.

Lunar phases depend on how the Earth, Moon, and Sun are positioned relative to one another. When the Moon is located between the Earth and the Sun, the side of the Moon that is illuminated is the side facing away from the Earth so you do not see the Moon.

Moon, Earth, Sun as viewed from above our Solar System

3

4

2

5

Earth

1

Sun

6

8

7

diagram not to scale

The relative positions of the Earth, Moon, and Sun determine the lunar phases.

This phase is called the *new* Moon. During the first half of the lunar cycle, you see a little more of the illuminated Moon each time it rises. When the Earth, the Moon, and the Sun are in the same plane and nearly in a line, you see either a new Moon or a *full* Moon.

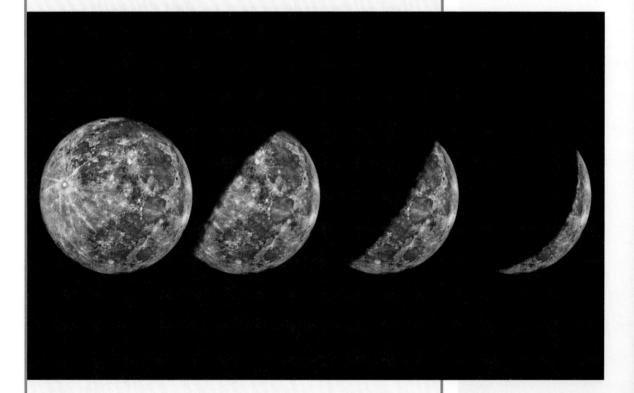

The cycle of lunar phases takes about 29.5 days to complete. After a new Moon, you gradually see more and more of the Moon until, about two weeks after the new Moon, a full moon appears in the sky. At this point, the entire visible side of the Moon is illuminated by the Sun. Over the two weeks that follow, you see less and less of the Moon until it is a new Moon again.

Review and Reflect

Review

1. Describe the main features of the Moon.

2. How can scientists predict lunar cycles?

Reflect

3. Explain why the lunar cycle is called a cycle.

Thinking about the Earth System

4. How can the craters on the Moon help scientists better understand the geosphere?

Thinking about Scientific Inquiry

5. How did you use modeling in this investigation?

6. Why do you think sharing findings is an important process in scientific inquiry?

Investigation 3:

The Relationship between the Earth and Its Moon

Key Question

Before you begin, first think about this key question.

What is the relationship between the Earth and its Moon?

Share what you know about the relationship between the Earth and the Moon with others in your group. Keep a record of your ideas in your journal.

Share your group's ideas with the rest of the class.

Investigate

GravLab

The purpose of this **Investigation** is to help you understand how the force of gravity works on the Earth. It will also get you to begin thinking about the role of gravity in the Solar System and beyond. As you go through each part of the **Investigation**, think about how you are building your understanding of gravity.

1. Think about the following question: What is gravity? Talk about this with other members of your group. Here are some questions to think about during your discussion:

   • How high can you jump off the ground? What happens to you when you get to the top of your jump?

- What happens when you throw a ball into the air? How can you explain this?

- Think about any rockets you have seen on television taking astronauts into space. Why do they need so much power to get off the launch pad?

- Think about pictures of astronauts in space capsules. What is unusual about the way they move around? Why do you think this is so?

a) When you finish the discussion, write down a whole-group explanation of what you think gravity is. Do your best to agree as much as possible, but it is alright if people have different ideas at this point.

2. When you feel comfortable with your explanation, share it with the rest of the class to see what ideas other groups can add to yours. Your teacher will record the class's definition of gravity on the board or on chart paper.

a) Record the class's definition in your journal.

You will now work with your group to investigate gravity in a number of ways. When you finish, you will revisit your class definition of gravity to see how it might need to change.

Mini-Investigation A: Gravity on the Moon

1. Look over the information in the table on the next page for this **Mini-Investigation**. It shows how much common objects weigh on Earth and how much they would weigh on the Moon.

a) Write a sentence that explains the relationship between the weight of an object on Earth and the weight of the same object on the Moon. You do not have to use an exact number; just write a description of how the weights compare.

2. When you have thought about the relationship, check with another group to see what they have discovered. Talk this over as a class with the help of your teacher. Write your answers to the following questions:

Table: Weight of Objects on Earth and on the Moon		
Object	Weight on Earth (kg)	Weight on the Moon (kg)
Adult male African elephant	6800	1134
Pair of adult man's tennis shoes, size 9	1.2	0.2
Gallon of paint	6.6	1.1
3-L tin of cooking oil	3.0	0.5

a) Why do you think there is this relationship? Think about the size of the Earth compared to the size of the Moon. Does that help?

b) As a group, write one sentence explaining what you think the relationship is between gravity on the Moon and gravity on the Earth.

Mini-Investigation B: You're on the Moon! Now, Jump!

In this part of the investigation, you will be figuring out how far you could jump if you were on the Moon. Think about **Mini-Investigation A** and the relationship you discovered between the gravity on the Earth and on the Moon. Now, imagine how that might affect how far you could jump on the Moon.

1. To get a better idea of this, first see how far you can jump from a standing position on the Earth.

Materials Needed

For this part of the investigation your group will need:

• masking tape

• measuring tape (metric)

• calculator

a) Make a data table for your group. The table should hold the following information for each student in the group: distance jumped on Earth, estimated distance on the Moon, estimated distance on Jupiter.

2. Take turns being *Jumper*, *Measurer*, and *Recorder*. Follow these steps:

   • In a hallway or the gym, use masking tape to mark a starting line.

   • *Jumper 1* stands with toes on the starting line and jumps as far as possible.

   • *Measurer 1* holds the end of the measuring tape on the starting line.

   • *Measurer 2* pulls the tape to where the Jumper lands and puts a second piece of masking tape on the floor.

   • *Measurer 2* records the Jumper's initials and length of jump in centimeters on the masking tape at the end of the jump.

   • The *Recorder* records the initials and distance in the data table for the group. The *Recorder* should also be on hand to steady the *Jumper* so that he or she doesn't fall at the end of the jump.

   • After *Jumper 1* jumps, everyone rotates roles so that all group members get a chance to jump.

3. Remember the relationship between the weight of objects on Earth and the same objects on the Moon. To find the weight of an object on the Moon, you can multiply the weight of that object on the Earth by 0.1667.

   For example:

   The weight of an elephant on Earth is 6800 kg.

   The weight of the elephant on the Moon is 6800 kg × 0.1667 = 1133.56 kg or about 1134 kg.

   Use this procedure to determine how far each person could jump on the Moon.

   a) Place this information in the data table.

4. Measure these distances for each *Jumper* on the floor. Mark each distance with a new piece of masking tape with initials and the new distance in centimeters. Label each of these tape pieces with MJ (Moon Jump).

Inquiry

Using Mathematics

Mathematics is often used in science. In this investigation you began by comparing the weight of an object on Earth to the weight of the object on the Moon. Then you used the mathematical relationship to calculate how far you can jump on the Moon.

5. Take it one step further and think about this. The planet Jupiter has a gravitational pull that is about $2\frac{1}{2}$ (2.5) times greater than that of the Earth. How far could each of you jump on Jupiter?

   a) Do the calculations and place this information in the data table.

6. Measure these distances on the floor and make tape markers for this as well. Label each JJ (Jupiter Jump).

Mini-Investigation C: Our Moon and the Earth's Tides

In this last part of the GravLab, you will pull together what you know about the Moon and gravity to explore a major effect that the Moon has on the Earth.

1. Look at the tide tables on the following pages. This table shows the level of the ocean tides during August 2004. It also shows the phases of the Moon for that same month.

2. Review what you learned in the previous investigation about the phases of the Moon and what you now know about gravity. Now, look carefully at the data in the table. Talk about the following questions. First, talk with your group and then with the rest of the class. Then answer the questions in your journal.

   a) What do you think is the relationship (if any) between the tides and the phases of the Moon?

   b) How might you explain this relationship knowing what you know about the Earth, the Moon, and the pull of gravity?

Sharing and Discussing Your Findings

1. When you finish all of the GravLab, summarize what your group has learned about gravity in several clear and complete sentences.

   a) Record these sentences in your journal.

2. When you have written them in your journal, compare them to the whole-class definition of gravity.

   a) Do you need to change anything about the class definition, or add to it? Work as a class, with the help of your teacher, to come up with as complete and accurate a definition as possible. Record this in your jounal.

Inquiry

Using Data Tables as Scientific Tools

Scientists collect and review data using tools. You may think of tools as only physical objects like telescopes and measuring tapes. However, forms in which information is gathered, stored, and presented are also tools for scientists. In this investigation you are using a tide table as a scientific tool.

Ocean City (fishing pier), Maryland 38.3267° N, 75.0833° W

August 2004

Day	High	Low	High	Low	High	Moon	Sunrise	Sunset
Sun 01		02:41 / -0.25 ft	08:29 / 3.50 ft	14:36 / -0.58 ft	21:03 / 4.75 ft		06:02	20:09
Mon 02		03:29 / -0.29 ft	09:22 / 3.61 ft	15:29 / -0.50 ft	21:52 / 4.53 ft		06:03	20:08
Tue 03		04:15 / -0.24 ft	10:13 / 3.68 ft	16:21 / -0.31 ft	22:39 / 4.24 ft		06:04	20:07
Wed 04		05:01 / -0.13 ft	11:02 / 3.69 ft	17:15 / -0.06 ft	23:25 / 3.87 ft		06:05	20:06
Thu 05		05:46 / 0.03 ft	11:51 / 3.65 ft	18:10 / 0.23 ft			06:06	20:05
Fri 06	00:10 / 3.48 ft	06:32 / 0.21 ft	12:42 / 3.58 ft	19:07 / 0.50 ft			06:07	20:04
Sat 07	00:58 / 3.12 ft	07:18 / 0.40 ft	13:35 / 3.50 ft	20:06 / 0.72 ft		Last Quarter	06:08	20:03
Sun 08	01:49 / 2.81 ft	08:05 / 0.57 ft	14:31 / 3.45 ft	21:06 / 0.88 ft			06:09	20:02
Mon 09	02:46 / 2.61 ft	08:54 / 0.68 ft	15:31 / 3.47 ft	22:07 / 0.96 ft			06:09	20:00
Tue 10	03:45 / 2.54 ft	09:46 / 0.73 ft	16:28 / 3.54 ft	23:08 / 0.96 ft			06:10	19:59
Wed 11	04:41 / 2.58 ft	10:39 / 0.70 ft	17:20 / 3.67 ft				06:11	19:58
Thu 12		00:00 / 0.90 ft	05:32 / 2.69 ft	11:31 / 0.61 ft	18:07 / 3.83 ft		06:12	19:57
Fri 13		00:43 / 0.79 ft	06:18 / 2.85 ft	12:20 / 0.48 ft	18:50 / 3.98 ft		06:13	19:56
Sat 14		01:21 / 0.67 ft	07:01 / 3.03 ft	13:04 / 0.34 ft	19:32 / 4.12 ft		06:14	19:54

Ocean City (fishing pier), Maryland 38.3267° N, 75.0833° W

August 2004

Sun 15		01:58 / 0.45 ft	07:44 / 3.21 ft	13:47 / 0.24 ft	29:12 / 4.21 ft	New Moon	06:15	19:53
Mon 16		02:33 / 0.42 ft	08:25 / 3.38 ft	14:28 / 0.17 ft	20:51 / 4.25 ft		06:16	19:52
Tue 17		03:08 / 0.33 ft	09:07 / 3.54 ft	15:09 / 0.16 ft	21:29 / 4.21 ft		06:16	19:50
Wed 18		03:45 / 0.28 ft	09:47 / 3.69 ft	15:52 / 0.20 ft	22:08 / 4.11 ft		06:17	19:49
Thu 19		04:22 / 0.26 ft	10:29 / 3.83 ft	16:38 / 0.29 ft	22:47 / 3.93 ft		06:18	19:48
Fri 20		05:02 / 0.28 ft	11:12 / 3.94 ft	17:28 / 0.40 ft	23:30 / 3.69 ft		06:19	19:46
Sat 21		05:45 / 0.31 ft	11:59 / 4.01 ft	18:35 / 0.52 ft			06:20	19:45
Sun 22	00:16 / 3.43 ft	06:32 / 0.36 ft	12:52 / 4.05 ft	19:23 / 0.63 ft			06:21	19:44
Mon 23	01:09 / 3.17 ft	07:25 / 0.38 ft	13:52 / 4.08 ft	20:28 / 0.69 ft		First Quarter	06:22	19:42
Tue 24	02:11 / 2.98 ft	08:24 / 0.37 ft	14:59 / 4.15 ft	21:35 / 0.67 ft			06:23	19:41
Wed 25	03:19 / 2.90 ft	09:27 / 0.30 ft	16:07 / 4.27 ft	22:43 / 0.57 ft			06:24	19:39
Thu 26	04:27 / 2.97 ft	10:33 / 0.16 ft	17:11 / 4.42 ft	23:47 / 0.39 ft			06:24	19:38
Fri 27	05:30 / 3.157 ft	11:37 / -0.04 ft	18:10 / 4.56 ft				06:25	19:36
Sat 28		00:43 / 0.18 ft	06:27 / 3.38 ft	12:37 / -0.23 ft	19:04 / 4.63 ft		06:26	19:35
Sun 29		01:33 / -0.00 ft	07:21 / 3.61 ft	13:32 / -0.37 ft	19:54 / 4.62 ft	Full Moon	06:27	19:33
Mon 30		02:18 / -0.13 ft	08:12 / 3.82 ft	14:23 / -0.41 ft	20:41 / 4.50 ft		06:28	19:32
Tue 31		03:01 / -0.17 ft	09:00 / 3.97 ft	15:12 / -0.33 ft	21:26 / 4.29 ft		06:29	19:30

Digging Deeper

As You Read...

Think about:

1. What does gravitational attraction depend on?

2. Why doesn't the Sun's gravity pull all the objects in our Solar System into the Sun?

3. How does the Moon affect the Earth's tides?

GRAVITY HOLDS THE SOLAR SYSTEM TOGETHER

It is impossible to talk about the relationships among the Earth, Moon, and Sun without first learning about gravity. Gravity is the attraction of all objects to all other objects. Gravitational attraction depends on the mass (amount of matter) of the objects and the distance between them. The greater the mass of the objects, the greater is the force. The greater the distance between the objects, the smaller is the force. You can't see gravity. As a force, it is invisible.

The Sun is very far away from the Earth (approximately 150 million kilometers), but it has tremendous mass. Because of its incredible mass, the Sun has the strongest gravity in the Solar System. As the planets orbit the Sun, gravity pulls them towards the center of the Sun. Although this pull exists, the planets do not move towards the Sun's center. This is because of their forward motion. The forward movement of each planet is balanced against the Sun's gravitational pull. As a result, the planets move constantly through their orbit just fast enough to stop them from being pulled toward the Sun.

The Sun's mass is so great that its gravity keeps the Earth (and all the other objects in the Solar System) orbiting around it. The Moon is much smaller in mass than the Earth.

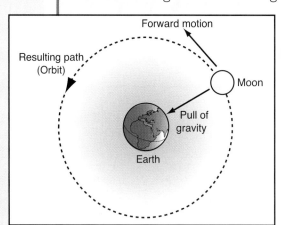

Like the planets around the Sun, the Moon's orbit around the Earth is controlled by its forward movement and the gravitational pull of the Earth.

However, it is relatively close to Earth and revolves around Earth. Just as the Earth's gravity keeps the Moon traveling around it, the Moon's gravity causes certain events on the Earth.

THE RISE AND FALL OF THE TIDES

The gravitational pull of the Moon is strong enough to cause the Earth's oceans to move slightly towards it. The ocean's rise in height forms a *tidal bulge* as water moves towards the Moon.

If part of the Earth's surface within the bulge has a coastline, then it will experience a *high tide*. A high tide also occurs on the opposite side of the Earth at the same time. During the Earth's 24-hour rotation, part of a coast can move into a tidal bulge. It will have a high tide inside the bulge. Then a *low tide* occurs after a coast has moved away from the bulge. Each coastal location has two high tides and two low tides daily. Together these make one *tidal cycle*.

The Sun's gravitational pull also affects the Earth's oceans. The Sun pulls the Earth's oceans in the same way as the Moon. When the Sun, the Moon, and the Earth are in alignment (during a new Moon or a full Moon), the highest high tides and the lowest low tides occur. During the half-Moon phases, the Sun and Moon pull the oceans in different directions. At this time, high tides aren't as high and low tides aren't as low.

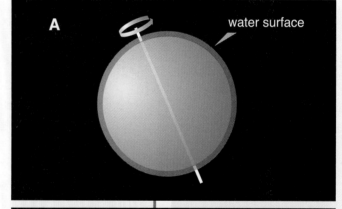

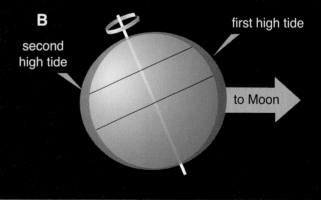

The gravitational pull of the Moon causes the Earth's oceans to form a tidal bulge.

The left image shows high tide and the right image shows low tide.

A SYSTEM IN MOTION

Despite the gigantic size of the Solar System, some of the most important processes that affect the Earth can be predicted. This is because different parts of the Solar System, such as moons or planets, move with regular cycles. Just as the Earth is a system with many parts, it is also part of a larger system involving the Sun and the Moon. Each planet and moon is also part of a larger system, called the Solar System. The key to the Solar System is the gravitational force that ties it all together.

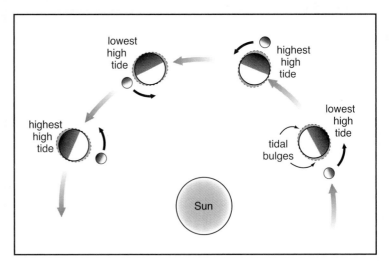

The Earth's tides are affected by the gravitational pull of both the Moon and the Sun.

Review and Reflect

Review

1. How does gravity affect our Solar System?
2. What factors affect gravity?
3. What effect does the Moon have on the Earth?
4. What effect does the Earth have on the Moon?

Reflect

5. How might motion on the Earth be different if the Earth was half its mass? Why do you think that?
6. How might motion on the Earth be different if the Earth was twice its mass? What reason do you have for that?

Thinking about the Earth System

7. How does the Moon's and Sun's gravity affect the hydrosphere?
8. How does this effect on the hydrosphere affect the other major systems. Remember to write connections, as you find them, on the *Earth System Connection* sheet.

Thinking about Scientific Inquiry

9. In which parts of the investigation did you:
   a) Make a prediction?
   b) Use tools to measure?
   c) Record your own ideas?
   d) Revise your ideas?
   e) Compare data to look for patterns and relationships?
   f) Share ideas with others?
   g) Find information from different sources?
   h) Pull your information together to make a presentation?

Investigation 4:

Finding Our Place in Space

Key Question

Before you begin, first think about this key question.

Where is the Earth in space and how do scientists know?

Materials Needed

For this investigation your group will need:

- drawing materials (colored pencils or markers and paper)
- diagram of Solar System
- long narrow roll of paper
- masking tape
- metric measuring tape
- access to a school hallway
- calculator

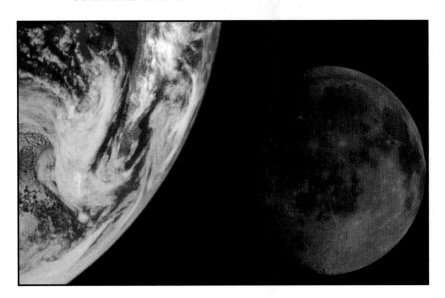

Think about what you know about the Earth in space. Share your thinking with others in your group and in your class. Keep a record of the discussion in your journal.

Share your group's ideas with the rest of the class.

Investigate

In the first **Investigation**, you learned some of the characteristics of Earth. In this **Investigation**, you will learn about where the Earth is in space and how people came to discover this over time. You might be surprised to see how ideas about the Earth's position in our Solar System have changed.

1. Without looking ahead, draw the Sun and the planets and the distances from the Sun to the planets as nearly to scale as you can. Compare your drawing to the diagram of the Solar System in this book.

   a) Make a list of all the differences you observe between your drawing and the diagram.

2. In this **Investigation** you will be making a scale model of the Solar System. To do this you need to be able to answer the following questions. You may use the information in the **Digging Deeper** section and the table on the next page to help you answer these questions.

   a) What is at the center of our Solar System?

   b) What are the names of all the planets in our Solar System?

   c) Where is the Earth in the Solar System?

   d) How far is the Earth's Moon from the Earth?

   e) How far is the Earth from the Sun and the other planets in the Solar System?

3. The objects in the Solar System are great distances away from one another. How can they be a "system"? A system is made up of parts that depend upon each other. Think of the cars, roads and bridges of a transportation system or the wires, signals, and receivers of a communication system.

   a) Can objects so far away from each other in space really be dependent on one another? In what ways?

4. You will now design and construct a model of the Solar System. The table shown on the next page will help you with the relative sizes of the Sun and planets and their average distances from the Sun. Your goal is to be able to make a model of the Solar System that you can place in the hallways in your school. This will give you enough space to be able to model the relative distances between the planets. You still may have some trouble modeling the different sizes of the planets and the Sun. Do the best you can to get the distances as much to scale as possible, even if you can't do the sizes of the planets.

5. Use this scale to make your model:
   1 cm (centimeter) = 1,000,000 km (kilometers).

Inquiry

Using Mathematics

Scientists often use mathematics in their investigations. In this investigation you used a scale to construct your model of the Solar System.

Table 1: Diameters of the Sun and Planets and Distances from the Sun						
Planet	Diameter (km)	Kilometers from Sun (multiplied by 1,000,000)	Astronomical Unit	Average Temperature (Degrees Celsius)	Number of Moons	Orbital Period (Earth Days)
Mercury	4879	57.9	0.39	167	0	88.0
Venus	12,104	108.2	0.72	464	0	224.7
Earth	12,756	149.6	1.0	15	1	365.2
Mars	6794	227.9	1.52	-65	2	687.0
Jupiter	142,984	778.6	5.20	-110	61	4331
Saturn	120,536	1433.5	9.54	-140	31	10,747
Uranus	51,118	2872.5	19.19	-195	26	30,589
Neptune	49,528	4495.1	30.07	-200	13	59,800

Inquiry

Modeling

To investigate the great distances between objects in the Solar System, you will be making a model. Models are very useful scientific tools. Scientists use models to simulate real-world events. Since you cannot travel from one planet to the next to discover how far apart they are, you will make a model that will let you make the journey in the hallway of your school.

Work in specialist groups in the class to draw the Sun and the planets. For example, one group might draw the Earth, another group Jupiter, etc.

6. When all the planets and Sun are complete, tape them in the hallway, adding labels with the planets' names. If you have a long roll of paper (such as adding-machine paper), you could put this on the wall from planet to planet, writing the distances between the planets on it with markers.

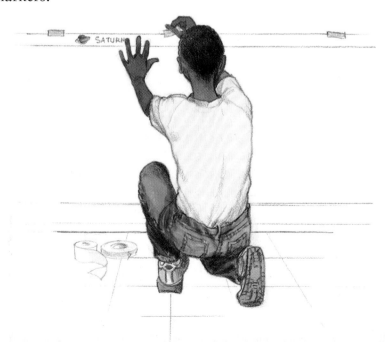

 Digging Deeper

THE SKY AT NIGHT

When you look up into the sky at night, what do you see? On a clear night, you might see some of the billions of stars that make up the *Milky Way Galaxy*. Light from these stars travels many hundreds of trillions of kilometers before it reaches your eyes.

The Moon is the closest object that you might see in the night sky. The Moon is approximately 384,403 km from Earth. Compared to other objects in the Solar System, this is not very far away. At certain times, the Moon appears quite large and bright. If you look carefully, you may notice some of the Moon's surface features, such as craters and maria. Maria are the dark flat areas covered by the black rock *basalt*.

You might also see some planetary neighbors. The nearest planet to the Earth that you might see is Venus. This planet can be as close as 38 million kilometers away when it passes Earth in its orbit, or as far away as 261 million kilometers! Mars is the next closest planet to the Earth with a distance that varies from 56 million kilometers to about 401 million kilometers.

In between the stars, the Moon, and the planets you would see blackness. This is space that fills the

When you look up into the sky at night, you can see planets and some of the billions of stars that make up the Milky Way Galaxy.

As You Read...
Think about:

1. What are some of the objects you can expect to see in the sky on a clear night?

2. How do astronomers measure distance between objects in the Solar System?

3. How do astronomers measure distance between objects outside the Solar System?

4. What are the names of the planets in the Solar System and where are they in relation to the Sun?

The Moon is a familiar object in the night sky. The dark areas are maria.

huge gaps between objects. It contains very little matter, except for a small amount of dust that is usually too small and far away to be seen.

EARTH'S NEAREST STELLAR NEIGHBORS

How far does light from the stars in the sky travel to reach the Earth? The Sun is the closest star to the Earth and is about 150 million kilometers away. The second nearest stellar neighbor is Proxima Centauri. Its light travels 40,000,000,000,000 km to reach the Earth!

The distances between objects in space are so huge that Earth-based units are not very useful measurements. Instead, scientists use distance units of measure that are more appropriate. For distances within the Solar System, astronomers use the astronomical unit (AU). One AU is the average distance between the Earth and the Sun or about 150 million kilometers. For distances between stars, astronomers use light-years. Light travels about 300,000 km per second. In one year it can travel 9,460,000,000,000 km. Light traveling from Proxima Centauri to the Earth takes 4.22 years. Using this measurement, you can say that Proxima Centauri is 4.22 light-years (LY) from Earth.

MODELING THE SOLAR SYSTEM

Scientists often use models when they examine the moons, planets, stars and other objects in space. A model can be a small object that represents a larger object. Since the sizes of stars and planets are so great, scientists build small models of space systems.

A composite picture of the planets in the Solar System.

These models give scientists a clearer idea of what objects are in space and how those objects interact. To

build a model, scientists must create objects and distances that are proportional to what is actually found in space. Because of the huge distances in space and the relatively small diameters of planets, making a scale model of the Solar System can take up a lot of space!

THE EARTH'S POSITION IN SPACE

The position of the Earth in space depends on its location in its orbit around the Sun. An orbit is the path and motion of one object around another object. If you look down on the Solar System from the North, with respect to Earth, each planet in the Solar System revolves around the Sun in a counter-clockwise direction. This is due to the gravitational force between the Sun and the planets. The relative position of the planets to one another depends on their positions in their orbits.

Another way to think of orbits is as a large racetrack with parallel lanes. The Sun lies near the center of the flat surface of the track. Planets race along in their lanes at different speeds and over different distances. The planets closer to the Sun on the inside lanes travel faster and over a shorter distance than the planets in lanes farther away from the Sun.

Can you imagine living on a planet that takes 165 years to orbit the Sun? This would be the case if you lived on Neptune. If you lived on Mercury, however, the closest planet to the Sun, your orbit would only take 88 days! On Earth, it takes us an average of 365.2 days to orbit the Sun.

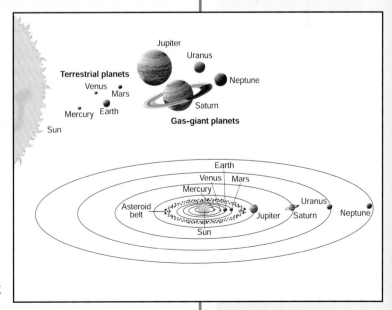

The orbits of the planets around the Sun.

Review and Reflect

Review

1. What was the most difficult part in making the model of the Solar System ? Why was this so?

2. If you traveled at the rate of 300 km/h (kilometers per hour), how long would it take you to get to Mars? To Jupiter?

Reflect

3. In what ways is the Solar System a true "system"?

4. What relationship do all of the planets have to the Sun? To each other?

Thinking about the Earth System

5. How does understanding the Earth System help you understand the Solar System?

Thinking about Scientific Inquiry

6. In which parts of the investigation did you:

a) Make a model?

b) Use mathematics to solve a problem?

c) Revise your ideas?

d) Use your imagination?

e) Share ideas with others?

f) Find information from different sources?

Investigation 5:

The Sun and Its Central Role in Our Solar System

Key Question

Before you begin, first think about this key question.

What are the characteristics of the Sun and why is it so important to the Solar System?

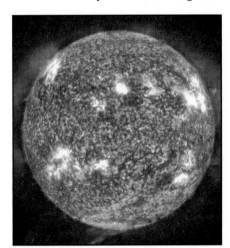

Think about what you know about the Sun. What is the Sun made of? Why is the Sun important to you?

Share your thinking with others in your group and with your class.

In this **Investigation**, you will become more familiar with three important facts about the Sun.

Investigate

Part A: What do you already know about the Sun?

1. You experience the Sun's energy every day. Take a minute and list in your journal all the ways you can think of that the Sun affects your life. (You might want to illustrate your list with pictures.) These sentence stems can help you in your thinking:

   a) The Sun is important because _____.

   b) If we didn't have the Sun, _____.

Inquiry

Charts and Tables

Charts and tables organize a lot of information in a small amount of space. They can be useful because they allow you to focus on important points. In this investigation you will be using a table to organize what you know about the Sun and compare it to what scientists know.

2. Exchange your ideas about the Sun with other members of your group. Think about these questions:

   • What do we get from the Sun?

   • What place does the Sun have in our Solar System?

   • Where is the Sun in our galaxy?

   • What would we lose if we didn't have the Sun?

   • What reasons can you think of for some ancient peoples worshipping the Sun? Why was it so important to them? (Use your imagination with this question – why would the Sun be so important to early humans who knew very little about science?)

3. Make a three-column table in your journal to organize your thinking about the Sun.

   a) Write your answers to the questions in the table.

Revisit this table when you finish the Solar Lab and have read the **Digging Deeper** section. The Solar Lab will help you to understand more about the Sun, how it works, and why it is important in the Solar System. The Solar Lab is set up in stations, so that you and members of your group can work together to explore the Sun's energy and how it produces that energy.

Thinking about the Sun		
Sun Questions	**My Answers**	**Scientists' Answers**
What do we get from the Sun?		
What place does the Sun have in our Solar System?		
Where is the Sun in our galaxy?		
What would we lose if we didn't have the Sun?		
What reasons can you think of for some ancient peoples worshipping the Sun? Why was it so important to them?		
Other questions about the Sun.		

Part B: Solar Lab

Solar Lab Station 1: The Electromagnetic Spectrum

You have probably already learned a little about light in other science courses. Visible light is part of the electromagnetic (EM) spectrum – the energy we receive from our star, the Sun.

You can see from the diagram that the longer wavelengths are on the left side of the spectrum and that the wavelengths get shorter as you travel to the right side. You feel infrared radiation as heat. You may also be familiar with black light, which is actually ultraviolet radiation.

1. Shine the flashlight through the prism onto a dark surface and see for yourself what colors are in the visible light spectrum.

   a) Use colored pencils to draw in your journal what you see.

2. Use your drawing and the explanation above to answer the following questions:

   a) Which color of light seems to be bent the *most* by the prism?

   b) Which color of light seems to be bent the *least*?

Materials Needed

For Station 1, your group will need:

- triangular prism
- flashlight with a strong narrow beam
- colored pencils

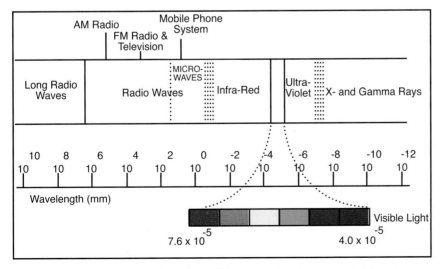

The electromagnetic spectrum shows how different wavelengths represent different types of energy.

c) Of the colors in the visible light spectrum you can see, which has the longest wavelength?

3. Look again at the diagram of the EM spectrum.

   a) In your journal, make a list of ways that you think life on Earth would change if we didn't have this energy from the Sun.

Materials Needed

For Station 2, your group will need:

- plant that has been kept in a closet for a week
- plant that has been kept in the sunlight

Solar Lab Station 2: Plants and the Sun's Energy

At this station, you will see two plants that have the same type of soil and were watered the same amount every day.

1. Observe the two plants. One plant has been exposed to sunlight on a day to day basis, and the other plant has been kept in a closet for a week.

   a) What differences do you observe between the two plants? How might you explain this?

   b) What do you think would happen to the plant kept in the closet if it were never put in the Sun again? Why do you think that is so?

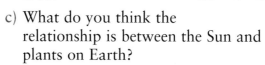

   c) What do you think the relationship is between the Sun and plants on Earth?

   d) How much do animals on the Earth depend on plants? What might happen to animal life on the planet without the Sun's energy?

2. As a group, design an experiment that you could do that would further test these ideas. Can you think of a way to test the impact of the sunlight on only the plant leaves?

   a) Write down your steps, the materials you would need, and your procedure for your teacher to review.

   b) Even if you do not conduct the experiment, what do you think you would be able to learn from this experience?

Solar Lab Station 3: Heat from the Sun

1. At this station, you will have the opportunity to investigate the Sun's infrared (heat) energy.

   a) Draw a table in your journal like the one below.

Temperature Readings (degrees Celsius)			
	0 minutes	5 minutes	10 minutes
Thermometer under paper			
Thermometer in direct sunlight			

2. There are two thermometers under a sheet of paper at this station.

   a) Lift the paper and record the temperatures of both thermometers.

   b) Place one thermometer back under the paper and put the second thermometer into direct sunlight. Wait five minutes, and then record the temperatures again.

Materials Needed

For Station 3, your group will need:

- two thermometers
- sheet of paper

Inquiry

Quantitative and Qualitative Observations

Observations dealing with numbers are called quantitative observations. An example of a quantitative observation is temperature recorded in degrees Celsius. Qualitative observations refer to the qualities of the object. Color is often recorded qualitatively as yellow or green, for example. Some observations can be made either qualitatively or quantitatively, depending on what tools are available and the level of accuracy needed. In this investigation you are making both qualitative and quantitative observations.

c) Wait an additional five minutes, and then record the final temperatures.

3. Write the answers to the following questions in your journal:

   a) What can you conclude about the effect of the direct sunlight on the thermometer?

   b) Did the energy of the Sun have any effect at all on the thermometer under the paper? Why do you think that?

Materials Needed

For this part of the investigation your group will need:

• poster board and colored pencils

Part C: Sharing and Discussing Your Findings

1. When you finish all the stations in the Solar Lab, return to your table of questions about the Sun, from the beginning of this investigation.

   a) Change any answers that were incorrect or incomplete.

   b) Work with your group to come up with as complete a picture of the role of the Sun in the Solar System as possible.

2. As a group, create an informative, yet interesting and colorful, poster about the Sun. The poster should focus on how the Sun and the energy from the Sun has an impact on life on Earth as well as general facts about the Sun.

3. Share your posters with the other students in your class.

Digging Deeper

OUR SUN: A FAMILIAR OBJECT

The Sun is the probably the most prominent object in the sky because of its great size and the enormous amount of energy it releases. The Sun contains 99% of all the matter within the Solar System. It has 300,000 times more mass than the Earth and more than 1,295,000 times more volume. During the day, you can watch what appears to be the Sun's journey across the sky as the Earth receives the Sun's energy. This energy is a strong driving force in the Earth system. It heats the surface of the Earth and makes life possible. At night, the Sun's rays illuminate the Moon. Without the Sun, the Earth would be a dark frozen mass drifting through space.

The Reason For the Seasons

The tilt of the Earth's axis changes over the course of about 41,000 years between an angle of 22° and an angle of 25° as the Earth revolves around the Sun. For part of

As You Read...
Think about:

1. *How is the tilt of the Earth's axis related to the seasons?*
2. *What is the result of the spreading effect of the solar energy over the surface of the Earth?*
3. *Why is noon usually the hottest part of the day?*
4. *Why is the Sun important to our Solar System?*
5. *Where is our Sun in the universe?*
6. *What are some of the Sun's special features?*

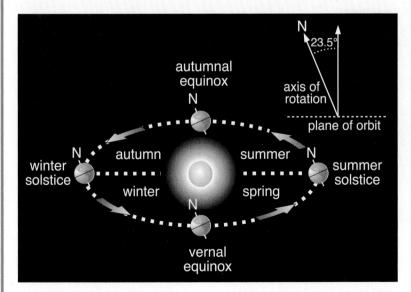

The tilt of the Earth on its axis and its rotation around the Sun cause the seasons.

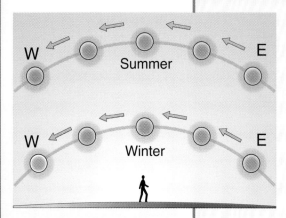

In the summer, the Sun is higher in the sky than in the winter.

the year (summer), the Northern Hemisphere tips towards the Sun. During that same time, the Southern Hemisphere is having winter, since it is tipped away from the Sun.

When either of the Northern or Southern Hemispheres is tipped towards the Sun, two things happen. First, the Sun is visible for more hours of the day, providing more heat energy. Second, the Sun is higher in the sky at noon and shines more directly on the Earth's surface than any other time.

Six months later, the Earth is halfway through its orbit and the same hemisphere is tilted away from the Sun. During this time, the Sun is lower in the sky and the days are shorter. Also, the Sun's energy is spread over the Earth's surface. These effects result in the cooler temperatures of winter. Each year, the cycle of the seasons repeats itself because of the regular and predictable orbit of the Earth around the Sun.

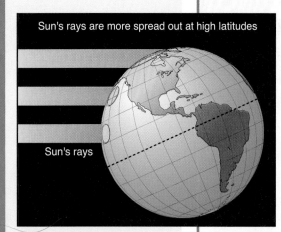

The Earth's tilt and curved surface cause the Sun's rays to be more spread out at high latitudes.

The Earth's curved surface affects how much of the Sun's (solar) energy the Earth receives. A greater angle between the Sun's rays and the Earth's surface causes energy to be spread over a larger area. When is the hottest part of day? It is usually around noon when the Sun is high in the sky and its energy is concentrated on the surface of the Earth.

The spreading effect of solar energy on the Earth's surface creates different temperatures at different points on the Earth. The direct concentration of solar energy on the Earth's Equator causes it to be much warmer than the poles. The spreading effect also causes the Northern and Southern Hemispheres to experience opposite seasons throughout the year.

What is the Sun?

The Sun, the center of our Solar System, is an enormous ball of glowing gas. Most of the Sun is made of hydrogen, one of the simplest atoms in nature. It has a nucleus with one proton at its center and one electron orbiting around it. In the core of the Sun, these protons combine to create new nuclei of helium. This reaction is known as hydrogen fusion. It produces huge amounts of energy that cause the Sun to glow.

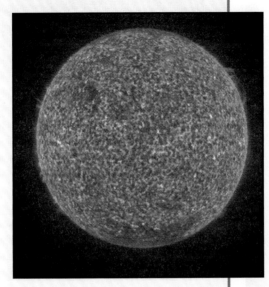

The reactions within the Sun produce a huge amount of energy that cause the Sun to glow.

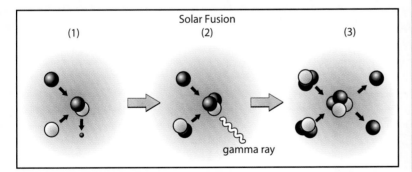

Solar Fusion

(1)   (2)   (3)

gamma ray

(1) Nuclei of two hydrogen atoms collide in a high-temperature environment. Particles and energy are released. A two-part atom is formed.
(2) Hydrogen nuclei collide with the two-part atom. A three-part helium atom is formed. More energy is released as well as gamma rays.
(3) Two three-part helium atoms collide to form a four-part helium atom. More energy is released as well as a pair of hydrogen atoms.

Structure of the Sun

Like the Earth, the Sun has a layered structure. The outer part of the Sun consists of an atmosphere known as the corona. This layer extends millions of kilometers into space. Temperatures in the corona can get as high as 1,000,000°C. Its gases are so hot that the Sun's gravity

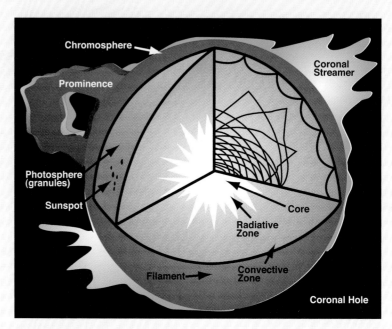

Temperatures vary in the Sun's different layers.

cannot hold them and they escape into space. Below the corona is the irregular surface of the Sun, called the photosphere. This is the visible surface of the Sun and the layer that produces light. Between these two layers is the chromosphere. The temperatures in this layer range from 6000°C to 20,000°C. This layer has a reddish appearance and extends about 2500 km above the photosphere.

Surface Features of the Sun

From the Earth, the Sun appears to have a smooth surface. This surface is actually not so smooth and contains a number of interesting features.

Sunspots are areas that have an irregular shape and are darker than other parts of the Sun. Sunspots are relatively cooler than the surrounding parts of the Sun, although they are still very hot. They develop in pairs and appear to travel across the surface of the Sun.

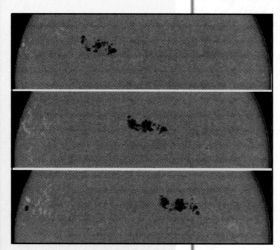

The dark irregular shapes on the surface of the Sun are sunspots.

Their movement is actually due to the Sun spinning on its axis. Because the Sun is made up of gas, it rotates more quickly at the Equator (about 25 days) than at the poles (about 33 days). Sunspots at the poles take longer to travel around the Sun than at the Equator. The number of sunspots on the Sun increases and decreases during cycles that last about 22 years.

A close-up of a sunspot

Solar flares are giant explosions of gas on the surface of the Sun. They occur near sunspots and erupt outwards with brilliant colors. During a solar flare, material is heated to millions of degrees Celsius in a matter of minutes. Then it is blasted off the surface. Many forms of energy are released during a solar flare. These include gamma rays and x-rays. Some of the most violent flares can produce enough radiation to be harmful to astronauts or damaging to satellites. Another

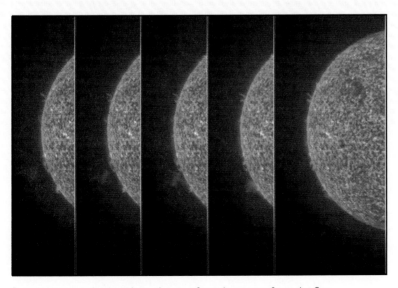

Prominences are huge arcing columns of gas that come from the Sun.

feature of the Sun's surface are huge rising columns of flaming gas called prominences. They are not quite as violent as solar flares and look like feathery red arches.

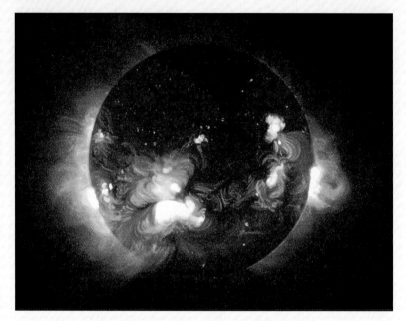

Hot gases in the corona of the Sun cause CMEs to occur.

Coronal mass ejections (CMEs) occur when gases in the corona are so hot that the Sun's gravity cannot hold them. The gases break free from the Sun and form a solar wind. In a single second, this wind can travel 400 km! CMEs take several hours to develop and create one of the largest features in the Sun's atmosphere. Each day, two or three CMEs can occur close to sunspot activity. The solar winds carry magnetic clouds with them. Some of the high-energy particles from these clouds reach the Earth. They can cause problems with communications equipment, including satellites.

Review and Reflect

Review

1. How does the tilt of the Earth produce the seasons?

2. Are the Sun's rays striking the Northern Hemisphere or the Southern Hemisphere more directly when it is summer in North America?

3. When is the hottest part of the day usually? Why?

4. What types of energy does the Sun produce?

5. What evidence do you have that plants need light?

6. What is the role of the Sun in our Solar System?

Reflect

7. How are you personally affected by the change in seasons?

8. Who would be affected more by the change in seasons, someone living close to the Equator or someone living in the far north? Explain.

9. How do humans use the different types of energy in the electromagnetic spectrum?

10. Do you think there would be life on Earth without the Sun? Why do you think that?

Thinking about the Earth System

11. The Sun is vital to the Earth System. How does the effect of the Sun on one Earth System affect the other systems?

Thinking about Scientific Inquiry

12. In which parts of the investigation did you:

    a) Read for understanding?

    b) Record your own ideas?

    c) Use tools to make measurements?

    d) Make inferences from data?

    e) Share ideas with others?

    f) Find information from different sources?

Investigation 6:

The Planetary Council

Key Question:

Before you begin, first think about this key question.

How are the planets in our Solar System the same and how are they different?

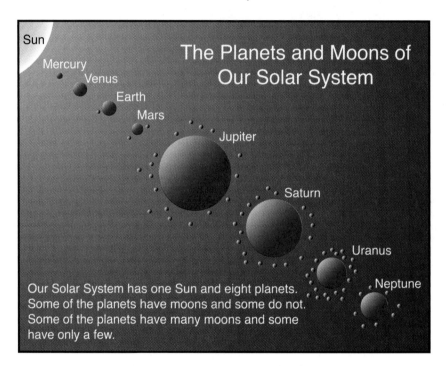

The Planets and Moons of Our Solar System

Sun
Mercury
Venus
Earth
Mars
Jupiter
Saturn
Uranus
Neptune

Our Solar System has one Sun and eight planets. Some of the planets have moons and some do not. Some of the planets have many moons and some have only a few.

Think about what you have learned so far about the planets in the Solar System. What are the names of the planets? Are they different sizes? Which ones are large and which ones are small?

Share your thinking with others in your group and in the class.

Investigate

In **Investigation 4**, you started to think about the planets in our Solar System. You studied their location in relation to one another and their different sizes. In this investigation, you will learn how the planets are alike and how they are different.

1. In this investigation, you will be role-playing researchers in a space program. Each group in your class will represent a different planet in our Solar System (excluding the Earth). There is only a limited amount of funding to explore the different planets. Each group wants as much research funding as possible for exploring "its planet." For this to happen, you will need to prove to the Planetary Council that your planet should be studied in depth. You will need to make a professional presentation that covers the following points:

   • the features of your planet (size, atmosphere, number of moons, rings, etc.);

   • what evidence there is for how your planet formed;

Materials Needed

For this investigation, your group will need:

• resource materials on the planets

• access to the Internet (optional)

• presentation materials (overheads and markers, presentation software, computer, computer projector, poster board and colored pencils, photographs, VCR and monitor)

- where the planet is in the Solar System in relation to the Sun and the other planets;
- what your planet looks like (use photographs, drawings, video, etc.);
- what interesting questions your research team wants to find out about your planet;
- what other objects in, or passing through, the Solar System might have an effect on your planet;
- what technology you think could be used to study and/or explore your planet.

2. Once groups have chosen their planets, you will need to decide on research assignments for each group member. Your teacher will have a list of web sites for you to use, and you can also use your school's media center and classroom resources.

3. Plan your presentation. Remember that you want to make the strongest case possible for your planet. You might want to use a computer program to present your information. You might also want to use posters, photos, videos, or overheads. As you research your planet, find out what questions scientists have been asking about it over the years. You will also need to know the latest discoveries that scientists have made about your planet.

4. When you finish your research, outline the important points you need to make in your presentation. Divide up the work fairly, put your presentation together, and rehearse it.

5. Your teacher will arrange a time for the presentations to the Planetary Council. You will need to do a convincing job, so look and act like professional scientists. Be sure to take notes on what the other groups present. That way you can identify what features are the same from planet to planet and what features are different.

6. After each presentation, answer the following questions in your journal:

   a) What is the size of the planet?

   b) How far is it from the Sun?

   c) What is its atmosphere like?

   d) How many moons does the planet have?

   e) What are the unique features of the planet?

   f) What does the planet look like?

   g) What kind of geologic action (if any) occurs on the planet?

7. When all groups have presented, the Planetary Council will decide which groups will receive the major funding.

Inquiry

Ways of Packaging Information

Scientists are often asked to provide information to the public or to make presentations. In doing so, they need to consider both the information they want to communicate and the person or groups that will be using the information. Then they must decide on the best method of packaging and delivering that information. These are decisions you need to make in this investigation.

As You Read...
Think about:

1. What is the difference between meteors, meteoroids, and meteorites?

2. What happens when a meteor strikes the Earth?

3. What are asteroids? Can an asteroid strike the Earth?

4. What are comets?

5. What is the relationship between a nebula and the objects in our Solar System?

Digging Deeper

METEOROIDS

Have you ever looked into the night sky and seen the bright streak of a shooting star? If you have, what you have really observed is a small meteoroid entering the Earth's atmosphere.

A shooting star streaking through the night sky

Meteoroids are small, rocky bodies that revolve around the Sun. If the Earth's orbit crosses the orbit of a meteoroid, the meteoroid may enter into the Earth's atmosphere. When this happens, the meteoroid starts to burn up and creates a streak of light. During its journey through Earth's atmosphere, the meteoroid is known as a meteor. If the meteoroid does not completely burn up and hits the Earth's ground, it is called a meteorite. Each year, the Earth gains about ninety million kilograms of matter from meteorites. Most are small specks, but some are quite large. The largest meteorite ever found was in Africa and weighed more than 54,000 kg!

Meteoroids enter the atmosphere at speeds of several thousand meters per second. The friction of the atmosphere slows down most meteoroids. Only meteoroids larger than a few hundred tons make craters when they strike the Earth. One example of a meteorite crater is in Arizona. This crater formed about 50,000 years ago and is 1200 m in diameter and 50 m deep.

ASTEROIDS

Asteroids are bodies of metallic and rocky material, sometimes called minor planets. They orbit the Sun like meteoroids, but are much larger in size. Most asteroids are located in a wide

The Barringer meteorite impact crater in Arizona.

region of the Solar System called the Main Asteroid Belt. This belt of asteroids is like a giant doughnut-shaped ring between the orbits of Mars and Jupiter. During the early development of the Solar System, the strong gravity of Jupiter kept the asteroids in the Main Asteroid Belt from forming into a planet.

Asteroids that come close to our planet are known as near-Earth asteroids. The largest near-Earth asteroid is called 1036 Ganymede, and is 41 km in diameter. Scientists think that near-Earth asteroids are produced by the collision of asteroids within the Main Asteroid Belt. At least a thousand asteroids larger than 1 km in diameter have orbits that cross the orbit of the Earth. Sometimes these near-Earth asteroids collide with the Earth. About 65 million years ago, an asteroid 10 km across struck the Earth. The after-effects of this collision may have been responsible for the extinction of the dinosaurs.

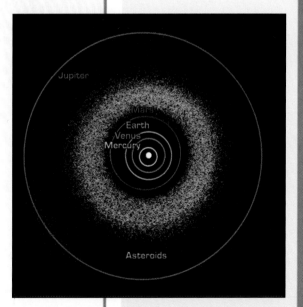

The Main Asteroid Belt is located between Mars and Jupiter.

A close-up of an asteroid.

Ice turns into a gas to form the streaming tail of a comet.

COMETS

Most comets can only be seen with a telescope but some pass close enough to Earth to be observed with the naked eye. A very bright comet can be seen in the night sky for days, weeks, or even months. A comet is a small body of ice, rock and dust that is loosely packed together. It can be thought of as an enormous snowball made of frozen gases that contains very little solid material. Comets, like planets, also orbit the Sun.

When a comet comes close enough to the Sun, the solar energy turns some of the ice into a gas. This vapor can be seen streaming behind the comet like a tail. Although very low in mass, comets are one of the largest members of the Solar System. The frozen part of a comet is only a few tens of kilometers at most. A comet's head can be as large as 100,000 km across. Its tail can be tens of millions of kilometers long.

One of the most famous of Earth's visiting comets is called Halley's comet, which was last seen in 1986. It passes by Earth every 76 years and will next appear in 2062.

NEBULAR THEORY

Most scientists agree that the objects in the Solar System formed about 4.6 billion years ago from a giant cloud of swirling gas and dust. This cloud is called a nebula, and its matter was probably thrown off from other stars in our region of the galaxy. Gravity caused the gases and dust to be drawn together, making the giant cloud fall inwards. As it collapsed, it got flatter,

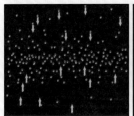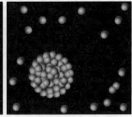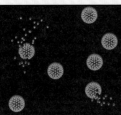

Particles within the nebula cloud were pulled together by gravity.

began to rotate and took the shape of a disk. The collapsing matter in the center of the disk eventually formed the Sun.

In the hot, inner part of the young Solar System, rock and metals with high freezing-point temperature remained solid. Here, the terrestrial planets formed as dense rocky worlds. The terrestrial planets include Mercury, Venus, Earth, and Mars. Farther from the Sun, the temperatures were lower. At this point, gas and icy particles (bits of matter) formed different types of planets. As the mass and gravity of these planets increased, they started to attract more particles. They

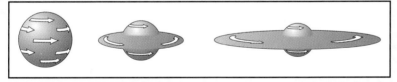

The Sun formed from a giant cloud of swirling gas and dust.

grew into the gigantic outer planets we call the gas giants. The gas giants include Jupiter, Saturn, Uranus, and Neptune.

Powerful telescopes have provided scientists with images of other stars and planets forming in the depths of giant clouds and rotating disks of gas and dust. Scientists have used the images as evidence of nebular theory.

Chandra is an x-ray telescope sent into orbit around the Earth in 1999.

Review and Reflect

Review

1. What did you learn about your planet that you did not know before?

2. What important and interesting questions have scientists asked about your planet?

Reflect

3. What explanation do you have for the similarities between the planets?

4. How are the planets different? Make a list of those differences as well.

5. How can you explain the differences between the planets?

Thinking about the Earth System

6. How are meteoroids and asteroids connected to the Earth System?

7. How does the Nebular Theory help you understand the structure of the Earth?

Thinking about Scientific Inquiry

8. In which parts of the investigation did you:

   a) Ask your own questions?

   b) Record your own ideas?

   c) Revise your ideas?

   d) Use your imagination?

   e) Share ideas with others?

   f) Find information from different sources?

   g) Pull your information together to make a presentation?

Investigation 7:

What Is Beyond Our Solar System?

Key Question

Before you begin, first think about this key question.

What are the other major objects in our universe and what are they like?

Think about what you have learned about the Solar System. What is beyond our Solar System?

Share your thinking with others in your group and in your class.

You have spent quite a bit of time in this module studying the objects in our own Solar System. You should now know about the role of the Sun, the names and characteristics of the planets (including the Earth), and the structure of the Solar System. You should also know the role of gravity in orbital paths, and how our Moon is related to and affects the Earth. In this investigation, you will move beyond our Solar System to learn about stars, galaxies, nebulae, and theories of how the universe was formed.

Investigate

Human beings have always been fascinated by stars and constellations. Constellations are the patterns stars make in the night sky. Knowing about the constellations and where they appear in the sky at different times of the year is useful in identifying individual stars.

Materials Needed

For this investigation, your group will need:

• star chart

• glow-in-the-dark stars

• large sheet of black construction paper

• small flashlight with a very powerful beam

• large flashlight with a dim beam

• metric measuring tape

• CD-ROM on the universe (optional)

Inquiry

Initial Experiments

Often, a scientific investigation begins with a simple informal experiment to test a prediction. The results may not solve the problem, but they may be useful in later investigations. In this part of the investigation, you did a simple demonstration to start you thinking about whether all the stars you see at night are the same distance from the Earth.

Part A: How Stars Look to Our Eyes

1. To get a sense of the relationship between the brightness of stars and their distance from Earth, your group will try a little demonstration. You will need a strong flashlight and a much weaker flashlight to do this.

2. Two members of your group will each take a flashlight. The other members will stand at a distance of at least 10 m away.

3. The students with the flashlights will turn on both flashlights, in a large darkened area. The observers will note the differences in the way that the flashlights appear.

4. As a group, brainstorm how the flashlights could be arranged so that they appear to be the same brightness to the observers. Try different ideas until the flashlights appear to be the same brightness to the observers.

   a) Record the steps you took and the end locations of each flashlight in your journals.

5. Answer the following questions in your journal:

   a) What did you have to do to make both lights look about the same?

   b) What might that tell you about the stars that you see in the night sky?

   c) Do you think all stars are the same distance from the Earth? What evidence do you have for or against this idea?

   d) If your class has access to computers with an Internet link-up, see what you can find out about stars and their distance from the Earth on the NASA web site: www.nasa.gov. Did this information match your group's ideas about stars and how they appear from the Earth?

   e) What else can you find from the NASA site about how stars appear to twinkle from the Earth? Find this out and share it with other groups in your class.

Part B: Your "Specialist" Constellation

1. Your teacher will give you a "map" of the night sky at a particular time of the year. Work with your group to decide on a constellation that you find really interesting. You may have heard about one in language arts studying mythologies of different cultures.

2. Once your group has agreed upon its constellation, find out the following information about it to share with other groups in your class.

   a) How did it get its name and is there any story behind that?

   b) What stars are in it?

   c) How does it appear to change its position with the seasons?

   d) What "famous" stars are in it?

3. Use glow-in the-dark stars to "make" your constellation on a sheet of black construction paper. You will also need to become aware of where this constellation is in relation to other constellations in the sky. Your teacher will later hang the constellation posters on the ceiling in their proper locations.

4. Once all the constellations are on the ceiling, turn off the classroom lights. Have a whole group session during which each group explains the facts about its constellation to the other groups.

   a) Make notes on the constellations so that you can ask questions about them later on.

Inquiry

Using References

When you write a science report, the information you gather from books, magazines, and the Internet comes from evidence gathered by others. You must always list the source of your evidence. This not only gives credit to the person who wrote the work, but it allows others to examine it and decide for themselves whether or not it makes sense.

Part C: Galaxies, Nebulae, and the Origin of the Universe

1. Examine the photographs of galaxies taken by one of the Great Observatories.

   a) Examine the pictures closely. What other galaxies do you see? How do the galaxies seem to be similar? How are they different?

   b) In your journal, make a table like the one below. As you study your galaxy photographs, fill in the table as best you can. You will also want to refer to the **Digging Deeper** on Galaxies and Nebulae to help you out.

Name of the Galaxy	Shape of the Galaxy	Important Stars in the Galaxy	Other Interesting Facts About the Galaxy

2. Now, examine the pictures that you have of nebulae (the plural of nebula) in the same way. You already know that nebulae are enormous clouds of dust and gas in the universe.

   a) How are the nebulae the same and how they are different?

   b) In your journal, make a table like the one below for nebulae. Complete the information, again, using the information on Galaxies and Nebulae for help.

Name of the Nebula	Shape of the Nebula	Type of Nebula	Other Interesting Facts About the Nebula

3. When you finish, compare what you have discovered about galaxies and nebulae with another group.

   a) Share your information and make your tables as complete and accurate as you can. Keep these tables handy for the **Review and Reflect** questions at the end of this investigation.

Part D: Theories About How the Universe Began

Over the years, scientists have had many theories about how the universe began. It has always been very difficult, however, to collect evidence that would support these theories. With advancing technologies, though, scientists have been able to collect data that seem to support one or two major theories. In this last part of the investigation, you will search the **Digging Deeper** section for evidence supporting one of these, the "Big Bang" Theory.

1. You will first need to find out what the Big Bang Theory is.

   a) What does it seem to explain about the universe and who came up with it in the first place?

2. Use the evidence about the Big Bang Theory in the **Digging Deeper** section.

   a) Work with your group to write an argument supporting the Big Bang Theory.

3. When you finish, share your argument with the class. Listen to what other groups say about the theory. They may have spotted evidence that your group missed.

   a) How complete, do you think, is the evidence of the Big Bang Theory?

   b) What appears to be missing in the evidence?

   c) How much sense does the evidence make to you? How useful is the theory in thinking about the universe?

Inquiry

Using References as Evidence

When you write a science report, the information you gather from books, magazines, and the Internet comes from science investigations. Just as in your experiments, the results can be used as evidence. Sometimes, enough new evidence accumulates that make ideas change drastically. This is true of the theories about how the universe began.

GALAXIES AND NEBULAE

Galaxies

Galaxies are large systems of stars, nebulae, and the matter between the stars (interstellar matter). A number of galaxies were discovered and cataloged by Charles Messier in the late 1700s. Messier's telescope did not have the resolution necessary to see individual stars in the galaxies and he referred to them as nebula.

Milky Way Galaxy (spiral): This is our own galaxy. It is 100,000 light-years in diameter.

Andromeda Galaxy (spiral): This is a relatively close spiral galaxy similar to our own (2–3 light-years away).

As You Read...

Think about:

1. What are galaxies and how are they classified?
2. Where are we in the Milky Way Galaxy?
3. What do scientists think "black holes" are?
4. What is the "Big Bang" Theory? What is the evidence for this theory?

M84 (lenticular): Sixty million light-years away.

Virgo A or M87 (giant elliptical): Sixty million light-years away.

Types of Galaxies

- **Spiral:** These galaxies have a large central disc with clusters of young stars and lots of matter between the stars and a bulge component of older stars.

- **Lenticular:** These galaxies are "smooth disc" galaxies of older stars. They have used up the material between the stars.

- **Elliptical:** These galaxies are football-shaped galaxies of older stars with little or no material between the stars.

- **Irregular:** These galaxies are those that don't fit into the other categories.

Nebula

A nebula is an enormous cloud of gas and/or dust in space. Nebulae are the birthplaces of stars.

Types of Nebulae

- **Emission Nebulae:** These are clouds of gas, which glow by re-emitting the ultra-violet radiation absorbed from young hot stars. These nebulae usually look reddish and are the source of recent star formation.
- **Reflection Nebulae:** These are clouds of dust that reflect the light of nearby stars. They usually look blue and are also the source of star formation.
- **Dark Nebulae:** These are usually about a few hundred light-years in width. Dark nebulae are clouds of dust that block the light from behind them.
- **Planetary Nebulae:** These are relatively small clouds of dust given off by dwarf stars as they near the end of their lives.
- **Supernova Remnants:** These are a relatively small (few light-years across) part of a massive star that is left over after the star ends its life in a supernova explosion.

Stars are formed from giant nebula clouds.

Horsehead Nebula (dark nebula at the center).

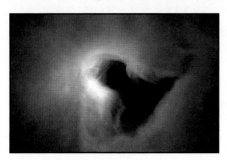

NGC 1999, a nebula in the constellation Orion. (reflection)

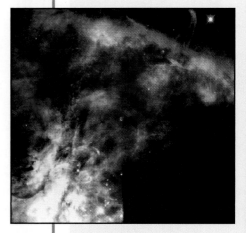

Orion Nebula (emission).

The Milky Way.

The Milky Way Galaxy

Our Solar System is located in a galaxy known as the Milky Way Galaxy. The Milky Way Galaxy contains more than 100 billion stars, each of which may have orbiting planets and other objects. The Milky Way Galaxy is shaped like a spiral, with arms that extend outwards from a bulge at its center. Each arm is full of dust, stars, and space. Our Solar System is located on the outside of one of these arms.

The arms of the Milky Way Galaxy rotate on an axis that goes through the middle of the galaxy. This means that just as the planets in our Solar System orbit the Sun, our Solar System orbits around the center of the Milky Way. It takes 240 million years for the Sun to orbit the center of the Milky Way Galaxy!

Scientists believe that many galaxies contain gigantic black holes in their centers. These black holes formed when stars collided as matter moved toward the center of the galaxy during its beginnings. The black holes produce "active" galaxies where there is more energy being emitted than would normally be expected.

The gravitational pull of a black hole is so intense that nothing can escape, not even light.

In contrast, "normal" galaxies give off energy from their stars without this additional source. Change takes place much more slowly in normal galaxies than in active ones. The Milky Way Galaxy is a normal galaxy.

THE UNIVERSE BEGAN WITH A BANG! (OR DID IT?)

The Big Bang Theory is the most widely accepted explanation among scientists for the origin of the universe. It states that the universe was formed 13.7 billion years ago. In the beginning, everything in the universe was concentrated into a volume that was incredibly small. The matter that made up this tiny universe was very hot and very dense (heavy for its size). The early universe began with space rapidly

Our Solar System is located in a spiral arm of the Milky Way Galaxy. The stars in the inner bulge of the spiral were the first to form when the Milky Way Galaxy began to develop. Stars in the arms of the spiral formed later and are younger than those in the bulge.

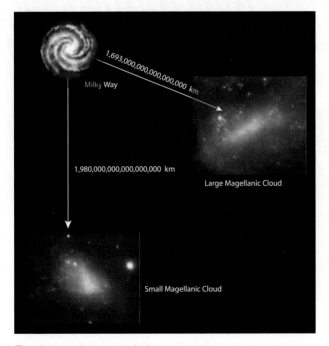

Milky Way

1,693,000,000,000,000,000 km

1,980,000,000,000,000,000 km

Large Magellanic Cloud

Small Magellanic Cloud

The distances between galaxies are great.

expanding carrying matter along with it. The Big Bang Theory also states that the universe is still expanding. Distant galaxies are traveling away from each other at great speeds.

Evidence of the Big Bang

The Big Bang Theory explains only the expansion of the universe. It does not attempt to explain how this process began. Nor does it explain what is beyond the edge of the universe. As with many strong theories, its strength comes from making a clear statement that is supported by solid evidence.

Stronger telescopes in the 20th century helped many astronomers investigate faraway galaxies and the Big Bang Theory. In 1929, Edward Hubble discovered that the more distant a galaxy is from our galaxy, the faster it is moving away from us. Specialized astronomers who study the origin and expansion of the universe are known as cosmologists.

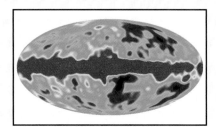

A microwave map of the Universe produced by the Wilkinson probe.

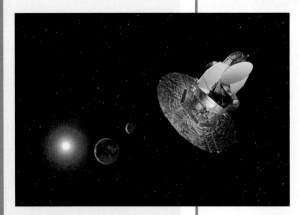

The Wilkinson probe mapping the edge of the universe.

Cosmologists study the universe by using probes that look out into space. These probes detect the energy released during the initial moments of the Big Bang. This energy has been detected by these probes coming in from all directions of the universe.

By studying the light from distant galaxies and the energy from the edges of the universe, scientists are actually looking back through time.

A STAR IS BORN

Astronomers believe that a star begins to form when particles in a dense region of a gas and dust cloud nebula are pulled toward each other. This collapse is caused by gravitation as the particles move inwards toward the center of the nebula to form the star. Eventually, enough particles collect to make the star dense enough to produce energy. Most of the energy produced is by hydrogen nuclei joining together, deep in the star's center to form helium nuclei. This process is called hydrogen fusion.

Main-Sequence Stars

The diagram shows the relationship between a star's brightness and its temperature. The stars in the diagram are categorized into one of three types: white dwarfs, main-sequence stars, and supergiants and giants. The stars in the main-sequence section show that as temperature increases, brightness increases. About 90% of the stars in the universe fit into this sequence. The

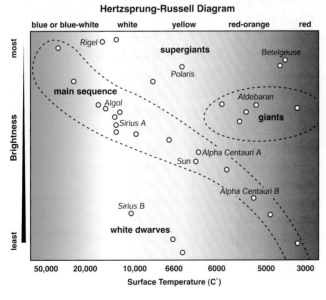

diagram also shows that as stars become cooler, they also become dimmer. As their brightness *decreases*, they change color from bright blue to dim red. The white dwarfs are small stars that are very hot, but not very bright. Supergiants and red giants are brighter than the hottest main-sequence stars. These stars are not as hot as the blue stars in the sequence.

The Life Cycle of a Star

The temperature of stars is so high that they cause nuclei of hydrogen to fuse together to create helium atoms in a process called fusion. For this reaction to occur, four hydrogen nuclei must combine to form a single helium nucleus. During this reaction, a small amount of mass is lost and converted into a massive amount of energy. All stars have a limited supply of hydrogen that can be fused into helium. Once the hydrogen is used up, the star goes through some big changes.

A picture of a giant galactic nebula, showing various stages of the life cycle of stars in one single view.

When main-sequence stars use up their hydrogen atoms, they become giant stars. It can take millions to billions of years for a star to deplete its supply of hydrogen. When a main-sequence star uses up its hydrogen supply, it starts to cool. As it cools, it begins to contract and become smaller. The contraction eventually makes the star heat up again causing the star to expand. During this process, its outer layers become much cooler than when it was a main-sequence star. The star is now like a car that is running out of gas. In its next cycle, it swells in size to become a giant star. Our Sun will

Impressions of supernova explosions in neighboring galaxies.

use up its supply of hydrogen and go through this process in about 5 billion years.

White dwarfs form after the hydrogen in a star's core is used up. The star starts to cool and contract and it loses its outer layers into space. Gravity continues to draw matter toward the core of the star and it becomes a hot, very dense star of low brightness.

Giant stars are more than ten times larger than the Sun and can go through violent explosions. In the super-hot cores of giant stars, some of the matter fuses together. The star expands rapidly to a gigantic size. Supergiants form from giant stars and are much larger than the Sun. Eventually, iron forms in the core and energy production comes to an end. Once their hydrogen supply is depleted, their high core temperatures cause violent reactions to occur. The core collapses violently, sending shock waves through the star. This creates a gigantic explosion called a supernova.

→

HOW DO SCIENTISTS INVESTIGATE OUTER SPACE?

The 2.5-meter reflecting telescope of the Sloan Digital Sky Survey. The box-like structure protects the separately mounted telescope from being buffeted by the wind.

The invention of the telescope during the time of Galileo was one of the most important events in the history of astronomy. This small instrument completely changed how people thought about the stars, planets, and moons in space. It was an extension of human senses and, for the first time, people could see things never before dreamed of. Since Galileo's time, countless telescopes have been designed, each one providing clearer images of objects in space.

Today's optical telescope magnifies objects in space, such as stars and planets, by concentrating the visible light waves they emit or reflect. These telescopes use lenses or mirrors to gather the light from an object. The light is then focused to create a magnified image of that object. There are optical telescopes that are small enough to be carried in your hand, while others are as big as buildings and weigh 300 tons!

The Zeiss 12-inch refracting telescope

The Earth's atmosphere can get in the way of the visible light gathered by optical telescopes. The gases, clouds, and particles in the atmosphere can make the visible light from stars appear blurry or flicker. To prevent this from happening, scientists put their telescopes on mountaintops, where the air is dryer and thinner. There is also less pollution to distort the visible light coming from space.

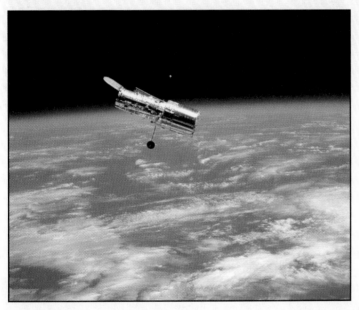

The Hubble Space Telescope (HST) orbiting above Earth.

In 1990, scientists put the Hubble Space Telescope into orbit above the Earth's atmosphere. In space, there is little to distort the visible light coming from distant objects. It has produced some of the most detailed and clearest images of space ever seen. Hubble is about the size of a large school bus. It travels at an orbital speed of nearly 8 km/s (kilometers per second), or 97 min per orbit. Hubble is powered by energy from the Sun and in an average orbit, uses about the same amount of energy as twenty-eight 100-W light bulbs.

The Arecibo Observatory located in Puerto Rico.

Other telescopes can collect different types of electromagnetic radiation from objects in space. The largest of these are the radio telescopes. They have huge surfaces to receive long radio wavelengths from space objects. Arecibo is the largest radio telescope in the world with its 300-m wide surface built into a hill! There are also ultraviolet telescopes, infrared telescopes,

The W. M. Keck Observatory on the summit of Hawaii's dormant Mauna Kea volcano. The twin Keck Telescopes are the world's largest optical and infrared telescopes.

gamma-ray telescopes, and x-ray telescopes. They work in space and collect radiation from above the Earth's atmosphere. Each of these telescopes creates its own image for the data that it is designed to collect.

A human-made object placed in orbit around the Earth is called an artificial satellite. Artificial satellites serve a variety of purposes, including the transmission of signals for television shows and cell phone calls. When a telescope is placed in space above the Earth's atmosphere, it is also an artificial satellite.

Scientists also send research instruments, such as telescopes, that travel into space away from the Earth. These unmanned spacecraft are known as space probes. The first probe was launched in 1959 to collect information about the Earth's Moon. Since that time, dozens of probes have been sent into space to collect information about all the planets of the Solar System, as well as asteroids, comets, and solar wind. Probes have even landed on the surface of Mars!

The first single crewmember EVA capture attempt of the Intelsat VI as seen from Endeavour's aft flight deck windows. EVA Mission Specialist Pierre Thuot standing on the Remote Manipulator System (RMS) end effector platform, with the satellite capture bar attempting to attach it to the free floating communications satellite.

The Mars Pathfinder lands on Mars. The Sojourner used the fully deployed forward ramp at far left, and rear ramp at right, to descend to the surface of Mars on July 5, 1997. Rover tracks lead to Sojourner, shown using its Alpha Proton X-Ray Spectrometer instrument to study the large rock Yogi.

Review and Reflect

Review

1. Explain why you think that stars, although they are incredibly large, can look so tiny to us here on the Earth. Why does our own star, the Sun, look so big?

2. What are constellations? How can you explain how they look different in the sky at various times of the year?

3. What are galaxies? How do scientists classify them?

4. Explain what nebulae are and how they are different from one another.

5. What is the Big Bang Theory? What is one piece of evidence supporting that theory?

Reflect

6. What do you think are the main problems in studying objects in the universe?

7. How has technology helped scientists to learn more about what is in the universe? What new technology do you think would be useful in studying the universe?

8. How well do you think the Big Bang Theory is supported? How confident are you that this theory explains how the universe began?

Thinking about the Earth System

9. What conditions would have to be in place for a planet similar to Earth to exist?

Thinking about Scientific Inquiry

10. In which parts of the investigation did you:

a) Make models?

b) Compare ideas?

c) Revise your ideas?

d) Use your imagination?

e) Share ideas with others?

f) Organize information?

g) Pull your information together to make a presentation?

Investigation 8:

Discovering the Difference Between Science Fact and Science Fiction

 Key Question
Before you begin, first think about this key question.

How can you tell the difference between science fact and science fiction?

Think about what you have learned so far about Earth and space. Think about the science fiction movies or television shows you have watched. How are they different?

Share your thinking with others in your class.

There are many ways of communicating information about science. There are scientific journals, conferences, books and web sites. However, these are not the only ways people learn about science. In this investigation, you will first explore ways in which people communicate scientific information. Then you will practice separating science fact from science fiction.

Materials Needed

For this investigation, your group will need:

- communications piece that combines astronomy fact with fiction (teacher's choice)

- materials to develop your own communications piece (video camera, presentation software, computer, poster board, colored pencils)

Investigate

1. With your group, think about and make a list of all the ways you find out about science information every day. Think creatively! There are a lot of choices!

   a) Write your list in your journal.

2. When you finish with your list, share it with other groups in your class to make a master list.

   a) On the master list, work with your class to make a check mark by any of the items on the list that might have science fact mixed with science fiction.

   b) Be sure to explain why you think that item on the list should be checked. It would help to give a specific example to make your explanation stronger.

Which photograph represents science fact and which is science fiction?

3. Your group's task is to create an interesting and creative presentation for the general public on an astronomy topic you have learned about in this module.

   You may present it in any form, such as a comic book, TV show, commercial, movie trailer, but be sure to mix fact and fiction in your piece.

   When you finish, you will present your piece. The job of the other groups in the class will be to figure out which astronomy information is fact and which is fiction.

   You might want to focus on some of the basic science you learned about astronomy, or you might prefer to deal with some of the exciting new findings coming out of the field.

4. To practice how to do this, you will first analyze astronomy fact versus fiction in a movie, story, television show, or some other medium.

   a) As you watch or read the communications piece, make notes on what you think is scientific fact and what appears to be science fiction.

5. When you finish, discuss your notes with your group. Sort the fact from fiction, and then meet with another group to talk over your thoughts. Answer these questions:

a) Why do you think the piece blends fiction with fact?

b) What do the producers of the piece seem to want the readers/viewers to believe?

c) How could you change the piece to make it more factual?

6. Use all of the resources in your classroom, plus your journals, to decide what content will be in your piece.

Divide up the work so that everyone in your group has a fair share of the effort. Some people might be better at artwork, while others are good writers or researchers.

a) Outline what you want in your piece, and then do the research you need to make sure that the science content is correct. Be as creative as you can, but don't try to cover a huge topic. Some ideas might be:

- Water on Mars
- Remote space travel to distant planets
- Search for extraterrestrial intelligence
- U.S. space program compared to other countries' programs
- Space Shuttle flights
- New planets
- The Apollo missions
- New technologies used for space observation
- History of astronomy (famous astronomers)
- Potential space hazards

7. Take your accurate information and decide how you will weave fiction into your piece. It might be useful to limit the fiction to just three or four items, so that your audience isn't overwhelmed.

a) Create your piece and your presentation. Check with your teacher to make sure that your "accurate" information really is accurate.

8. When everything is ready, your teacher will set up a presentation schedule. You will be responsible both for presenting your piece and analyzing other groups' pieces for fact versus fiction.

Review and Reflect

Review

1. How did other groups capture your interest with science fact?

2. How did they capture your interest with science fiction?

Reflect

3. What use do you think science fiction has in the world?

4. How can you tell science fact from fiction in your everyday life? What would you look for? What resources could you use to help you figure out fact from fiction?

Thinking about the Earth System

5. In what ways can the factual parts of the Earth System combine with fantasy to make science fiction?

Thinking about Scientific Inquiry

6. In which parts of the investigation did you:

   a) Analyze information?

   b) Compare ideas?

   c) Revise your ideas?

   d) Use your imagination?

   e) Share ideas with others?

   f) Organize information?

   g) Pull your information together to make a presentation?

Reflecting

Back to the Beginning

How have your ideas about the Earth in space changed from when you started? Look at following items carefully. Draw and write down the ideas you have now about these items. How have your ideas changed?

- Your original sketch of the Solar System with labels.
- Your explanation of what gravity is.
- Your list of all the objects you know about that are outside the Solar System.
- The explanation of two of the items from your list of objects in space and the explanation of what they are.

Thinking about the Earth System

The investigations in this module have had you looking at the Earth, the Solar System, and beyond. Think about the idea of "systems within systems." Answer the following question in your journal:

- What connections can you make between *Earth in Space* and the Earth System?

Thinking about Scientific Inquiry

Review the investigations you have done and the inquiry processes you have used. Answer the following questions in your journal:

- What scientific processes did you use?
- How did scientific inquiry processes help you learn about *Earth in Space?*

A New Beginning!

Not so much an ending as a new beginning!

This investigation into *Earth in Space* and astronomy is now complete, but that's not the end of the story! As time goes by, you will see, and hear about, many new space-science events and discoveries. Maybe you will actually travel in space one day. Be alert for opportunities to add to your knowledge and understanding.

The Big Picture

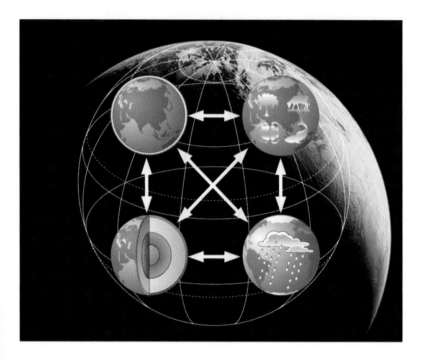

Key Concepts

Earth is a set of closely linked systems.

Earth's processes are powered by two sources: the Sun, and Earth's own inner heat.

The geology of Earth is dynamic, and has evolved over 4.6 billion years.

The geological evolution of Earth has left a record of its history that geoscientists interpret.

We depend upon Earth's resources—both mined and grown.

INVESTIGATING

WATER
AS A RESOURCE

Unit 6

What you will be investigating in this Unit:

Introducing Water as a Resource

Did you ever drink water from a well?

Have you ever seen a stream trickling from the side of a mountain?

Have you ever wondered what happens to water after you have used it?

Have you ever thought about how water enters the atmosphere?

Why is Water an Important Resource?

Water is such an important part of your everyday life that it is easy to take it for granted. Getting a drink of water is as simple as turning on the tap. However, this is not the case everywhere. Safe drinking water may be scarce in arid regions or because of drought, floods, and other natural disasters. Of course, water is used for more than drinking, but other uses of water may not be so obvious. You may be surprised to learn that wastewater treatment requires water. Farming, raising livestock, manufacturing, mining, power generation: all of these processes require water.

If you look at a world map, you will see that much of the Earth is covered with water. It would seem as though there should be an endless supply. However, most of this water is in the oceans and is not suitable for human use. The water that you rely on for drinking and other uses comes from rivers, lakes, streams, and below the ground. Evaporation and precipitation replenish this supply in a process called the Water Cycle.

What Will You Investigate?

You will discover how water as a resource is part of the Earth System.

Here are some of the things that you will investigate:

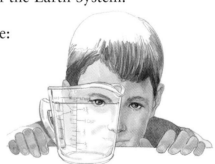

- how water is used;
- where your water supply comes from;
- how water moves through the Earth System;
- properties of water;
- water management.

You will need to practice your problem-solving skills and be good observers and recorders as you work together with other members of your class.

In the last investigation you will have an opportunity to apply all that you have learned about water resources. You will develop a plan to monitor and conserve the water supply in your community.

Investigation I:

Use of Water in Your Home

Key Question
Before you begin, first think about this key question.

How is water used in your home?

Think about all the ways that you and your family use water. How do you use water at home every day? Record your thoughts in your journal.

Share your thinking with others in your small group and in your class. Make a list that combines the ways that everyone in the class uses water in their homes.

Materials Needed

For this investigation your group will need:

• empty 2-L cardboard drinking container

• very small sewing needle

• metal rack

• measuring cup or graduated cylinder

• stopwatch or watch with a second hand

• calculator

Investigate

Part A: Estimating Home Water Use

1. Imagine hearing an announcement on the radio that a water shortage in your area has reached a crisis. There are plans to ration the amount of water that each household can use. You have to reduce your water consumption drastically.

Inquiry

Exploring Questions to Answer

Scientific inquiry starts with a question. Scientists take what they already know about a topic, then form a question to investigate further. The question and its investigation are designed to expand their understanding of the topic. You are doing the same.

Using Mathematics and Measurements

Measurements are important when collecting data. In this investigation your group will need to agree on the measurement units you will use. Consider the U.S. system of measurement (cups, pints, quarts, gallons, cubic feet) or metric measurement (milliliters, liters, cubic centimeters, cubic meters). Be sure to have good reasons for what you decide.

In your group, discuss how you would deal with the crisis. Here are some questions you could discuss:

- What would you need to find out?
- How could you find out what you need to know?
- What could you do to handle this situation?

a) Write the main ideas from your group discussion in your journal.

2. One important piece of information that you need to find out is how much water you and your family use in one day.

In your group discuss a plan for calculating the amount of water used daily in your home. Use the list that combined the ways that everyone in the class used water to help you.

a) Write your plan in your journal.

3. Share your plan with other groups and the class.

Decide on the best way to calculate the amount of water used in each home.

You may wish to make measurements in your home. You can also use the table, shown below, to help you get started.

Common Household Water Uses		
Type of Use	**U.S. System of Measurement**	**International System of Units (approximation)**
Water from a tap	1.5 gallons/minute	5.7 L/minute
Clothes washer	30–35 gallons/cycle	110–130 L/cycle
Dishwasher	25 gallons/cycle	95 L/cycle
Shower	2.5 gallons/minute	9.5 L/minute
Bathtub	50 gallons	190 L
Toilet	3.5 gallons/flush	13 L/flush
Low-flow toilet	1.6 gallons/flush	6 L/flush

4. Use your plan to calculate the amount of water used in your home each day.

a) Record your findings in your journal.

5. Organize a way of sharing your results. This could take the form of a large, wall-size chart that would show how much water different families use for different things in one day.

6. Look at the results for your class. Answer the following questions in your journal:

a) Where are there similarities and differences? How could you explain these?

b) For what purposes do people seem to use the most water? Why is that?

c) Which water uses around the house do you think you could cut back on? Explain your reasoning.

d) Calculate the average household water usage for your class.

Part B: Calculating Water Wasted in the Home

1. In many buildings, water taps have slow leaks, resulting in dripping faucets. Such leaks might seem very small, but the water losses can add up to be surprisingly large.

   Use a sewing needle to punch a small hole in the bottom of an empty cardboard drinking container. Make the hole as small as you can.

2. Support the container on a rack.

   Place a measuring cup under the container to catch the dripping water.

   Fill the container half to two-thirds full of water.

3. Leave the cup under the container for a measured time, in minutes, long enough to fill the cup to a depth of 3 to 5 cm.

a) In your journal, record the length of time.

Use caution when poking the hole. Wipe up any spills immediately.

4. Measure the volume of water caught in the cup. Make sure that the cup is resting on a flat surface when you make the measurement. Your sight line should be at the same height as the water level in the cup.

   Estimate the volume to the nearest milliliter.

   a) Record this measurement.

5. Calculate the rate of water loss (volume per unit time) in milliliters per minute.

   Write this measurement in liters per day.

   a) Show your calculations, conversion, and your results in your journal.

6. As a class, compare the values obtained by all of the groups.

   a) Why might the results vary from group to group?

7. In your group discuss how to deal with the water shortage described in Part A. Assume that it is a temporary shortage but that it will last at least a week. Try to be as creative as you can in your approach to the problem.

   Write a commercial to educate and inform citizens about the local water shortage and to explain your proposed solution.

   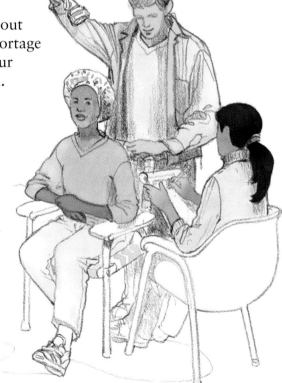

   a) Record your commercial in your journal.

8. Present your commercial to the class.

Wash your hands after the activity.

USING WATER AS A RESOURCE

In most parts of the world, water is a scarce resource. That might seem strange to you because there is so much water on Earth. Almost all of the water on Earth, more than 97% of it, is seawater in the oceans. The rest is called fresh water, because it does not have a high salt content. Most of the world's fresh water is frozen solid in large glaciers in Antarctica and Greenland. Almost all of the fresh water that is available for human use is either contained in soil and rock below the surface, called groundwater, or in rivers and lakes.

As You Read...
Think about:

1. Why is water a scarce resource for humans if more than half the Earth is covered by water?

2. Where on or near the Earth's surface is fresh water located?

3. Where are water shortages most likely to occur? Explain.

4. Why can some groundwater not be used as a supply of water for human consumption?

In most areas of the United States there is enough fresh water for human use. Yet usable fresh water is not as abundant as you might think. In some areas, like the arid Southwest, there is not enough water. In those areas,

water has to be transported long distances from other places in human-made channels called aqueducts. Even in areas with plenty of fresh water there are sometimes

An aqueduct in California.

shortages. Rainfall is the only way that water supplies are replenished. During times of drought, when rainfall is below average for several weeks, months, and even a number of years, water supplies can become dangerously low. Even when rainfall is adequate, water from rivers and lakes might be unusable because of pollution. In some areas, groundwater cannot be used because when it is removed from the ground, nearby wetlands would be damaged by drying up. As the population of the United States continues to grow in the future, water shortages will become more common, because the supply of available water remains the same. Water conservation will become more and more important as time goes on.

Your investigation of the amounts of water used and possibly wasted in your home for these purposes might have surprised you. Most people do not think much

about how much water they use. Perhaps this is partly because you don't pay for it each time you use it, except when you buy bottled water.

There are many ways to conserve water in your home. Some are easier than others. Leaky faucets and leaky toilets waste very large amounts of water, because even though the flow rates are small, they leak all the time. New designs of toilets and washing machines use much less water than older designs, but replacement is expensive. Water-saving shower heads save a lot of water, and they are relatively easy and inexpensive to replace. The most effective ways to reduce water use, however, might be the most difficult. Taking "navy showers" (turning off the water while you're soaping yourself), not planting lavish lawns in areas that are normally arid, and driving an unwashed car are examples of effective and simple ways to conserve water.

Landscaping with plants that require little water can conserve water.

Review and Reflect

Review

1. What surprised you the most about how much water a family uses? Why?

2. Describe three ways to reduce water consumption at home.

3. Based upon what you learned about water conservation in the home, suggest three ways that the school might conserve water.

Reflect

4. Refer to your calculations for the average daily household water use for your class. If water costs as much as milk, how much would the average weekly household water supply cost? Show your calculations and describe how you obtained your numbers.

5. List 10 ways that you and your classmates use water at home.

   a) Rank the list in order of importance.

   b) Justify your ranking system.

6. Could there ever be a water shortage in your area? Explain when or how it could occur, or why you think it could never occur.

Thinking about the Earth System

7. What connections did you find in this investigation that tied water to the biosphere? Be sure to record your findings on your *Earth System Connection* sheet.

Thinking about Scientific Inquiry

8. How did you use measurement in this investigation?

9. In what part of the investigation did you show evidence and reasons to others? Why is this an important part of scientific inquiry?

Investigation 2:

Tracing Water in Your School

Key Question

Before you begin, first think about this key question.

From where does the water supply in your school come, and where does it go?

You have investigated how you and your classmates use water in your homes. Think about how water is used in your school. From where does the water you use come? Where and how does it leave your school when everyone is done with it?

Record your thoughts in your journal. Share your ideas with others in your small group and in your class.

Materials Needed

For this investigation, your group will need to decide what materials you will require.

Investigate

1. In your group think about the following:
   - How and where does water get into your school?
   - Where does water go once it enters the school?

Inquiry

Dividing Tasks

This investigation provides you with an opportunity to mirror the teamwork that often happens in scientific studies. Different groups often take on responsibility for different parts of the study.

Do not enter maintenance areas of the school without permission and adult supervision.

- How much water is used in your school, and how is it used?
- How and where does the water leave the building after it has been used?
- Where does the water go after it has left your school?

Discuss ways you could find out this information.

a) Record the key points of your discussion in your journal.

2. Devise a plan to find out answers to these questions. Things to consider while designing your plan include:

- How will responsibilities be divided among groups and within your own group?
- How will you gather and record the information?
- How will your group present its findings to the rest of the class?

Once you have agreed on a method that will help answer the questions, share it with others in your class.

As a class, develop a plan to find the answers.

a) In your journal record the plan developed by the class.

3. Carry out your plan.

4. When you have found the answers to your questions, present them to your classmates.

   Listen carefully to what others in your class have to say.

   a) In your journal record the information from each presentation that helps you answer the questions.

5. Review your notes from the presentations. Using your notes, answer the following questions:

   a) How many different places does water enter the school?

   b) How is the use of water in your school different from the use of water in your home? How is it the same?

   c) Where does wastewater leave the school?

   d) Where does wastewater go after it leaves the school?

   e) What new questions could you ask about your school's water supply?

Inquiry
Learning from Others

Because different groups may have concentrated on different aspects of the school's water supply, you need to ensure that everyone fully understands the whole picture. You have a responsibility to present your findings to others.

Digging Deeper

WATER DISTRIBUTION SYSTEMS

In rural areas, most homes and businesses get their water from groundwater. Long ago, wells had to be dug by hand and reached only shallow groundwater. Now, wells can be drilled by machinery to as deep as several hundred feet. In urban and suburban areas, most water is piped in from a central water supply. The water supply might be a river, a natural lake, a reservoir behind a dam, or a number of deep wells. In many big cities, reservoirs are located far away, and the water is brought to the city through aqueducts.

If you have ever tried to stop the flow of water from a hose or pipe with your thumb, or if you have seen a hose or a pipe burst, you know that water pressure is very high. The high pressure ensures that the flow of water is adequate wherever and whenever it is needed. ➡

As You Read...
Think about:
1. What is the main source of water in rural areas?
2. What is the role of pressure in ensuring a supply of water for homes and schools?
3. How is water supplied to homes and businesses in larger towns and cities?

Storing water at a high elevation in a lake or reservoir can produce pressure. Where water is pumped from the ground it is stored in special tanks on hilltops. In home water systems pumps produce the pressure needed.

In urban and suburban areas, water is distributed from the source through large underground pipes, called water mains, under the streets. A map of the water mains in your town would look something like the pattern of branches on a tree or the pattern of tributaries in a

river system. The water mains keep branching out into smaller and smaller pipes until they reach a home or other building, where they enter the building and pass through a water meter. In areas with cold winters, the mains and pipes have to be buried as deep as several feet below the surface to keep them from freezing.

Most of the water that is used inside your home or school remains liquid. It flows through drainpipes into a municipal sewer system or into a septic system connected to the building. A septic system consists of a large tank buried in the ground. The solids in the sewage are slowly digested by microorganisms and converted to sludge. The sludge settles to the bottom of the tank and is pumped out occasionally by special trucks. The wastewater flows out of the tank and into underground pipes that leak water into the ground over a large area.

Municipal sewer systems are the opposite of municipal water systems: they collect the used water and carry it through a network of underground sewer pipes to a central treatment plant. Sewage treatment plants differ in how much they treat the sewage. Some do nothing more than filter out the solid materials. Others treat the sewage in several stages and end up with water that is pure enough to

drink! The treated sewage is usually returned to rivers, lakes, or the ocean, or is spread on the ground to soak in. In some places untreated sewage, called "raw sewage," is still dumped directly into rivers, lakes, or the ocean.

Some of the water that is used in your home and school evaporates. Most of the evaporation happens when water is spread over a large area, as in cleaning floors or pavement, or in watering a lawn or garden.

Review and Reflect

Review

1. Look again at the key question for this investigation. What did you learn about your school's water system?

2. What surprised you the most about how water is used in your school? Explain.

3. Draw a diagram showing how water is supplied to your school, and where it goes when it has been used. Label the diagram to show the flow of water.

4. What surprised you the most about how water is supplied or removed from your school? Explain.

Reflect

5. Do you think trends of water use would be the same in a school in another town? In another country? Explain.

6. What do you think your school could do to reduce its water usage?

Thinking about the Earth System

7. How does your school's water supply depend on the hydrosphere?

8. How does your school's water supply depend on the atmosphere?

Thinking about Scientific Inquiry

9. How did you use mathematics as a tool for inquiry?

10. What did you do to present findings in a form that others could see and understand?

Investigation 3:

Sources of Water

Key Question

Before you begin, first think about this key question.

Where does your water come from?

You have seen where water is used, both at home and at school. You have also looked at where it enters and exits the school. Imagine you are a drop of water in a tap at your school. What journey did you have to make to get where you are today?

Write your ideas in the form of a first-person story. For example: "I started my journey as a tiny drop many…" Share your stories with your small group and the rest of the class.

Materials Needed

For this investigation your group will need:

• topographic map of your local area

• map showing industrial sites, waste dumps, etc.

• colored pencils or transparency markers

Investigate

1. Look at a topographic map of your local area.

   Lay a piece of tracing paper or a clear piece of plastic over the map, or obtain a copy of the map.

   a) Using a blue pencil or marker, carefully trace all of the major streams and bodies of water in your community. This is your local stream network.

b) Draw arrows with one of your colored pencils, showing the direction in which the water flows.

c) Lightly shade over the land area drained by your local stream network. This is called your watershed.

Inquiry

Using Maps as Scientific Tools

Scientists collect and review data using tools. You may think of tools as only physical objects such as measuring cups. However, forms in which information is gathered, stored, and presented are also tools for scientists. In this investigation you are using a topographic map as a scientific tool. A topographic map shows the hills and valleys with contour lines. A contour line connects places at the same elevation. Elevations are labeled, usually in feet or meters above sea level.

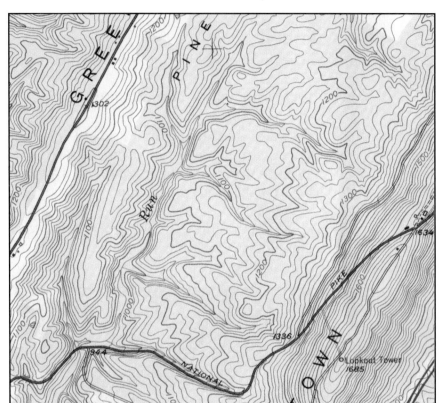

Scale 1:24,000 Contour interval: 20 ft.

2. Locate each of the following on your map:

- water treatment and wastewater treatment facilities
- industrial sites
- waste sites and landfills
- mines or excavations
- farms
- new, large communities
- recreational areas
- any other places that you think might affect the local water supply.

a) Draw and label each on your map.

3. Use your map to answer the following questions:

   a) Through which areas does the water flow?

   b) What does the water encounter along the way?

   c) Where and how could pollutants enter the watershed?

4. In your group, think of questions about your local water sources that you want to try to investigate.

   Post your questions to share with the class.

   a) Write down other groups' questions and compile a master list.

5. Choose questions for your group to investigate. Think about who you would consult to find answers to your questions.

   a) In your journal write down the question that your group will be investigating.

   b) Write down the answers that you find. Be sure to include the source of your information.

Inquiry

Representing Information

Communicating findings to other scientists is very important in scientific inquiry. In this investigation it is important for you to find good ways of showing what you learned to others in your class. Be sure your maps and diagrams are clearly labeled and well organized.

As You Read...

Think about:

1. **How does gravity control the flow of water?**

2. **What is the main source of water supply for humans?**

3. **What is a watershed?**

4. **What are possible sources of pollution in a watershed?**

6. When everyone has their information, decide on a method of sharing it with others. You might consider making up a "class magazine," in which each group submits an illustrated article about their research (possibly with maps and diagrams).

Digging **Deeper**

WATERSHEDS

Everybody knows that water flows downhill. The reason is that the force of gravity pulls everything downward toward the center of the Earth. Groundwater also flows from high areas to low areas, but its motion is much more difficult to observe. Water in the pipes in your home can flow upward as well as downward, because the high pressure in the pipes is much greater than the force of gravity.

The source of almost all of the water supplies for human civilization is rainfall or melted snowfall. When rain falls on the land, it either runs off into streams and rivers or it soaks into the ground to become groundwater. The groundwater flows slowly underground and eventually comes back out to the surface at the beds of lakes and rivers.

Every stream or river drains a particular area of the land surface. The land area that is drained by a given river is called the watershed of that river. Watersheds are also called drainage basins. The imaginary line on the land surface that separates the watershed of one river from the watershed of another river is called a divide. Divides follow along the crests of hills and ridges. You can stand on a divide and pour a glass of water from one hand into one watershed and a glass of water from the other hand into another watershed! There are watersheds for groundwater as well as for surface water. Divides between groundwater drainage basins are usually in about the same place as divides between river drainage basins.

Most towns and cities get their water from their own watershed. In some places, especially in large cities, the demand for water is greater than the supply in the local watershed. Then water has to be transported from distant watersheds.

Many substances that are hazardous to human health can enter water supplies. Chemical waste from factories is sometimes dumped into rivers and lakes, or directly into the ground. Pesticides (chemicals that kill insects) applied to farmland enter surface water and groundwater, often in large quantities. Leaks from underground storage tanks for liquids like gasoline go directly into groundwater. Salt put on icy roads in winter pollutes water also, although it is not as hazardous to human health.

Once a pollutant enters a water supply, it is difficult to get rid of it. Some pollutants slowly break down into harmless chemicals. Once the input of pollution is stopped, the pollutant gradually travels downstream and is replaced by unpolluted water. The problem is that it usually takes a long time for pollution to clear up in that way.

➤

As the pollutant travels downstream it is diluted by the addition of water. This causes the concentration of the pollutant to decrease. Often, the concentration becomes low enough for the water to be judged safe for use, but the pollutant is still there.

Review and Reflect

Review

1. Describe the watershed in which you live.

2. Where does your local water come from?

3. Where is your local water treatment facility?

Reflect

4. How does the direction of water flow help you to understand what can get into the watershed?

Thinking about the Earth System

5. On your *Earth System Connection* sheet, write any connections that you have made between water as a resource and the Earth system.

Thinking about Scientific Inquiry

6. How did you use a question as a starting point for inquiry?

7. How did you use tools to collect data?

8. How did you use evidence to develop ideas?

9. Provide at least one new question about water resources that your investigation has raised.

Investigation 4:

Water Movement on the Planet

Key Question

Before you begin, first think about this key question.

How is water recycled in nature?

You have seen where your local water supply comes from. How else does water move through your community? Discuss your ideas with your classmates.

Materials Needed

For this investigation the materials your group will need are listed with each part of the investigation.

Investigate

Part A: Visualizing Water in the Environment

1. Draw a picture of a cloud with rain falling from it, mountains, a stream coming from a mountain, and a body of water. Use the diagram on the following page as an example.

2. Think about places in the picture that water would be in one of its three forms: solid (ice), liquid, or gas (vapor).

   a) Label these places on your diagram.

3. Share your labeled drawings with your group members and then with your class.

   Discuss any differences in the ways you have labeled your drawings.

   a) What evidence do you and your classmates have for your ideas?

   b) What changes might you make to your diagram, based on your discussion?

4. Imagine you are a drop of water.

   a) Describe how you would move throughout the environment pictured in your sketch.

   b) What forces cause you to move?

Part B: Modeling Water in the Environment
I Flow of Groundwater

1. Set up the materials as shown in the diagram to model the flow of groundwater through gravel, coarse sand, fine sand, and a mixture of all three. Before you begin, develop a hypothesis about the rate of flow through sediments of different sizes.

   a) Record your hypothesis in your notebook. Be sure that your hypothesis includes a prediction and a reason for your prediction.

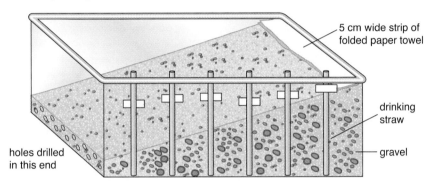

5 cm wide strip of folded paper towel

drinking straw

gravel

holes drilled in this end

2. Suppose you were to spray water onto the paper towel long enough for water to completely soak the gravel so that water flows out the base. Predict the level of water in each of the wells.

   a) On a copy of the experimental setup, indicate the water level you predict in each well. Explain your prediction.

3. With a watering can or spray hose, spray water onto the paper towel. Move the spray back and forth across the paper towel to water the whole width of the box equally.

   Keep on spraying until water flows out from the lower end of the wedge of gravel.

4. Continue to spray.

   Measure the heights of the water levels in each of the straws or tubes through the side wall of the container with the ruler.

   a) Record your measurements.

Materials Needed

For this part of the investigation your group will need:

- clear plastic box (about 40 cm x 20 cm, and at least 15 cm deep)
- package of transparent plastic drinking straws, or six 15 cm lengths of transparent plastic tubing, 6 mm to 12 mm in diameter
- tape
- centimeter ruler
- 2.5 kg aquarium gravel
- paper towel
- watering can or kitchen spray hose
- food coloring
- plastic sheeting
- 2.5 kg coarse sand
- 2.5 kg fine sand

Wear safety goggles. Be sure water draining from the plastic box will be caught by the sink or large container. Wipe up spills immediately.

Inquiry

Modeling

To investigate the flow of groundwater in the environment, you have set up a model. Models are very useful scientific tools. Scientists use models to simulate real-world events and processes. They do this when it is difficult to study the real thing in a controlled way. It is important that you try to model what happens in the real world as accurately as possible.

Using Mathematics

Mathematics is a key tool for scientists. Accurate measurement with suitable units is very important for collecting and analyzing data. In this investigation you must measure time. You also are measuring length. You need to decide on the best unit of length measurement to use.

Dispose of the straws or mark them as contaminated. Wash your hands after the activity.

5. While spraying, note the time, and put four drops of food coloring in the middle of the paper towel. Continue spraying.

   Watch for colored water to emerge from the lower end of the wedge of gravel.

   a) Record the time when you first see the colored water, and record the later time when the water again becomes clear of coloring.

6. Stop spraying and note the time.

   a) Record this time and then record the later time when the flow of water out the open end of the container has slowed down to a trickle.

7. Remove the gravel and clean up the setup.

   Spread the gravel out on a plastic sheet to allow excess water to drain away.

8. Repeat Steps 2 through 7 with the coarse sand and then with the fine sand in the container.

   a) Record all your observations and data.

9. Repeat Steps 2 through 7 with the mixed material in the container.

   a) Record all your observations and data.

10. Use your results from all parts of the investigation (gravel, coarse sand, fine sand, mixed materials) to answer the following questions:

    a) Describe the pattern of water heights in the tubes you observed. How did it compare to your predictions? How can you account for the pattern you observed?

    b) In which part of the investigation (gravel, coarse sand, fine sand, or mixed material) were the water levels in the straws or tubes the highest? In which part were the water levels the lowest? Why?

    c) In which part of the investigation did it take longest for the water flow to stop after you stopped spraying? Why?

    d) In which part of the investigation did the colored water reach the open end of the container the soonest? In which part did the colored water reach the open end of the container the slowest? Why?

e) How can you explain why there was a nonzero period of time between when you first saw the colored water flow from the open end of the container and when you saw the water become clear again?

II Distillation

1. Set up the equipment for modeling distillation as shown in the diagram.

   Equipment used for distillation is called a still. Since you will be using sunlight as a source of energy, your setup is called a solar still.

   a) Write a prediction of what you think will happen inside the still when you place it in sunlight. Give the reasons for your prediction.

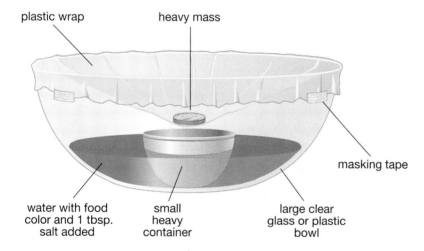

plastic wrap   heavy mass

masking tape

water with food color and 1 tbsp. salt added   small heavy container   large clear glass or plastic bowl

2. Place the still where it will receive direct sunlight, or under a sun lamp.

   Leave the still in the light for a few hours.

   a) Record your observations.

3. When about a teaspoon of water has collected in the small container, open up the still and remove the small container.

4. Observe the color of the water in the container.

   Your teacher will arrange a taste test of the water.

   a) Record your observations in your journal. How do your predictions compare with what you observed? Explain any differences.

Materials Needed

For this part of the investigation your group will need:

- small but heavy container, like a small drinking glass or coffee mug
- large clear plastic or glass bowl
- water
- food coloring
- tablespoon of salt
- clear plastic wrap
- masking tape
- heavy mass, such as a coin
- sun lamp, or a place where there is direct sunlight for at least a few hours

Be sure all materials are clean prior to use. Do not use beakers or other scientific equipment for either the bowl or the small container. Be sure that the bowl is placed in a safe location where it will not be broken. Follow the teacher's instructions with respect to the taste test. Wash your hands after the activity.

Inquiry

Using Evidence

Evidence is very important for scientists. They use evidence that other scientists have collected, as well as evidence they collect themselves.

b) Distillation is the process of making pure water by evaporating impure water and then condensing the water vapor. What evidence do you have distillation occurred?

III Transpiration

Wash your hands after the activity.

1. Obtain a potted plant that needs watering.

   Water the plant until excess water runs out of the bottom of the pot.

   Wait until all of the excess water has drained.

2. Wrap the pot tightly in plastic wrap. Be sure to cover the entire soil surface.

   Fit the plastic wrap snugly around the stem of the plant.

3. Find the mass of the potted plant on a balance or scale.

   a) Record the mass of the potted plant in your journal.

   b) Write a prediction of what you think will happen to the mass of the potted plant over the next few days. Give the reasons for your prediction.

   Let the pot sit in a warm, bright area of the classroom for at least one day.

4. Find the mass of the potted plant again.

   a) Record the mass in your journal.

   b) Calculate the decrease in the mass of the potted plant.

   c) Explain any difference that you find in the mass of the potted plant.

Part C: Analyze and Present your Findings

1. In your group, discuss how the drawing you created in Part A could be changed to reflect any new information you discovered in this investigation.

   a) What forces drive water movement?

   b) Where else is water located?

2. As a group, decide on a means to show the rest of the class your findings.

   Present your findings.

   Consider using a chart, a report, a revised drawing, a poster, or a model.

   Revise your findings based on feedback for your classmates.

THE WATER CYCLE

Water exists at the Earth's surface as liquid, solid, and vapor. It is forever changing from one of those three states to another. You can easily observe how water changes from liquid to solid by freezing and from solid to liquid by melting. Water also changes from liquid to vapor by evaporation and from vapor to liquid by condensation. Condensation is how clouds and raindrops form. Water can even change from vapor directly into solid; by the process of sublimation. That is how snowflakes are formed, high in the atmosphere.

As You Read...
Think about:

1. *How does water change from one form to another on Earth?*

2. *Where is water stored near the surface of the Earth?*

3. *What does an example of a "loop" in the water cycle involve?*

4. *What properties of Earth materials affect the flow of groundwater?*

5. *Why does groundwater flow so much more slowly than water in a river?*

6. *What conditions make groundwater a nonrenewable resource?*

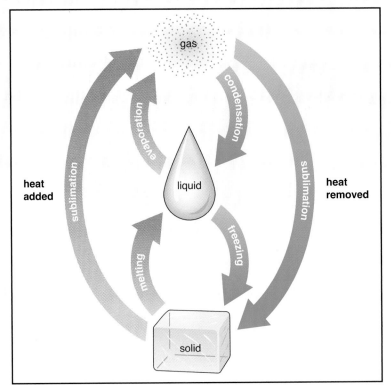

Change of state of water.

The total amount of water near the surface of the Earth stays almost the same through time, but water is always moving from place to place. You can think of places

where water resides, like the ocean or lakes or glaciers, as "reservoirs." Water moves from reservoir to reservoir in various ways. It can move in the form of liquid, solid, or vapor. This complicated movement of the Earth's water is called the water cycle.

One of the most important "loops" in the water cycle involves evaporation of water from the ocean surface, transport in the form of water vapor to the continents by winds, and precipitation as rain or snow on the continents. The rainfall then runs off by way of streams, rivers, and groundwater back to the ocean. You modeled a similar loop with your distillation setup. Another important "loop" in the water cycle involves condensation of water vapor in the atmosphere to form rain, soaking of the rain into the ground, uptake of the water by plant roots, and return of that water, in the form of water vapor, back into the atmosphere by transpiration through the leaves of the plants. You modeled transpiration using a potted plant in this investigation. There are many other "loops" as well. The Earth's water cycle is very complicated in its details.

Groundwater Flow

Most of the materials beneath the Earth's surface are porous. That means that they contain tiny open spaces as well as solids, just like a sponge. The porosity of a material is the percentage of open pore space it contains. Loosely packed sand and gravel can have porosities as high as 25%. Solid rock is much less porous. Many rocks have a porosity of only a small fraction of a percent.

Another important property of Earth materials is their permeability. The permeability describes how easy it is to force a fluid to flow through the pore spaces of the material. Loose sand and gravel have high permeability. Solid rock usually has low permeability. The best sources of groundwater, called aquifers, have high porosity and also high permeability. Sand, gravel, and fractured rock make the best aquifers.

Groundwater flow is much slower than flow in streams and rivers. That is because the passageways through the pore spaces are very small, so there is a lot of friction with the solid walls of the pores. Speeds of flow in streams and rivers are often greater than a meter per second. Groundwater flow is often as slow as several meters per day.

For a large town or city to obtain its water from groundwater, there needs to be a large aquifer. Several widely spaced wells are used to pump water from the aquifer, all at the same time. If the groundwater is replaced as fast as it is pumped, then it is a renewable resource. If the groundwater is pumped faster than it is replaced, however, then the level of the groundwater falls. It becomes more and more difficult to obtain the required water. Then the groundwater is not really a renewable resource, because the replacement might take far longer than a human lifetime!

Review and Reflect

Review

1. How does the size of particles in a material affect the movement of groundwater through the material?

2. How might your model of distillation be used as a source of fresh water?

Reflect

3. Choose one of the processes that you modeled in this investigation. Explain how you could improve the investigation so that your observations could be more easily repeated by others.

4. Describe the movement of water through a "loop" of the water cycle.

Thinking about the Earth System

5. What new connections between water and the biosphere did you notice in the investigation of transpiration?

6. What new connections between water and the atmosphere did you notice in this investigation?

7. What new connections between water and the geosphere did you notice in this investigation?

Thinking about Scientific Inquiry

8. Why are predictions helpful in scientific inquiry?

9. Describe how your examination of evidence is similar to what scientists do.

10. What new questions could you investigate?

Investigation 5:

The Special Properties of Water

Key Question
Before you begin, first think about this key question.

Why is water special?

Materials Needed

For this investigation the materials your group will need are listed for each station.

Think about your previous experiences with water. What unique properties does it have? How do other materials interact with water? How does water change when it is heated or cooled? How do its special properties make life possible?

Write your thoughts in your journal. Share and discuss your thoughts with your group and with the rest of your class. Make a class list of your ideas.

Investigate
1. Each group will investigate a special property of water at each station.

Here are the questions you will be investigating:

Station A: What happens when water interacts with other common substances?

Station B: What happens when objects are placed in water?

Station C: What happens when water is cooled?

Station D: What kind of particle is a water molecule?

Station E: How is frozen water different from liquid water?

Station F: What kind of particle is a water molecule? (Part 2)

Station A

1. You will add a small quantity of each of the following items to water, one at a time:

   - vegetable oil
   - food coloring
   - dry fruit drink mix
   - sand

   Before you add the material to the water, write a prediction of what you think will happen.

   a) Record your prediction in your journal. Give the reasons for your prediction.

   Observe the water after each addition.

   Stir the water and observe again.

   Observe how the substances interact with the water.

   b) What items dissolved in water?

   c) What items did not dissolve?

   d) How did stirring affect each trial?

Inquiry

Hypothesis

When you make a prediction and give your reasons for that prediction, you are forming a hypothesis. A hypothesis is a statement of the expected outcome of an experiment or observation, along with an explanation of why this will happen. A hypothesis is not a guess. It is based on what you, as the "scientist," already know.

Materials Needed

- four 500-mL beakers or similar containers
- vegetable oil
- food coloring
- dry fruit drink mix
- sand
- stirrers
- source of hot water
- ice

Wear goggles.
Do not eat or drink any materials used in investigations. Hot water should not be scalding hot. Dispose of all materials properly. Wash your hands after the activity.

Materials Needed

- granite chips
- pumice
- leaf
- dry soil
- plastic item
- five 500-mL beakers or similar containers

Clean up spills immediately.

Wash your hands after the activity.

Materials Needed

- two soda cans
- two thermometers
- two 1000-mL beakers
- sand
- container of ice
- timing device
- graph paper

Wash your hands after the activity.

2. Repeat Step 1 using ice water and hot water. Be sure to make a prediction. If you think that the temperature of water will affect what happens, explain why.

a) Record your predictions and reasons in your journal.

b) How did hot water affect the ability of each substance to dissolve?

c) How did cold water affect the ability of each substance to dissolve?

d) What properties of water does this station demonstrate?

Station B

1. You will add a quantity of each of the following items to water, one at a time:

- granite chips
- dry soil
- pumice
- plastic item
- leaf

Before you add the material to the water, predict what you think will happen and why.

a) Record your prediction in your journal. Give the reasons for your prediction.

b) After you have added each item, record your observations.

c) What did you find surprising about your results?

d) What properties or characteristics of water does this station demonstrate?

Station C

1. Fill a soda can halfway with water and a second soda can halfway with sand. The sand and water should be at room temperature.

Use a thermometer to measure the temperature of the water and the sand.

a) Record the initial temperatures.

2. Place each soda can and thermometer in a 1000-mL beaker of ice water.

3. Observe the temperature every minute for 25 minutes. Add ice to the ice water as needed

   a) Record your observations.

   b) Graph your results. Plot time along the horizontal axis (*x*-axis) and temperature on the vertical axis (*y*-axis).

   c) Describe the two graphs. Which substance cools faster, sand or water?

   d) What properties or characteristics of water does this station demonstrate?

Station D

1. Inflate a balloon and rub it against your hair or a sweater. You have put an electric charge on the balloon.

2. Put the "charged" balloon near a thin stream of running water.

   a) What do you notice about the interaction between the balloon and the water?

   b) How do you explain this?

   c) What properties or characteristics of water does this station demonstrate?

Station E

1. Put some water in a container.

   Put a piece of ice in the water and observe what happens.

   a) Compare and contrast ice with liquid water.

2. Measure the mass of a graduated cylinder or measuring cup.

   Pour 100 mL of water into the cylinder.

   Measure the mass of the cylinder and the water sample.

   Calculate the mass of the water.

   Calculate the density of the water in grams per milliliter by dividing the mass by the volume.

   a) Record your observations and your calculations.

3. Fill a graduated cylinder two-thirds full with very cold water.

   Note the volume in your notebook.

   Measure the mass of a block of ice.

Materials Needed

- balloon

- water faucet

Wipe up spills immediately. Wash your hands after the activity.

Materials Needed

- container of water

- ice cube

- 100-mL graduated cylinder or measuring cup

- 100 mL water

- balance scale

- block of ice

Wipe up spills immediately. Wash your hands after the activity.

Inquiry

Quantitative and Qualitative Observations

Observations dealing with numbers are called quantitative observations. An example of a quantitative observation is mass, measured in grams, and volume, measured in milliliters. Qualitative observations refer to the qualities of the object. Observing whether an object floats or sinks in water is a qualitative observation. Some observations can be made either quantitatively or qualitatively. In this investigation you are making both quantitative and qualitative observations.

Materials Needed

• sewing needle

• container of tap water

• capillary tube

• container of colored water

Handle the needle with care. Wipe up spills.

Wash your hands after the activity.

Without spilling or splashing the water, tilt the graduated cylinder and slide the ice block into the water. Hold the ice just below the surface of the water with a toothpick or pencil point. Note the new volume of the water.

a) Subtract the volume of water from the volume of "ice plus water" to obtain the volume of the ice block.

b) Calculate the density of the ice in grams per cubic centimeter by dividing the mass of ice by the volume (1 cc of water = 1 mL of water).

4. Use your observations in Steps 1 to 3 to answer the following questions:

a) How does the density of ice compare to the density of water? (Note that 1 mL is equivalent to 1 cm^3.)

b) How does the difference between the density of ice and water explain your observations in Step 1?

Station F

1. Try floating a needle on the surface of a container of tap water.

a) How did you place the needle on the water surface to get the needle to float?

b) How do you explain this property of water?

2. Place a capillary tube in a solution of colored water.

a) Record your observations.

b) Explain your observations.

Summary

1. Revisit your answer to the key question of this investigation.

   a) Add any new information that you now have as a result of the activities you have completed. Summarize your findings in the form of a table.

2. Present your findings to the class.

 Digging   Deeper

THE PROPERTIES OF WATER

You probably take water for granted because it is so common, but water is a very unusual substance. Its most spectacular property is that ice floats in water. You probably think that's no big deal, but water is almost the only substance in the universe for which the solid floats in the liquid!

As You Read...
Think about:

1. *How does the heat capacity of water compare with the heat capacity of rock?*

2. *How effective is water as a solvent?*

3. *Why is the water molecule called a polar molecule?*

4. *Why is the density of ice less than the density of water?*

5. *What special property of water allows certain insects to walk on water?*

Water is also very unusual in several other ways. For example, the heat capacity of water is higher than just about any other substance. The heat capacity of a substance is the amount of heat you need to add to a mass of material to raise its temperature by a given amount. The heat capacity of water is more than twice the heat capacity of natural mineral and rock material. This tends to even out temperature differences on Earth, from day to night and from summer to winter. Water is also the best all-around solvent. More solid substances dissolve in water than in any other liquid.

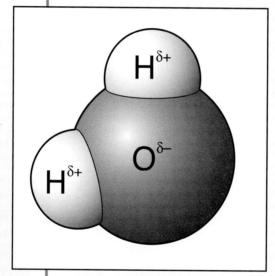

Molecule of water.

Water consists of molecules with the composition H_2O (two small atoms of hydrogen and one larger atom of oxygen). The two hydrogen atoms are bonded very strongly to the oxygen atom. The three atoms are not arranged in a straight line; instead, they form an angle, as shown in the diagram. The electrons that orbit around the three atoms are more strongly attracted to the oxygen atom than to the hydrogen atoms. Electrons have a negative electric charge. This gives the oxygen "side" of the water molecule a slightly negative electric charge. The hydrogen "side" of the water molecule has a slightly positive electric charge. Molecules like this, with one side positive and the other side negative, are called polar molecules. This is why the stream of water was affected by the electric charge on the balloon in Station D of this investigation.

In nature, electric charges of the same sign repel, and electric charges of different signs attract. When water molecules bond together in a regular structure to form solid ice, the positive sides of the molecules are attracted to the negative sides of adjacent molecules. The bond that is formed is called a hydrogen bond. It is weaker than the bonds between the hydrogen and the oxygen but still strong enough to cause water to freeze into ice.

Why does ice melt when the melting temperature is reached? In nature, every atom or molecule undergoes a vibration, or "jiggling," because it has thermal energy. The strength of the vibration increases with temperature. When the temperature is high enough, the ice melts, because the thermal vibration of the molecules becomes so strong that the hydrogen bonds are broken. In the ice structure, the molecules have a relatively open arrangement. When the ice melts, the molecules become free to pack together more closely. That is why water is denser than ice.

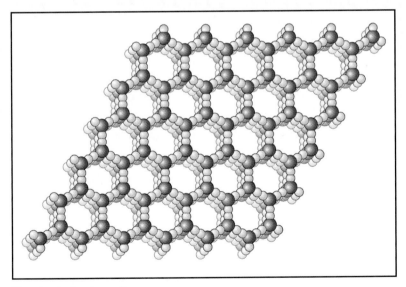

The atomic structure of ice.

The water molecules in liquid water attract each other. Inside the liquid, any particular water molecule is acted on by attractive forces from all directions. It is different for a molecule right at the water surface, however. It is attracted by molecules below it and beside it, but not from above. This makes the surface tend to shrink parallel to itself. This shrinkage force is called surface tension. Have you ever watched a soap bubble being made by waving a bubble wand? It is stretched out at first, but as soon as it leaves the wand, it becomes a sphere. That is because surface tension is making the whole bubble pull inward on itself. You were able to float the needle in the water because, as the needle started to sink downward, the surface tension pulled it upward, almost as if the water surface had been a thin sheet of rubber.

The rise of water you observe in a thin tube is called capillary action, or capillarity. It is another effect of surface tension. If you looked closely, you noticed that the surface of water in the tube curves upward around its edge. (This curved surface is called the meniscus.) To understand capillarity, you need to know that there is more to surface tension than just at the water surface. There is also surface tension in the film of water that is in contact with the glass of the tube, and also in the film of air that is in contact with the glass of the tube. The surface tension of the air film is stronger than the surface tension of the water film. That causes the meniscus to be pulled upward along the glass surface, and water rises up in the tube. Capillarity explains why a piece of cloth or a paper towel gets wet when you hang its lower edge in water. The tiny passageways between the fibers act as capillary tubes! When the material is treated with a water repellent the surface tension between the air and the material is reduced. Then water is no longer drawn up into the fibers.

Review and Reflect

Review

1. Explain what happens when oil is spilled on water.

2. Name at least three substances that dissolve in water.

3. What special properties of water did you investigate that provide evidence that water is a polar molecule?

Reflect

4. Water is a good solvent. How does this fact relate to water pollution?

5. You live on the shore of a large lake. Would you expect the temperature of the air near your home to be cooler or warmer than inland during the winter months? During the summer months? Explain your answer.

6. Why would the fact that ice is less dense than water be important for the survival of freshwater fish and other organisms that live in cold climates?

7. Use what you learned about water in this investigation to convince someone that water is a very valuable resource.

Thinking about the Earth System

8. How do the properties of water influence its role in the Earth System?

Thinking about Scientific Inquiry

9. Use examples from this investigation to explain the difference between qualitative and quantitative observations.

10. Describe two pieces of evidence that you have that water is a special substance.

Investigation 6:

The Quality of Your Water Resources

 Key Question
Before you begin, first think about this key question.

How healthy is your local watershed?

Materials Needed

For this investigation your group will need:

- water samples
- water-testing kits and tools

As you found in the last investigation, water is a good solvent. Many materials readily dissolve in it and are carried along as the water flows from the source to its destination. Professionals who monitor your water supply test the water for impurities at key points along the way. Where could your water supply pick up impurities? What impurities do you think you might find in your water supply?

Share your thinking with others in your group and with your class.

Investigate

1. Before you begin this investigation, you need to revisit what you did when you mapped the watershed for your area in Investigation 3.

Determine exactly:

- what feeds into your local watershed;
- what is the condition of your watershed;
- whom you can contact with any questions.

2. Water analysis is performed at various stages of the water distribution system to ensure that the quality of water is safe. The analysis might include tests for:

- dissolved oxygen
- turbidity (clarity)
- pH (acidity or alkalinity)
- hardness
- chemicals
- bacteria.

As a group, decide which tests you could perform in the classroom.

a) In your journal record the test that you plan to perform, the reason that you chose the test that you did, and the exact testing procedure. Have it checked by your teacher for safety and accuracy and make any changes necessary.

3. Use your local watershed map to determine where you should take and test water samples.

Remember that you are trying to find out what your local water quality is like at key points in the watershed.

a) Write down your sampling plan, and why you made your decisions. Have it checked for safety and feasibility. Make any necessary changes to your plan.

4. You will need to acquire a collection of the water samples.

Your class might go on a field trip to key areas, or someone may be able to collect the samples (with the accompaniment of an adult) for the entire class.

5. When your samples arrive in class, conduct your tests.

a) Record the information for each part of the watershed that you are testing. You might find it particularly useful to record your data directly onto a map of your local watershed.

Do not proceed with any test until the teacher has approved it. If using test kits or equipment, follow all instructions carefully. Wash hands when finished.

Inquiry

Consider Evidence

In this investigation you are asked to answer questions about water quality in your community. You have gathered some evidence that can help you answer these questions. However, the evidence you have may not answer all the questions. Looking for patterns and relationships within the evidence may lead to new questions to investigate.

6. Review what you have found out about the water quality in different parts of your watershed.

   Answer the following questions. Provide the evidence that you have.

   a) How does the water change as it proceeds downstream?

   b) How would you describe the quality of your water as it heads toward you?

   c) What do you think needs to be done in your area to ensure a regular supply of clean fresh water?

   d) What do you think are the water quality issues in your area? What is your evidence for that?

   e) What other questions still need to be asked?

7. An important piece in identifying a water supply issue in your area is public knowledge and perception of that issue.

   Ask a selection of adults in your community if they know of any water supply issues in your area.

   a) Record the responses to this informal survey for later use.

 Digging Deeper

WATER QUALITY
What Is "Good" Water?

The term "water quality" is used to describe how good a water source is for human use. The idea of water quality would be easy to deal with if all water sources were either "good" or "not good." The real world is more complicated than that. There are all degrees of "goodness" of water. That is because many substances can affect water quality, and their concentrations can range from very low to very high. The quality of water required also depends on its intended use. For example, the quality of water that is meant for drinking ("potable" water) is different from the quality of water that can be used for the irrigation of fields.

Pollutants

Some of the substances that affect water quality are called pollutants. Pollutants are mostly substances that get into water by human activities. The number of toxic chemicals that are produced and used by humans is enormous. Many of these toxic chemicals are used in ways that cause them to be added to surface water or groundwater.

Cleaning up sources of pollution takes enormous sums of money. Contaminated soil or sediment has to be removed. Sometimes it is just put in special places that are sealed off from the environment forever. (We hope!) Sometimes the toxic substances are converted into nontoxic substances by chemical processes.

Have you ever thought about what happens to the salt that is put on roads in winter in the northern areas of the United States? It is dissolved by later rainfall. Some of it enters

As You Read...
Think about:
1. Why is it difficult to decide if water is "good" or "bad"?
2. What is meant by "potable" water?
3. What are possible sources of chemicals in water? Name at least two sources.
4. What are possible sources of harmful bacteria in water?

rivers and is carried to the ocean, and some of it is added to groundwater. Pollution by road salt is a major problem in some watersheds.

Harmful Microorganisms

Microorganisms that cause illnesses also affect water quality. Bacteria are single-celled animals that cannot be seen with the human eye except through a microscope. Some kinds of bacteria are the most dangerous microorganisms. They usually get into water supplies when untreated sewage mixes with the water supply. It is not only a matter of human wastes from leaky sewer pipes. Dog and cat droppings are also deposited on land inside and outside the city.

Natural Solutes

Naturally occurring substances also affect water quality. Even raindrops are not pure water. As they fall they pick up tiny dust particles and also harmful substances like acid that are in the atmosphere. Gases in the atmosphere (carbon dioxide, sulfur dioxide) can also dissolve in raindrops to form acid rain. When the rainwater comes in contact with soil and rock material, some of that material dissolves in the water. Substances that are dissolved in water are called solutes. The concentration of natural solutes depends mainly on two factors: the composition of the soil and rock material, and how long the water is in contact with that material. Calcium makes water "hard," although not harmful. Hard water has a noticeable taste, and it can leave deposits inside pipes and tanks. The softest and purest water comes from areas that are far from where humans live, and have rock like granite or quartz sandstone that does not dissolve easily in water.

Review and Reflect

Review

1. What did your tests reveal about the local water?

2. What surprised you the most about what substances entered your water-supply system?

3. Where do polluting chemicals come from in a water-supply system? Name a source in your community, and one in a community different from yours.

Reflect

4. Why is it important to know what chemicals are in water?

5. How did the quality of water change as it headed toward your community?

6. What are the water-quality issues in your area? What is your evidence for that?

Thinking about the Earth System

7. On your *Earth System Connection* sheet, write any new connections you found between water as a resource and Earth Systems.

Thinking about Scientific Inquiry

8. Give an example of how you used each of the following inquiry processes in the investigation:

   a) forming a question;

   b) making a prediction;

   c) collecting evidence.

Investigation 7:

Cleaning up Water Resources

Key Question

Before you begin, first think about this key question.

How is your water supply cleaned and tested?

In the previous investigation you discovered that impurities of many kinds can enter the water system. What can be done to remove these impurities before the water reaches your home? What is done with the water after you have used it?

Materials Needed

For this investigation your group will need:

- water filtering materials
- containers for water
- water-test kit

Investigate

1. Check the telephone book to find out what agencies in your area are responsible for cleaning up the water supply. You need to look for the water purification plant, and the wastewater-treatment facility.

   If possible, contact these agencies and ask for a person from the facility to visit your classroom.

An alternative would be to take a field trip to your local water or wastewater-treatment plant.

2. You will need to prepare questions for your visitor before he or she comes to visit (or before you go on a field trip to the plant). Remember to focus on the local water-quality issues that you have discovered from your own research.

   Think about these points as you generate your list of questions for your visitor:

   • Where is water cleaned?

   • How is water cleaned?

   • Who makes sure that the water is clean?

   • What assurance do you have that your water supply is clean?

   • What particular issues of water quality or supply are important in your area?

   a) List your questions in your journal and save them for later.

3. Before your visitor comes to your class, it is also important for you to have experience with the process of cleaning up a sample of "contaminated" water.

   Each group will be provided with a sample of simulated wastewater. There will not be anything in the water that is harmful, but the water will not look or smell like water that anyone would want to drink!

4. Before you get started with purifying your water sample, you need to get a good sense of what is in it. Use your senses (except for taste!) in a safe and careful way to find out what might be in your sample.

   a) Record your results.

5. Once you have used your senses to get a good idea of what might be in your water sample, take a good look at the water-purification materials on the supply table.

   Discuss the following points with your team and record your answers in your journal:

   a) Which tools might be useful for getting particular contaminants out of the water sample?

Follow the teacher's instructions for how to smell the sample safely.

b) What type of device could you set up that would allow the water to come in contact with the water-cleaning materials?

c) What types of devices already exist for cleaning up water? How do these work?

d) How will you know that the contaminants are no longer there?

e) What will you do with the waste materials?

Inquiry

Designing and Conducting an Investigation

Scientists must think very carefully about the design of their investigations to make sure that the results are reliable. Often, they repeat a test several times to ensure reliable results. When designing a system for cleaning and testing water it would be very critical to have consistent and accurate results.

6. Design and make your system for cleaning and testing water. Be sure that you can defend your method of cleaning the water sample to others.

a) Record your cleaning and testing system in your journal. Have your teacher check it for safety and workability. Make any modifications necessary.

7. With the approval of your teacher, clean up the water sample using the system you designed.

   Decide how you will collect evidence that your cleaning system removes specific contaminants from the water.

   a) Record your observations in your journal.

8. When you have cleaned up your water sample as well as you can, prepare a display showing what the problems were with your sample, how you cleaned up the water, and the evidence that you collected for demonstrating that the water is clean.

   Be prepared to present your display when you have your visitor from the local water-cleaning facility in the class or to the rest of the class.

Do not proceed with any plan for cleansing the water until the teacher has approved it. Do not drink water samples, even if they appear to be clean. Clean up spills. Wash hands when finished.

Digging Deeper

TREATMENT OF DRINKING WATER AND WASTEWATER

Most people in the United States get their water from municipal (city and town) water systems. Most people in rural areas, and also some in suburbs, get their water from their own wells, which tap shallow or deep groundwater.

The water that is supplied from municipal water systems comes mainly from three sources: streams and rivers; natural lakes or artificial reservoirs; and groundwater, pumped from large wells. Lakes and reservoirs that are located in unpopulated areas far from cities and towns usually have the highest-quality water. That is also true for streams and small rivers in unpopulated areas. Large rivers usually have lower-quality water, because of pollution from upstream areas. Groundwater is contained in underground materials called aquifers. The quality of groundwater varies a lot from place to place, depending on the quality of the surface water that supplies the aquifers.

➡️

Treatment of Drinking Water

Some sources of drinking water are of such high quality that not much treatment is needed. Usually, an addition of small amounts of chlorine are sufficient to kill any harmful bacteria or other microorganisms. Other water sources, especially large rivers, have higher levels of pollution. Such sources require more to bring the water up to the needed level of quality. River water usually contains fine sediment particles in suspension. The water can be passed through filtration materials, like sand, to remove the fine sediment. Filtering the water also tends to remove bacteria. Another way of removing the fine sediment is to let the water sit in large basins while the sediment slowly settles to the bottom. Sometimes this settling process is speeded up by adding certain chemicals that cause the fine sediment particles to clump together into larger particles. The larger particles settle faster than the original fine particles.

One problem in any system for water treatment is the difficulty of removing dissolved salts. All natural waters contain some dissolved substances, like sodium, calcium, magnesium, and iron. When the concentrations are too high, however, the water may taste salty. Calcium and magnesium make the water "hard," which makes washing with soap or detergents more difficult. Salt can be removed from water by various processes in what are called desalination plants. Drinking water produced by desalination is considerably more expensive than natural fresh water. It is used mainly in developed countries, like the United States, Israel, and Saudi Arabia, where fresh water is scarce but the ocean is nearby. Some coastal cities in California are beginning to use desalination for part of their water supply.

Wastewater Treatment

Most of the water that is used in homes and businesses is put into either municipal sewers or home septic

systems. Most of that water is polluted to some extent, because it comes from washing clothes, bathing, and toilets. In earlier times, sewage was put directly into the ground, into rivers, or into the ocean, without any treatment. As populations have grown, however, the need for wastewater treatment has increased as well.

Home septic systems consist of a large underground tank, where anaerobic bacteria (those that do not need oxygen) gradually break down most of the solids. The remaining liquid waste flows out into what is called a leach field, where the water flows out from porous underground pipes into the ground. This water still contains pollutants and harmful microorganisms. Some of these are removed as the water flows through soil and rock, but in many places they reach groundwater supplies and add to problems of water pollution.

Municipal sewage is treated in special wastewater-treatment plants. There are several common methods of treatment. Also, the level of treatment varies greatly.

- In primary treatment, all that is done is to put the water in large tanks or ponds to let the solid material, called sludge, either float to the surface or settle to the bottom. The water is then usually chlorinated, and the sludge is treated and disposed of in various ways.

- Most wastewater undergoes secondary treatment as well. The most common method is to sprinkle or trickle the water over a bed of sand or gravel. As the water filters downward, it is put into contact with oxygen and microorganisms, which work together to break down the organic matter in the water.

- In a few places, the water undergoes tertiary treatment, which involves a variety of processes to purify the water even further. After tertiary treatment, the water can be pure enough to drink!

1. Streams, rivers, lakes, and artificial reservoirs are sources of municipal water.

2. Screens are used to remove debris.

3. Settling removes fine sediment. Chemicals are added to speed the process.

4. Filtration also removes fine sediment.

5. Chlorine is added to kill microorganisms.

6. Water is pumped through water mains.

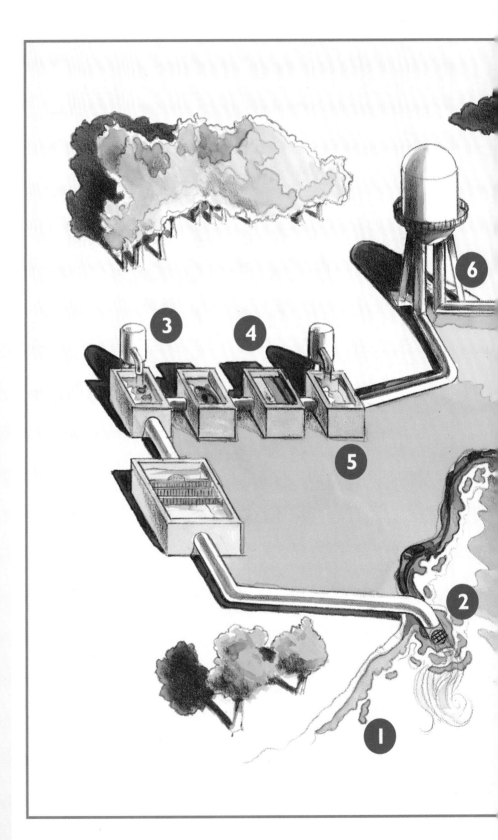

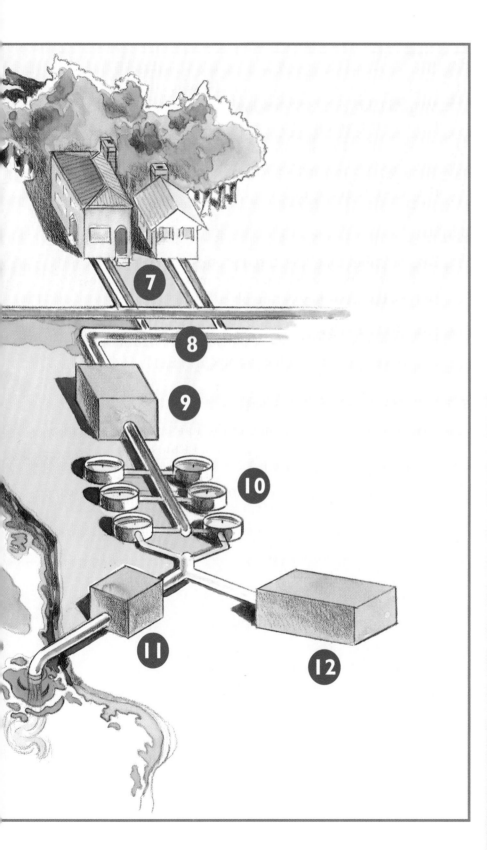

7 Clean drinking water is delivered to homes.

8 Pipes carry wastewater away.

9 Primary treatment takes place in large tanks. Solid materials settle as sludge.

10 During secondary treatment air and bacteria break down sewage.

11 Water is returned to the lake or river.

12 Tertiary treatment uses chemicals, filters, and radiation to purify water even further. It can be pure enough to drink.

Review and Reflect

Review

1. Look again at the key question: How is your water supply cleaned and tested? Write down what you have learned from your investigation that provides answers.

2. What kinds of things do water treatment facilities test for?

3. What kinds of problems can certain pollutants cause if they get into the water supply?

Reflect

4. Do you think that residential groups (everyday citizens) should become involved in water management issues? Why? How can they get involved?

5. How can a developed country such as the United States help others in developing countries that might not have a consistently clean water supply?

Thinking about the Earth System

6. How do you think a change in the Earth's water system (hydrosphere) affects other systems (atmosphere, geosphere, and biosphere)?

7. How do the atmosphere, geosphere, and biosphere affect the hydrosphere?

Thinking about Scientific Inquiry

8. Why is a carefully designed and reliable test for water quality important?

9. Where in this investigation did you:

a) Use tools?

b) Show evidence and reasons to others?

Investigation 8:

Water Conservation Partnership Plan

Putting It All Together

Key Question
Before you begin, first think about this key question.

How can you maintain your water resource?

You have investigated and read about water. What can you do in your community to maintain it as a resource?

Materials Needed

For this investigation your group will decide what materials are needed.

Investigate
1. At this point in the module, you should have a good understanding of the following key ideas:
   - where fresh water comes from;
   - what the properties of water are that make it such a valuable substance;

- where fresh water can be found on the planet;
- what a watershed is, and what your local watershed is like;
- what contaminants can get into the water supply;
- how contaminants in the water supply can be detected;
- some of the natural and commercial methods of cleaning a water supply;
- why water quality is important, and to whom it is important.

Review the work that you have produced over the course of the module, as well as all of the entries in your journal to check your knowledge of these points.

a) In your journal record any additional information you need to answer the above questions.

2. In this final investigation, you are going to pull together all of your knowledge about water and your experiences with the water supply in your area to develop a water quality partnership plan for your community.

Because there are so many different issues related to water quality, you may decide that it would be more beneficial if each group in your class specialized in just one part of the plan.

You can then put everyone's work together at the end to have a complete plan for the community.

3. To begin your work on your plan, you need to return to your water-issues survey from your previous investigation (Investigation 6, Step 7). As a class, list what you found to be key water-supply issues in your area.

Review these issues, and decide in which part of the plan each group will specialize.

a) List the name of the responsible group after its issue.

Before you begin any work on your plan, you may need to get help on ways in which you can develop it.

One useful way could be to make a flowchart of the issue and all key points which have an impact on the issue.

Here is one example:

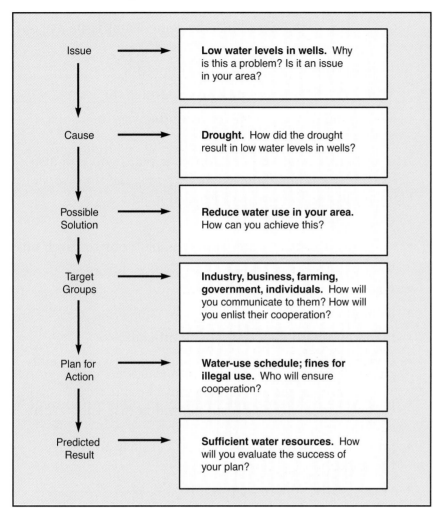

4. As you can see from the sample flowchart, your role as students must be a realistic one. You can come up with a well-thought-out plan and present it to those in authority over the water supply in your area. However there is only so much that you as an individual can do to carry out the plan.

    It is important that you have realistic expectations of what you can and cannot do with regard to maintaining your local water supply before you begin your plan.

5. Once you have agreed on which group is doing what issue, focus on making a flowchart (or other outline) of your plan.

    You have a number of resources already collected, but you may find that you need to do more research as you

develop your plan. For example, you may find, through searching on the Internet, that another community in another part of the world has the same water issue as your community.

Be sure to consult for advice as you need it.

a) What did that community do to resolve the issue?

b) What guidance can you get from the way they solved their water problem?

6. As you think about and develop your plan, you will also need to be thinking about what goes into the final version. Here are items that you will need to include:

- your water supply issue;
- why this is a local water supply issue (your research on the Internet);
- water test results;
- local news items;
- interviews with water authority officials;
- survey information from the community (water quality standards for your area, etc.);
- past work on this or similar issues in other geographic areas;
- how members of the community can help to resolve the issue;
- your specific role to help resolve the issue;
- timeline for the plan;
- who will implement and enforce the plan;
- what your plan will accomplish (impact on the water supply);
- who will receive your plan;
- approximately how much money you think it will take to get your plan started. (How could you find out?)

With your colleagues, discuss all these points, and form a plan that will include them. Consult your teacher if you need advice.

a) Record your plan in your journal.

7. When you have finished your plan, you need to present it to your classmates and, ideally, the person or persons for whom the plan is intended (local government official, water treatment operators, or community members). You may also want to share your findings with a wider audience (the whole school, parents, and the community).

You need to prepare your presentation in such a way that all the items included in your plan are clear and easily understood. You might choose to do this in a variety of ways.

8. After you have done what you can about your water quality plan (and this may take quite a long time), think back on the science that you needed to know to identify your issues, make your plan convincing, carry it out, and evaluate its success. For example:

a) How did you know what fed into your watershed?

b) How did you know what the water quality was in your area?

c) How did you figure out possible substances that could have gotten into any local groundwater?

d) What could account for any drought-related or flood-related issues?

e) What properties of water could explain why water quality and quantity are such important and controversial issues?

Review and Reflect

Review

1. According to the plans proposed by all of the groups, who were the important target groups for maintaining water as a resource?

2. What are important water issues in your community?

Reflect

3. Is your water plan realistic? Explain your answer.

Thinking about the Earth System

4. What effects would your water quality plan have on the biosphere? Atmosphere? Hydrosphere? Geosphere?

Thinking about Scientific Inquiry

5. How would you continue the inquiry process in this investigation?

Reflecting

Back to the Beginning

You have been investigating water as a resource in many ways. How have your ideas about water as a resource changed from when you started? Look at the following questions and write down your ideas now:

- How is water used?
- Where is water found?
- How is water part of the Earth system?
- How is a supply of safe, usable water ensured?

Thinking about the Earth System

At the end of each investigation, you thought about how your findings connected with the Earth System. Consider what you have learned about the Earth System. Refer to the *Earth System Connection* sheet that you have been building up throughout this Unit.

- What connections between *Water as a Resource* and the Earth System have you been able to find?

Thinking about Scientific Inquiry

You have used inquiry processes throughout the Unit. Review the investigations you have done and the inquiry processes you have used.

- What scientific inquiry processes did you use?
- How did scientific inquiry processes help you learn about *Water as a Resource?*

A New Beginning!

Not so much an ending as a new beginning!

This investigation into *Water as a Resource* is now completed. However, this is not the end of the story. You will see water where you live, and everywhere you travel. Be alert for opportunities to observe water as a resource and add to your knowledge and understanding.

The Big Picture

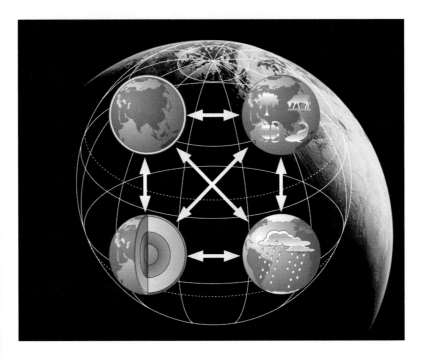

Key Concepts

Earth is a set of closely linked systems.

Earth's processes are powered by two sources: the Sun, and Earth's own inner heat.

The geology of Earth is dynamic, and has evolved over 4.6 billion years.

The geological evolution of Earth has left a record of its history that geoscientists interpret.

We depend upon Earth's resources—both mined and grown.

Glossary

A

Absolute time scale – The scale of geologic time, measured in years.

Acid rain – Rain that has a pH of less than 4.

Adaptation – A change in a plant or animal species, by the process of natural selection, that makes the species more successful in its environment.

Anaerobic bacteria – Bacteria that are able to live in an environment without oxygen.

Analogy – A correspondence or similarity between two things that otherwise are not exactly the same.

Anemometer – An instrument used to measure wind speed.

Aneroid barometer – An instrument that measures change of atmospheric pressure by its effect on the thin sides of a partially evacuated short hollow cylinder.

Aqueduct – A system of large surface pipes and channels used to transport water.

Aquifer – Any body of sediment or rock that has sufficient size and sufficiently high porosity and permeability to provide an adequate supply of water from wells.

Asteroid – A small planetary body in orbit around the Sun, larger than a meteoroid but smaller than a planet. Many asteroids can be found in a belt between the orbits of Mars and Jupiter.

Asthenosphere – A region of the Earth's interior immediately below the lithosphere where mantle rocks are hot enough and under enough pressure to deform, change shape and flow.

Astronomical unit – A unit of measure equal to the average distance between the Sun and the Earth, about 149,600,000 km (1.496×10^8 km).

Atmosphere – The layer of gas that surrounds the Earth. The atmosphere is a mixture of several gases.

Atmospheric pressure – The force per unit area exerted by the atmosphere.

Atom – A unit of matter composed of a nucleus and orbiting electrons; the smallest indivisible form of an element that maintains that element's chemical characteristics.

B

Bacteria – One-celled microorganisms that do not have a formal organization of their nuclear material.

Barrier island – A long, narrow coastal island, representing a barrier beach. It commonly has dunes on the ocean side with vegetated zones, and swampy areas extending on the lagoon side, toward the mainland.

Bay – A recess in the shore or an inlet of a sea or lake between two capes or headlands. A bay is smaller than a gulf but larger than a cove.

Beach – A gently sloping mass of sand or gravel along a shoreline, shaped by wave action.

Bedrock – Solid rock that is connected continuously down into the Earth's crust, rather than existing as separate pieces or masses surrounded by loose materials.

Below freezing – Temperature below 0°C (Celsius) or 32°F (Fahrenheit) at which water freezes from liquid into solid ice.

Big Bang Theory – The theory that all matter and energy in the universe was compressed into an extremely small volume that suddenly, billions of years ago, began expanding in all directions.

Biological weathering processes – The processes of weathering by which living things, both animals and plants, break down rock into smaller pieces or particles, at or near the Earth's surface.

Biosphere – The part of the Earth System that includes all living organisms (animals and plants) and also dead and decaying plant matter.

Black Hole – A hole in space formed by the collapse of a very large supernova. Its gravity is so great that not even light can escape.

Bluff – A high, steep bank along a river, a lake, the ocean, or at the edge of a low plain.

Body fossil – A fossil that consists of the preserved body of an animal or plant or an imprint of the body.

Breakwater – A man-made structure that is designed to protect a shoreline from the action of storms and waves.

C

Capillarity – The rise of water in a thin tube. Also called capillary action.

Cast – Mineral material that fills a hole that was left when a fossil shell dissolved.

Chemical weathering processes – The processes of weathering by which chemical reactions break down mineral particles in rocks into new minerals and chemicals in solution, at or near the Earth's surface.

Chemicals – Elements or compounds. The smallest part of an element that retains its characteristics is an atom. The smallest part of a compound that retains its characteristics is a molecule.

Chlorine – A substance used to kill harmful microorganisms in water.

Chromosphere – A reddish layer in the middle of the Sun's atmosphere; the transition between the outermost layer of the Sun's atmosphere, or corona, and the photosphere.

Cliff – A high, steep face or slope of rock; a precipice.

Climate – Condition of the atmosphere over a long period at a place on Earth.

Climatologist – A scientist who studies the causes and effects of climate.

Clouds – A visible mass of condensed water vapor suspended in the atmosphere and made up of minute water droplets or ice crystals.

Coastal cliff – A high, steep face of rock at the shoreline of an ocean or lake, caused by wave action.

Comet – A mass of frozen gases, ice, and rocky debris that orbits the Sun.

Compaction – The reduction in bulk volume or thickness of fine-grained sediments, or snow, owing to increasing weight of overlying material that is continually being deposited.

Condensation – The process of changing from a gas to a liquid.

Conserve – To save.

Constellation – A pattern of stars in the night sky.

Continent – One of the Earth's major landmasses.

Continental drift – A theory proposed by Alfred Wegener (1912) that proposed that the continents' positions on the globe are not fixed and that the continents have moved (and continue to move) about the globe during the course of geologic time.

Contour interval – The vertical distance between adjacent contour lines on a topographic map.

Contour line – A line (actually, a curve) on a topographic map that connects the positions of all points at the same elevation.

Control – Part of an experiment that is not altered which allows the experimenter to compare results to a standard.

Controlled test – A controlled test, or experiment, is one in which all other variables are held constant except for one. This procedure allows the experimenter to find out which variable in the test is giving a particular result.

Convection – The density-driven movement of a fluid material. Often, convection is driven by either heating from below or cooling from above the fluid.

Convection cell – A pattern of fluid movement where at one side material rises, moves laterally, then eventually sinks again to return back to its starting point.

Core – The central part of the Earth, beginning at a depth of about 2900 km, and consisting of iron-nickel alloy. It consists of a liquid outer core and solid inner core.

Corona – The outer layer of a star's atmosphere, such as that of the Sun's, extending millions of kilometers, and consisting of gas heated to very high temperatures.

Coronal mass ejections – (CMEs) Gases in the corona of the Sun that break free because they are so hot that the Sun's gravity cannot hold them. The gases form a solar wind.

Cosmologist – A scientist who studies the origin and dynamics of the universe.

Crater – A round depression, or pit-like feature found on the surface of some planets and moons that is formed by the impact of a meteorite. Similarly shaped features can be found on volcanoes and the sites of explosions.

Cross section – A diagram showing features along a vertical plane.

Crust – The outermost layer of the Earth, including the continents and ocean floor. Crust is composed of rock, sediment, and soil, representing less than 0.1% of the Earth's total volume.

D

Data – Observations, both quantitative and qualitative, from which conclusions can be inferred.

Decomposition – The chemical change when the material of a dead animal or plant decays.

Delta – The nearly flat area of land composed of sedimentary deposits supplied by a river and accumulated at its mouth, commonly forming a triangular or fan-shaped plain. A delta resembles the capital Greek letter "delta," "Δ" in shape, from which it gets its name.

Density – A measure of matter calculated as mass divided by volume, expressed as g/cm^3 or g/mL.

Dependent variable – In an experiment, a variable that is determined by the values of the independent variables that are imposed by the researcher. The researcher cannot set the values of the dependent variables directly.

Deposition – The process of settling of sediment particles onto a sediment surface beneath water or air; also, the process of precipitation of sedimentary minerals from a body of water.

Design – A plan for investigation. This could be a laboratory experiment, model, simulation, field study, or other type of investigation.

Dew point – The temperature at which air becomes saturated with moisture.

Dissolve – To put a solid into solution.

Distillation – The removal of impurities from liquids by boiling.

Distributary channel – One of two or more channels that branch from a main river channel where the river approaches a large body of water such as a lake or the ocean.

Drainage basin (also watershed) – The land area from which rainfall collects to reach a given point along some particular river.

Drainage divide – An imaginary line on the land surface that separates one drainage basin from another.

E

Earth System – A term used to describe the Earth as a set of closely interacting systems. Earth has four major subsystems; the geosphere, the atmosphere, the hydrosphere, and the biosphere.

Earthquake – A sudden motion or trembling in the Earth caused by the abrupt release of slowly accumulated strain.

Ecological niche – A kind of place or site where there is a particular combination of conditions needed for a species of animal or plant to live.

Electromagnetic spectrum – The complete range of wavelengths of radiation that travel through space.

Electron – A subatomic particle with a negative electrical charge.

Elevation – The vertical distance (height) from mean sea level to a point on the Earth's surface.

Erosion – The wearing away of soil or rock by weathering, mass wasting (downhill movement of material under the influence of gravity), and the action of streams, glaciers, waves, wind, and underground water.

Erosional landform – An area of the land surface that has been shaped by erosion or deposition.

Estimate – A mathematical approximation.

Evaporation – The process of changing from a liquid to a gas.

Evidence – Data that support or contradict a scientific hypothesis or conclusion.

Evolution – The development of new species of animals or plants from existing species by biological processes like natural selection.

Experiment – A fair and objective test of a hypothesis.

Extinction – The disappearance of a species of animal or plant when all of the members of that species die without reproducing.

Extrusive igneous rock – Igneous rock that has formed by rapid cooling of lava (melted rock that has reached the Earth's surface). Extrusive igneous rock is usually very fine-grained.

F

Fair test – A fair test (a test that is objective and systematic) is an experiment in which only one variable is tested at a time. A fair test also involves a control, a well-defined research question, collection and verification of data, and repeated trials.

Fault – A fracture through rock, along which the masses of rock on either side of the fracture move relative to one another.

Field work – Field work is observation or testing done in a "real world" setting outside the laboratory. It can include collecting samples, testing on-site, observing nature, and many other aspects of non-laboratory science.

Findings – Experimental results or conclusions.

Flatland – A tract of low-lying, level land, such as a level wetland, a swamp in a river valley, or a plain.

Flawed test – A flawed test is one in which the rules of fair testing have not been observed. A test could be flawed for a number of reasons: the test didn't have a control, more than one variable was altered at a time, the test didn't fit the research question, the data were not recorded accurately, or only one trial was done.

Floodplain – A flat area of a river valley, next to the river channel, that is built of sediments deposited by the river and covered with water when the river overflows its banks at flood stages.

Fold – A wavelike structure in a body of rock, caused by forces within the Earth.

Fossil – Any remains, trace, or imprint of a plant or animal that has been preserved in the Earth's crust since some past geologic time.

Fossil record – All of the evidence of past life that is preserved in the rocks of the Earth.

Freezing rain – Rain that falls as liquid and freezes upon impact to form a coating on the colder ground or other exposed surfaces.

G

Galaxy – A very large-scale system that contains a group of star clusters, with hundreds of billions of stars.

Gamma rays – Electromagnetic radiation with a wavelength of about 10^{-12}m, a shorter wavelength than visible light.

Gas giant – The name given to the first four outer planets: Jupiter, Saturn, Uranus, and Neptune. These large planets are not composed mostly of rocky or solid material, and consist mostly of gaseous matter.

Genes – The chemical units in organisms that transmit heredity from one generation to the next.

Geologic cross section – A diagram that shows rock units and their geological structures on a vertical plane downward from the land surface.

Geologic map – A map that shows the distribution, nature, and age relationships of rock units and structural features in the rocks.

Geologic time scale – The scale of time through Earth history, arranged in terms of officially defined units.

Geologist (or geoscientist) – A person who is trained in and works in any of the geological sciences.

Geology – The study of planet Earth: the materials of which it is made, the processes that act on these materials, the products formed, and the history of the planet and all its life forms since its origin.

Geoscientist – A person who is trained in and works in any of the geological sciences.

Geosphere – The part of the Earth System that includes the crust, mantle, and inner and outer core.

Giants – Very large, bright stars, that are dimmer than supergiants, and cooler than Main-Sequence Stars.

Glacial advance – The forward movement of the position of the terminus (front edge) of the glacier. Advance occurs when the speed of movement of the glacier is greater than the rate at which the ice is melted at the terminus.

Glacial retreat – The backward movement of the position of the terminus (front edge) of the glacier. Advance occurs when the speed of movement of the glacier is less than the rate at which the ice is melted at the terminus.

Glacier – A large and long-lasting mass of ice that is formed on land by compaction and recrystallization of snow. Glaciers flow downhill or outward under the force of their own weight.

Gravitation – The force of attraction of all matter to all other matter. The gravitational force between two bodies of matter depends on the masses of the two bodies and the distance between them. The smaller the masses, the smaller the force of gravity. The greater the distance, the smaller the force.

Gravity – A force that Earth exerts on any body of material on or at the Earth's surface.

Great Observatories – NASA's series of four observatories in space, designed to study the universe over the entire electromagnetic (EM) spectrum, so cosmologists can see the same object in different ways.

Greenhouse gases – Gases in the Earth's atmosphere that absorb certain wavelengths of the long-wavelength radiation emitted to outer space by the Earth's surface.

Groin – A rigid structure built out from a point on a shoreline to protect the shore from erosion by currents and waves.

Groundwater – Water contained in pore spaces in sediments and rocks beneath the Earth's surface.

H

Habitat – The place where an animal or plant species lives and grows.

Hail – Small rounded pieces of ice that sometimes fall during thunderstorms.

Hard water – Water that has a high concentration of calcium and magnesium ions.

Heat capacity – The amount of heat you need to add to a mass of material to raise its temperature by a given amount.

Helium – A light, colorless, odorless, nonflammable gaseous element.

High elevation – A point on a land surface where the vertical distance (height) from mean sea level to that point is large.

Hill – A high area of the land surface, rising rather prominently above the surrounding area, generally considered to be less than 300 meters (1000 feet) from base to summit.

Hydrogen – The lightest of all gases and most abundant element in the universe. It is colorless, odorless, and highly flammable.

Hydrogen bond – A weak chemical bond between a hydrogen atom in one polar molecule and an electronegative atom in a second polar molecule.

Hydrosphere – The part of the Earth System that includes all of the planet's water, including oceans, lakes, rivers, ground water, ice, and water vapor.

Hypothesis – A statement that can be proved or disproved by experimental or observational evidence; a scientist's best estimation, based on scientific knowledge and assumptions, of the results of an experiment.

I

Ice cap – A small ice sheet. The arbitrary division between ice sheets and ice caps is at a surface area of 50,000 square kilometers.

Ice sheet – A dome-shaped or sheet-like mass of glacier ice that covers a large area of a continent. The glacier ice of the ice sheet flows outward in all directions under its own weight.

Igneous rock – A rock that has solidified from molten or partly molten materials (magma).

Independent variable – In an experiment, a variable which can be controlled by the researcher and which determines the values of other variables (called dependent variables).

Infrared radiation – The electromagnetic radiation with wavelengths between about 0.7 μm to 1000 μm. Infrared waves are not visible to the human eye.

Inquiry – The process of finding answers to questions through a variety of methods. These can include research, fair testing, using models, asking experts, or many other methods.

Inquiry processes – The methods used by scientists to find answers to questions. They include hypothesizing, observing, recording, analyzing, concluding, communicating, and others.

Inquiry questions – Questions designed to be answered through a systematic, scientific process.

Interpolate – To find a value that falls in between two other values.

Intrusive igneous rock – Igneous rock that has formed by slow cooling of magma (melted rock) deep within the Earth. Intrusive igneous rock is usually coarse-grained.

Ion – An atom that has an electric charge.

Isobar – A line on a weather map connecting points of equal atmospheric pressure.

Isotherm – A line drawn on a weather map connecting points of equal temperature.

J

Jetty – A long structure that is built into the ocean or a lake to influence the current or to protect a harbor.

K

Karst topography – In areas of limestone bedrock, a kind of topography, with steep-sided local depressions and small, steep hills, that is formed by dissolution of the limestone by percolation of rainwater into the subsurface, to form open cracks, caves, and collapsed rock.

L

Landform – A part or area of the Earth's surface that has a distinctive shape or topography. Examples are major features like plains, plateaus, and mountain ranges, and also smaller features like hills, valleys, slopes, canyons, flatlands, wetlands, deltas, shorelines, and so on.

Landscape – A term commonly used to describe a person's view of landforms in an area or region.

Latitude – The north–south position of a point on the Earth's surface, relative to the Equator. The latitude is measured in degrees, from 0° at the Equator to 90° at the North Pole or the South Pole.

Law of Original Horizontality – The principle that sediments are usually deposited on a horizontal surface.

Law of Superposition – The principle that younger sediments are usually deposited upon older sediments.

Layers of sediment – Planar bodies of sedimentary material, with width much greater than thickness, that are formed by deposition of new sediment. The layers can be as thin as a millimeter or as thick as many meters.

Lightning – A sudden and visible discharge of electricity produced in response to the buildup of electrical potential between cloud and ground, between clouds, within a single cloud, or between a cloud and surrounding air.

Light-year – A unit of measure equal to the distance light travels in one year, 9.46 trillion kilometers (9.46×10^{12} km). Light-years are used to measure the great distances in space.

Limestone – A sedimentary rock that consists mostly of a calcium carbonate mineral, usually the mineral calcite.

Lithosphere – A term used in plate tectonics that refers to the rigid outer portion of the Earth. The lithosphere is composed of the crust and the uppermost portion of the mantle.

Lithospheric plates – A term used in plate tectonics that refers to the distinct and separate portions into which the lithosphere is subdivided.

Longitude – The east–west position of a point on the Earth's surface, relative to an arbitrary line on the Earth's surface that stretches from the North Pole to the South Pole and passes through Greenwich, England. The longitude is measured in degrees (0° to 180°) east or west from the arbitrary line.

Lunar cycle – The orbit of the Moon around the Earth. This process takes an average time of 29 days and 12 hours.

M

Magma – Naturally occurring molten rock material, generated within the Earth from which igneous rocks are derived through solidification and related processes.

Main Asteroid Belt – A band of rocky space debris located close to the orbit of Neptune and including Pluto, the largest of an estimated 30,000 objects.

Main-sequence stars – A star with characteristics that place it within a band running through the middle of the H-R diagram, and includes more than 90% of all stars.

Mantle – The zone of the Earth beneath the crust and above the core. It is divided into the upper mantle and the lower mantle.

Marshland – A saturated, poorly drained area, intermittently or permanently covered with water, and usually with dense vegetation.

Mass – The amount of matter in an object, measured in kilograms.

Melting – The process by which a solid material changes state to a liquid because of an increase in temperature.

Melting point – The temperature at which a solid material melts to a liquid.

Meniscus – The curved shape of the top surface of a liquid in a narrow container.

Metamorphic rock – Rock that has been changed (metamorphosed) into a different rock type, without actually melting, by an increase in temperature and/or pressure, and/or the action of chemical fluids.

Meteor – A streak of light in the sky at night that results when a meteoroid hits Earth's atmosphere and melts, vaporizes, or explodes (commonly known as a shooting star).

Meteorite – A meteor that is large enough to survive its passage through Earth's atmosphere and hit the ground.

Meteoroid – A small rocky body that revolves around the Sun.

Meteorologist – A scientist who studies the weather.

Mid-oceanic ridge – A continuous median mountain ridge extending through an ocean, which is seismically active and often has a central rift valley and rugged topography. Mid-oceanic ridges are divergent plate boundaries and are the site of sea-floor spreading and the formation of new oceanic crust.

Milky Way Galaxy – The galaxy which contains the Sun and our Solar System, and approximately 100 billion stars.

Mineral – An inorganic, naturally occurring solid material that has a definite chemical composition consisting of atoms and/or molecules that are arranged in a regular pattern.

Model – A representation of a process, event, object, or system that is too big, too distant, too small, too unwieldy, or too unsafe to observe or test directly.

Modeling – The process by which a representation of a process, system, or object is used to investigate a scientific question.

Mold – An impression made in sediment or rock by the outer surface of a fossil shell.

Molecule – Smallest individual unit of a compound formed by two or more atoms.

Mountains – Any part of the Earth's crust higher than a hill, elevated at least 300 m (1000 feet) above the surrounding land.

Multicellular organism – An organism that consists of a large number of specialized cells.

Mutation – A permanent change in one or more of the genes of a plant or animal, resulting in offspring that are unlike the parents.

N

Natural hazard – An event that arises from dynamic processes on Earth that can affect the lives, livelihood, and property of people (for example, earthquakes, volcanic eruptions, landslides, hurricanes).

Nebula – A term used to describe an enormous cloud of gas and dust in space. Nebulae are the birthplace of stars.

Nebular theory – The theory that the Sun and the planets condensed out of a spinning cloud of gas and dust.

Neutron star – A very small star formed from the imploded core of a massive star produced by a supernova explosion.

O

Observations – Data collected using the senses.

Oceans – Huge bodies of salt water that cover about three-quarters of the surface of the Earth.

Organic compounds – Chemical compounds that consist of atoms of carbon bonded to one another and to atoms of other elements like hydrogen or oxygen.

Organisms – Living things with parts that work together as a whole.

Overland flow – The flow of water on the Earth's surface in the form of thin, slow-moving sheets, rather than in localized channels.

P

Paleoclimatologist – A climatologist who studies evidence from the past (ice cores, ocean bottom cores, tree rings, rocks, and fossils, among others) to find out more about climate in the past.

Paleontologist – A scientist who studies past life.

Paleontology – The study of past life.

Pangea – A supercontinent that existed 200 to 300 million years ago and included most of the continental crust of the Earth.

Particle – A separate or isolated piece of material, usually small, such as a piece of a mineral or a rock.

Permeability – A measure of the ease with which a fluid can be forced to flow through a porous material.

Pesticide – A chemical that kills insects.

pH – A number between 0 and 14 that indicates how acidic a solution is. The lower the number the more acidic a solution is.

Photon – A unit of electromagnetic energy, regarded as a discrete particle having zero mass, no electric charge, and an indefinitely long lifetime.

Photosphere – The visible surface of the Sun, lying just above the uppermost layer of the Sun's interior, and just below the chromosphere.

Physical weathering processes – The processes of weathering by which rock is broken down by physical forces or processes, including gravity, water, ice, wind, or human actions at or near the Earth's surface.

Pilot testing – In an experimental program, one or more initial tests to determine whether the experiments will work the way they were designed.

Plate – A segment of the Earth's lithosphere.

Plate boundary – A zone of seismic and tectonic activity along the edges of lithospheric (tectonic) plates.

Plate tectonics – The theory in which the lithosphere is divided into a number of plates, and the study of how the plates move and interact with one another.

Polar molecule – A molecule with a negative charge on one side and a positive charge on the other.

Porosity – A measure of the percentage of pores (open spaces) in a material.

Precipitate – A solid chemical substance that is formed by growth from materials dissolved in water.

Precipitation – Water in the form of rain, snow, or sleet falling from the sky.

Prediction – A reasonable estimate of the outcome of a scientific test. Predictions are based upon prior knowledge, previous experimental results, and other research.

Pressure – Force exerted across a surface divided by the surface area of that surface. A familiar unit of measuring pressure is psi (pounds per square inch), but scientists usually use metric units, like newtons per square meter.

Prominence – Huge columns of glowing gases rising from hotspots that arc high above the Sun's surface.

Q

Qualitative properties – Features that are described without using numbers, such as color, odor, and so on.

Quantitative properties – Features that are described by making measurements using numbers, such as mass (number of grams), length (number of meters), and so on.

R

Radar – An electronic instrument used to detect distant objects and measure their range by how they scatter or reflect radio energy.

Radioactive element – A chemical element whose atoms occasionally change into atoms of other chemical elements, giving off energy in the process.

Radiosonde – A device for measuring physical properties of the atmosphere at high altitudes.

Rain – Precipitation in the form of liquid water droplets greater than 0.5 mm.

Raw sewage – Untreated sewage.

Record – To make a note of observations and events. Recording can be done on paper, electronically or through other means of communication such as video, sound recording, or photography.

Refraction – The deflection (or change in direction) of a ray of light or wave due to changes in its velocity as it passes from one medium to another.

Relative humidity – A type of humidity that considers the ratio of the actual vapor pressure of the air to the saturation vapor pressure.

Relative time scale – The scale of geologic time expressed in terms of officially defined units but without reference to the age of the units in years.

Relief – In a local area of the land surface, the difference in elevation between the high areas of the land surface and the low areas.

Research report – A record of the processes and results of an investigation.

Resolution – The process of making an object or sources of light observable.

Results – Findings from an investigation.

Rock – A naturally occurring solid material which is either a collection of one or more minerals, a body of mixed mineral matter, or solid organic matter.

Rock abrasion – The wearing away of rock by the rubbing of two rock surfaces together to loosen or break away mineral particles. Abrasion happens between two pieces of rock that are in motion in a waterflow or a landslide, or between a moving piece of rock and an underlying bedrock surface, as in a river or a glacier.

Rock cycle – A sequence of processes or events involving the formation, alteration, destruction, and reformation of rocks as the result of such processes as uplift, subsidence, erosion, transportation, deposition, lithification, melting, crystallization, and metamorphism.

S

Sandstone – A sedimentary rock that consists of particles of sand that are cemented together to form a solid rock.

Scientific inquiry – The process of investigating scientific questions in a systematic and reproducible manner.

Scientific processes – The methods used by scientists to investigate questions, record data, and analyze results.

Sediment – Particles of solid material that have been moved from their place of origin by wind, running water, or glacier ice and deposited on a surface.

Sedimentary rock – A rock, usually layered, that results from the consolidation or lithification of sediment. For example, a clastic rock like sandstone, or a chemical rock like rock salt, or an organic rock like coal.

Sedimentary sequence – A succession of different layers of material, oldest at the bottom through youngest at the top, each deposited in turn by the settling of sediment in water, or the precipitation of minerals from solution.

Seismic wave – A general term for all elastic waves produced by earthquakes or artificially through explosions (Syn: earthquake wave).

Seismograph – An instrument that detects, magnifies, and records seismic waves.

Shoreline – The place where a sea or lake meets the land. There are many kinds of shorelines, including beaches, rocky cliffs, and reefs.

Sleet – Partly frozen rain, or rain that freezes as it falls.

Sludge – The solid waste material that is separated from water in the treatment of wastewater.

Small-scale representation – A model of a process, system, or object that is not as large as the actual thing. A stream table, for example, can show a small-scale representation of a river.

Snow – Frozen precipitation in the form of frozen ice crystals.

Solar flares – Giant explosions of gas on the surface of the Sun. These can only be observed using specialized scientific instruments that can detect radiation released during a flare.

Solar fusion – The process by which the Sun creates energy by the nuclear fusion of hydrogen to produce helium.

Solar system – The Sun together with the planets, asteroids, meteors, moons, comets, and all other celestial bodies that orbit the Sun.

Solar wind – A flow of hot charged particles leaving the Sun, some of which can reach the Earth.

Solute – The substance dissolved in a solution.

Solvent – A substance, usually liquid, that can dissolve another substance.

Sounding – A plot of the atmosphere, using observations from radiosondes.

Species – A group of animals or plants that are capable of producing offspring, that themselves can reproduce.

Spit – A long and narrow body of sand or gravel that projects from the shore into a body of water.

Stratigraphic correlation – The process of establishing the time equivalence of rocks that exist in areas that are far apart.

Stratigraphic section – A stack or sequence of sedimentary rock layers that are exposed at a given place on the Earth.

Stratosphere – The layer of the atmosphere that extends upward from the troposphere to an altitude of 50 km.

Subduction zone – A long belt on the Earth where one plate dives down beneath another plate at some angle.

Sunspots – Cool, dark areas of gas within the photosphere that have intense magnetic activity.

Supercontinent – A term for a large landmass formed by the collision and joining of several continental landmasses into a single, large continent.

Supergiants – Extremely large, very bright, cool stars close to the end of their lives.

Supernova – The death explosion of a massive star whose core has completely burned out. Supernova explosions can temporarily outshine a galaxy.

Surface tension – The property of liquids in which the exposed surface tends to contract or shrink to the smallest possible area.

Surface water – Liquid fresh water that resides temporarily on the Earth's surface in the form of rivers and lakes.

Survey geologists – Scientists who conduct geological studies of regions for a government organization. Their work includes, but is not limited to, constructing geologic and topographic maps and assessing the quality and quantity of natural resources.

Synoptic map – A plot that shows data on weather and atmospheric conditions over a wide area at a given time.

T

Tectonic plates – Another term for lithospheric plates.

Temperature – The measure of molecular motion or the degree of heat of a substance.

Terrestrial planet – A small, dense planet similar to Earth that consists mainly of rocky and metallic material. Terrestrial planets include the inner Solar System planets Mercury, Venus, Earth, and Mars.

Theory – An explanation of why and how a specific natural phenomenon occurs that has been based on the support of considerable evidence and testing. Hypotheses that have been subjected to considerable testing and scrutiny, but have not been disproved, can evolve into theories. In turn, theories may be redefined as new hypotheses are tested.

Thermometer – An instrument used to measure temperatures.

Thunder – The sound emitted by rapidly expanding gases along the channel of a lightning discharge.

Topographic map – A map showing the natural and man-made configuration of a land surface, other features of the land surface, commonly by use of contour lines, colors, and symbols.

Topography – The configuration of a land surface, including its relief and the position of its natural and human-made features.

Trace fossil – Any evidence of the life activities of a plant or animal that lived in the geologic past (but not including the fossil organism itself).

Transpiration – The emission of water vapor from pores of plants as part of their life processes.

Transport (transportation) – The movement of sediment by natural agents such as flowing water, ice, wind, or gravity, either as solid particles or in solution, from one place to another on the Earth's surface.

U

Ultraviolet radiation – Electromagnetic radiation at wavelengths shorter than the violet end of visible light; with wavelengths ranging from 5 μm to 400 μm.

Unicellular organism – A plant or animal that consists of only a single cell.

Urbanization – A term used to describe the change in a region from rural or country-like to urban or more densely populated and developed.

V

Valley – Any long area of low-lying land bounded by higher ground. Valleys are usually occupied by a stream or river, which receives drainage from the surrounding slopes.

Vapor – A substance in the gaseous state.

Variables – The things about an experiment that can be changed by the researcher. In a fair test, only one variable is changed at a time.

Verify – To check and confirm data for its reliability. In science, this means that someone checks your procedures and findings.

Vestigial structures – Organs or structures in an organism that once served a purpose earlier in the history of the species, but now have no useful function.

Volcanic ash – Fine volcanic material (less than 2 mm in diameter) that can be ejected from a volcanic vent during an explosive eruption. Volcanic ash is the finest category of pyroclastic material (material ejected through the air during a volcanic eruption).

Volcano – A vent in the surface of the Earth through which magma and associated gases and ash erupt.

Volume – The amount of space taken up by an object.

W

Wastewater – Water after it has been used.

Wastewater treatment – A series of physical, biological, and chemical processes used to remove impurities from wastewater.

Water – A pure substance consisting of molecules of two hydrogen atoms bonded to one atom of oxygen.

Water cycle – A model of the circulation of water between the oceans, atmosphere, land, and living things.

Watershed – A drainage basin. The direction in which water drains from land.

Water treatment – Physical and chemical methods of removing impurities from the drinking water supply.

Wave – A motion that travels through a material and carries energy from one place to another; also, an undulating movement in a body of water shown by an alternating rise and fall of the water surface.

Wave action – The process by which land is eroded and sediment is moved by water waves.

Wavelength – The distance between the crests of two waves in succession.

Weather – The temporary condition of the atmosphere and the changes that occur within hours or days at a given location or region.

Weathering – The complex of natural processes, both physical and chemical, that act to change exposed rock into mineral and rock particles and chemical compounds in solution.

Weather forecast – A prediction that details what the weather is likely to be in the future.

Weather map – A graphic model of the state of the atmosphere over a given area.

Weather report – A report that details the weather conditions at the time.

White dwarf – A relatively dim star that has exhausted most or all of its nuclear fuel and has collapsed to a very small size.

Wind – The horizontal movement of air caused by pressure differences.

Wind direction – The compass direction from which wind blows.

X

X-rays – Electromagnetic radiation with a wavelength of about 10^{-10}m, a shorter wavelength than visible light.

Index

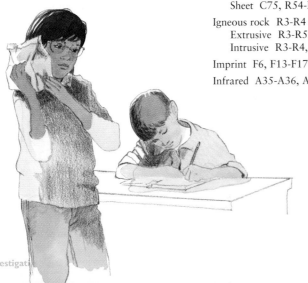

Illustration and Photo Credits

Unit 1

Our Dynamic Planet

P5, P13, P15, P18, P19, P20, P23, P24, P25, P27, P28, P31, P33, P36, P37, P38, P39, P43 (map), P45 (map), P52, P54 (source: Edwin Colbert, "Wandering Lands and Animals." Dover Publications, 1985), P55 (map), P57, P58, P67, illustrations by Stuart Armstrong; P41, Eric Bergmanis; P8, technical art by Burmar Technical Corporation; P22, Bob Christman; Pxi (lower left), Digital Vision Royalty Free Images: North America; P30, Perle Dorr; Pxii, P2, P9, P11, P33, P43, P53, P63, illustrations by Dennis Falcon; P4, courtesy of Fisher Science Education Co.; P61, Jim D. Griggs, U.S. Geological Survey Hawaiian Volcano Observatory; P68, Roger Hutchison; Pxi (top left), Pxii, P51, Martin Miller; P1, courtesy of the Paleontological Research Institute; P6, PhotoDisc; P37, John Shelton; P46, P66, J.K. Nakata; Pxi (upper right), H.G. Wilshire: from the "The October 17, 1989, Loma Prieta, California, Earthquake – Selected Photographs," U.S. Geological Survey; P49, Barbara Zahm

Unit 2

Rocks and Landforms

R43 (top), Marge Beaver, National Oceanic and Atmospheric Administration; R5 (bottom), R13 (top), R35, R36, R37, R38, R39, R47 (top), R53, illustrations by Burmar Technical Corporation; R4 (sedimentary rocks: a, b, d; igneous rocks: a, c), R5 (metamorphic rocks: a, b), Rich Busch; R27, Joel Dexter, Illinois State Geological Survey; Rxii, R2, R9, R12, R17, R19 (top), R21, R22, R30, R47 (bottom), R60, illustrations by Dennis Falcon; R4 (igneous rock: b), R5 (metamorphic rock: d), Ron Perkins; R49, Bruce Molnia; R42, Orrin Pilkey; R5 (metamorphic rock: c), Kent Ratajeski, University of North Carolina; R43 (bottom), Peter Scholle; R4 (sedimentary rock: c), R19 (bottom), Mike Smith, American Geological Institute; R8, R10, R13 (bottom), R46, U.S. Geological Survey; Cover, Rxi, Rxii, R1, R7, R15, R25, R26, R29, R32, R34, R40, R41, R45, R50, R52, R56, R58, R61, PhotoDisc

Unit 3

Fossils

Cover photo, courtesy of the Smithsonian Institution; Border photo, Doug Sherman, Geo File Photography; F9, F10, F21, F23, F30, F43, F44, technical art by Burmar Technical; F47 (top photo), Caitlin Callahan; F19, Digital Vision Royalty Free Image (North American Scenics); F8, James Edmunds; Fvii, Fxiv, F2, F12, F20, F29, F42, F51, F52, F59, illustrations by Dennis Falcon; F54 (diagram modified from "Fossil Horses in Cyberspace") with permission of the Florida Museum of Natural History; Fxiii (upper left), Geological Survey of Western Australia; F35, Bruce S. Grant; F6, Albert M. Hines; F39, Micromass UK LTD; F5, F47, Bruce Molnia; F15, NASA; F26, OAR/National Undersea Research Program; Fxiii (upper right), Fxiv, F17 (top), F28, Paleontological Research Institution; F1, Peabody Museum of Natural History; F36, F48, (photograph montage) F51, F53, PhotoDisc; Fxiii, (lower right), Fxiii (lower left), F4, F17 (top), F25, F32, F37, F58, Doug Sherman, Geo File Photography; F16, F41, F46, F57, Smithsonian Institution; F22 (map), F61 (map), U.S. Geological Survey; F55, Washington State University, College of Veterinary Medicine

Unit 4

Climate and Weather

C23, American Meteorological Society; C10, Annapolis Weathervanes; C54, illustration by Stuart Armstrong; C6, C7, C23, C25, C26, C27, C33, C34, C35, C39, C50, C51, C52, C61, C70, C75, C83, C84, C85, illustrations by Burmar Technical Corporation; C12, Cody Mercantile Catalog; C65 (left), Corbis Royalty Free Images; C24, C30, C31, C40, C42, C43, The DataStreme Project, American Meteorological Society; C11 (2nd down, right), (2nd from bottom right), Digital Royalty Free Images; C44, Digital Vision Royalty Free Images; C66 (bottom), Digital Vision Royalty Free Images; Cv, Cxii, C2, C15, C25, C28, C41, C49, C63, C70, C82, illustrations by Dennis Falcon; C72, (bottom), Geoff Hargreaves, USGS/National Ice Core Laboratory; C67, John Karachewski; C11 (2nd from bottom, left), (top right), James Koermer, Plymouth State College; C11, (top left) Ralph Kresge, NOAA; C73 (bottom), Laboratory of Tree-Ring Research, University of Tennessee; C71, Steven Manchester; courtesy of Oregon Department of Geology and Mineral Industries; C65, Martin Miller; C11 (bottom photos), C56, C66, (top), C69, C72 (top), C79, C85, Bruce F. Molnia; C11 (2nd from top, left), C28, C45, Joe Moran; C37, NASA; C22, NOAA; C1, C8, C14, C20, C48, C57 (top, bottom), C73 (top), C76, C77, PhotoDisc; C9, C18, Doug Sherman, Geo File Photography; C54, source, U.S. Geological Survey

Unit 5

Earth in Space: Astronomy

A60 (Left), A61 (Top), A63 (Bottom Left Composite) Anglo-Australian Observatory/David Malin; A5, A6 (Bottom), A12, A22, A23, A24 (Bottom), A39, A40 (Top and Bottom), A41, A46, A53 (Middle and Top), A65 by Stuart Armstrong; Av (Top and Bottom), Axii, A2, A10, A16, A17, A28, A36, A37, A47, A48, illustrations by Dennis Falcon; A68 (Top) Fermilab Visual Media Services; A38 Getty Images; Axi (Bottom Right), A68 (Bottom) Griffith Observatory/Anthony Cook; A24 (Top) Tom McGuire; A70 (Top) courtesy of the National Astronomy and Ionosphere Center - Arecibo Observatory, a national research center operated by Cornell University under a

cooperative agreement with the National Science Foundation; Axi (Top Right and Bottom Left), A4, A5, A6 (Top), A9, A15, A30 (Top and Bottom), A33, A41, A42 (Left), A43 (Top and Bottom), A53 (Bottom), A69, A71 (Top and Bottom), NASA; A66 NASA, Wolfgang Brandner JPL-IPAC, Eva K. Grebel; A60 (Top and Middle), A63 (Top and Bottom Left Composite) NASA/CXX/M. Weiss A1 NASA Goddard Space Flight Center; A62 (Middle Left) NASA Headquarters-Greatest Images of NASA (NASA-HQ-GRIN); A67 NASA, The Hubble Heritage Team; A26, A51 (Right), A70 (Bottom) NASA Jet Propulsion Laboratory (NASA-JPL); A51 (Bottom) NASA/JPL-Caltech/R. Hurt (SSC-Caltech); A42 (Top) NASA, Courtesy McRel; A55 NASA, Robert Williams and the Hubble Deep Field Team (STScl); A64 (Left and Middle) NASA/WMAP Science Team; A8 Courtesy Nasco, © Safari Ltd.; Axi (Top Left), A8 (Top), A13, A14, A44, A50, A51 (Top), A52, A57, A60 (Middle), A61 (Bottom), A62 (Top Right, Bottom Left and Right), A73, A74 (Middle) Photodisc; A29 Wojtek Rychlik

Unit 6

Water as a Resource

W3, W22, W23, W25, W26, W28, W34, W35 (bottom), W59, technical art by Burmar Technical Corporation; Wxii, W1, W6, W9, W13, W19, W42, W45, W46, California Department of Water Resources; Wxi (top right), Caitlin Callahan; Wv, Wxii, W4, W10, W17, W27, W33, W36 (top), W39, W44, W50, W54-W55, W61, illustrations by Dennis Falcon; Wxi (bottom right), W5, W12 (bottom), Bruce Molnia; W12 (top), John Nordland; Wxi (top left), W15, W29, W37, W48, W57, PhotoDisc; Wxi (bottom left), W21, Doug Sherman, Geo File Photography; W7, South Florida Water Manangement District; W32, Robert Suter, Vassar College; W16, U.S. Geological Survey

HERFF JONES EDUCATION DIVISION

84 Business Park Drive, Armonk, NY 10504
Phone (914) 273-2233 Fax (914) 273-2227
www.its-about-time.com

President
Tom Laster

Director of
Product Development
Barbara Zahm, Ph.D.

Creative Director/Design
John Nordland

Managing Editor
Maureen Grassi

Project Editor
Ruta Demery

Production/Studio Manager
Robert Schwalb

Production Specialists
Sean Campbell / Doreen Flaherty / Bernardo Saravia / Kadi Sarv / MaryBeth Schulze

Illustrator
Dennis Falcon

Safety Reviewer
Edward Robeck, Ph.D.

Senior Photo Consultant
Bruce F. Molina

Photo Research
Caitlin Callahan / Bernardo Saravia / Jennifer Von Holstein

Technical Art
Armstrong / Burmar